A SELF-HELP GUIDE TO IRS ISSUES

TAXJAMS
Simple Solutions

GREGORY M. MCCAULEY

Esquire

Published in the United States of America by
Gregory M. McCauley, Esquire and Taxjams, Inc.
510 Kennett Pike, P.O. Box 115
Chadds Ford, PA
Phone: 610-388-4474 Fax: 610-388-4476
www.taxjams.com

Library of Congress, cataloging-in-publication data.

McCauley, Gregory M.
        TAXJAMS: Simple Solutions. A self-help guide to IRS issues
ISBN 978-0-9851351-0-2 print book

ISBN 978-0-9851351-1-9 (E-book) First edition: e-book 2012
Taxation textbook – United States.
Taxation – enforced collection/audits/audit reconsideration/tax   problem/solutions.
Personal finance-tax issues
Debt – credit card settlement and mortgage foreclosure.

Editor: Victoria Wright, http://bookmarkservices.net
Cover design and interior layout: Jerry Dorris, http://authorsupport.com
Cover photo: Paul Facenda, www.facendaphoto.com

To Maureen

WAIVER & RELEASE

This book is intended to provide accurate and authoritative information to assist individuals in resolving their tax issues. The purchaser, reader, or end user has not engaged the author or publisher as an attorney or representative for tax matters by using this textbook. If representation is required, the user should engage the services of a qualified and authorized representative. The author and publisher will not be responsible for any liability, loss, increase in tax, penalties or interest, or risk incurred as a result of the use and application of any of the information contained in this book, forms, or web links.

The author and publisher have made every effort to provide accurate information, including but not limited to, forms, publications, telephone numbers, and Internet addresses at the time of publication. Neither assumes the responsibilities for any errors or changes that occur before or after the date of publication.

Table of Contents

HOW TO USE THIS BOOK

Perhaps my personal favorite and the best feature of this text is the brief explanation (titled "In Brief") at the beginning of certain chapters. "In Brief" is designed to give you a summary of the chapter so that you can determine if the chapter is applicable to your case and is necessary or mandatory reading. If the chapter is not relevant then you will be able to skip over the information and move to another topic, thus saving yourself a lot of time. In short, if you think you may be an innocent spouse or an injured spouse but do not know which is applicable, you can read the description to determine which is appropriate for you. There is a forms index in the back of the text. If you need a copy of a form to complete for mailing to the IRS or the case analysis form, you can go right to the Taxjams website and print a copy. Go to www.taxjams.com.

I use pronouns and subjects for simplification. Generally "he" is used to describe the taxpayer because in my experience the vast majority of taxjam clients are male. I have used "she" as the revenue officer simply for distinction from the taxpayer.

This book contains language used in the tax arena and I try to define the terms in ordinary words that you will understand. There is a small glossary in the back. I explain the same term in several chapters because a reader may not read the entire text but will need to know the specific meaning of the word or phrase being used.

When initials are used for a term such as Collection Information Statement (CIS), I try to repeat the term in the beginning of each chapter the first time the acronym is used. You may not use every chapter in the book, so I try to reintroduce the acronym or initials in each section it appears. I have included a list of all acronyms used in the book, and what they stand for, at the end of the book (List of Acronyms) just before the Forms Index.

Depending on your specific case and the amount of tax you owe, the time frame for how quickly you will achieve your case resolution will vary. Some cases take longer and are much more complicated than other cases. This book was written to produce results in as quick and efficient a manner as possible. For example, you may enter an installment agreement to pay the tax liability and file for penalty abatement later. You may attain currently not collectible status then file for an offer in compromise (OIC) and if not successful with the OIC, file bankruptcy to end the liability. Be prepared: Your route through this book may be roundabout.

I highly recommend that you begin the book and read the first three chapters through case analysis. After you understand your case, you will be able follow the logical steps towards tax compliance, reduction of the liability and, eventually, case resolution. As you move forward, you will begin to understand your taxjam, and you will find the path to its logical conclusion. Now it is your turn to invest a little time learning and exploring your case and this textbook will help you.

It is important for you to keep notes and organize your documents as you proceed. I want you to keep all of your tax information organized by year. When you are finished with your case, you will have all of your tax returns in folders arranged by tax year in one plastic waterproof or fireproof container. This is your important tax document **retention register**.

I will not mince words with you; you took the first step to solve your taxjam when you purchased this book. You want to stop looking over your shoulder. You want a good night's sleep. You want to begin saving for your future. Well, I want to help you achieve all of your goals.

By representing yourself and using this book as a guidepost, you can save yourself thousands of dollars and you will be represented by someone who sees your case as a priority—you. Your case will not be placed on a shelf or in a file cabinet. Your life will not be put on the proverbial backburner. Your tax case will be your most important goal.

With this book you can move your case as quickly as possible. By moving quickly, you can be both aggressive and successful with your results. Remember, the revenue officer will be able to close your file and get it off of her desk when you achieve success on your end of the case. The focus of this textbook is to get you tax compliant as quickly as possible.

You might ask, What does this mean? How do I become tax compliant?

Let's begin with your personal tax returns. Going forward, you will become and remain tax compliant by making certain all your future tax returns are accurately prepared, signed, filed on time, and paid. If you are a W-2 employee you will assure yourself you are declaring the right number of exemptions and if not, you will provide a new Form W-4 to your employer so that the proper withholding is made on your paycheck.

On the other hand, if you are self-employed, you will begin making quarterly estimated tax payments by filing Form ES quarterly. It may be easier to make a monthly or bi-weekly ES payment. There is nothing wrong with smaller more frequent ES payments. Some people find quarterly payments too high, or they have spent the funds in their account. Therein lies the inception of another taxjam.

Remember, your goal is to stay tax compliant. You must stay tax compliant moving forward or the revenue officer will not be able to work with you. Instead, she will resort to enforced collection—that is, she will file tax liens, issue bank levies, and a wage garnishment.

Resolving your case will benefit you in many ways. You will be healthier, both financially, mentally, and physically. You will be able to focus on the future. You will begin to feel the powerful and positive attitude that will help carry you through the end of your tax case.

This journey will require patience and perseverance. Each step that you take on the journey will bring you closer to your goal. Remember, your taxjam belongs to you. You are responsible for making sure all your taxes are filed and all payments are made on time. There are a few exceptions, which are explained in more detail later in this book. As you move forward with your case analysis you will decide which paths you want to pursue; if they don't work, you can come back to the case analysis and choose other paths to follow.

Trust me when I tell you that when your tax issues are behind you, you will feel a remarkable sense of relief. You will be proud of yourself for having dealt with these issues and putting them behind you. As a result of resolving your tax issue(s):

- You will owe nothing;
- You may receive refunds again;
- You may owe money and come to some type of agreement to pay back some or all of the liability;
- You will begin to increase your credit score;
- You will build a stronger financial future for you and your family;
- You will become more aware of your finances;
- You will have a chance to save for your retirement;
- You will make better financial decisions; and
- You will prioritize and purchase necessary items for you and your family.

Credit Cards and Mortgage Debt

Many people find themselves overwhelmed by credit card debt or falling behind in the payments on their home and facing mortgage foreclosure. There are two chapters in this text (Chapters 20 and 21) that teach you what it has taken many years to learn. These issues have tax implications because they significantly affect your financial status, and any relieved credit card or mortgage debts can have tax consequences.

I am not encouraging you to stop paying your credit cards, but if you are in an installment agreement with the IRS, they will expect to be paid first.

In fact, if you owe more than $50,000 in tax then the IRS will demand that you pay the liability before you pay your credit cards. In this connection, I will tell you what the credit card companies would want you to pay them and what you can offer them.

I will also illustrate for you the issues related to the tax implications of settling debts with credit card companies. This cancellation of debt income can tarnish what at first glance appears to be a great deal. I will show you how to negotiate the best deal.

The issues of mortgage foreclosure are similar to those of credit cards. If you walk away from your house you may have a substantial tax liability. When the mortgage company takes back your home or agrees to a short sale, the lender will issue you a Form 1099-C for the cancellation of the debt, the amount of the mortgage, which you did not pay.

You will learn that mortgage foreclosure or a deed in lieu of foreclosure may have a significant tax liability to you for the cancellation of debt. Moreover, you will learn about the secret law that allows you to eradicate the cancellation of debt tax by filing a simple form most people ignore or just don't know exists. I will tell you the specific calculations you need to know for insolvency and home mortgage credit, too. If you are behind on your mortgage or if you have already had a foreclosure, this is a must-read chapter.

Congratulations! You have started a new era in your life. You are going to be successful.

I wish you the best in solving your taxjam and in your future without it.

Best regards,
Gregory M. McCauley

ACKNOWLEDGMENTS

First, I thank my wife, Maureen, for her countless hours of work with me on this project. There were drafts and drafts of each chapter, which we read and reread, discussed, and changed countless times. In addition, Maureen is the author of the chapter on credit cards; she developed the settlement formula that we use in our practice and that we share with you in this book.

I also want to thank our sons, Gregory, Michael, Liam, and Aidan, for not only being the test subjects and proofreading, but more importantly, for sacrificing so much time that we could have spent together. Last summer, I asked them to read part of the book I had completed. I left the room and waited for the verdict, which came swiftly. In short, they said, "Start over, Dad." Aidan, the nine-year-old, did not know the word "panacea." If they were going to need a dictionary, they weren't going to read the book.

There are many people I want to acknowledge as being indispensable—some in helping me learn about civil and criminal tax cases and others in helping me write this book. There are several who helped me research and write, working beyond the call of duty. In no particular order, they are Daniel Barrett, Daniel S. Heller, Robert Lohr, Daniel P. Boyle, and John Rabil.

Daniel Barrett, Esquire, helped me with the research on the book and has been protecting taxpayer's rights in cases for years. I am sure he is tired of proofreading the book and seeing the boxes of research he helped me assemble. Dan Heller joined the firm over a year ago and has helped the first half of the book to grow to the end product you have in your hands. Dan did exhaustive research and study in tax, an area of the law in which he probably never thought he would be spending so much time. Dan helped with writing, editing, and keeping the project moving forward.

When I reached the point in the book where I was going to discuss income taxes and bankruptcy, I sought the assistance of bankruptcy attorney Robert J. Lohr II, Esquire. I called Bob's office late one night, thinking I was going to leave him a message, only to find out that he was burning the midnight oil, too. After I drafted the bankruptcy section analyzing how income tax is treated in bankruptcy, I asked Bob to edit it. Bob not only rewrote the bankruptcy chapter but he added the bankruptcy explanation and analysis.

Daniel P. Boyle, Esquire was the first to help me begin this project. He developed the list of subjects, and we began research and reading cases. John Rabil, Esquire was there in the early days, too.

Moreover, there has been a constant inner circle of support in my office including Michele Luzetsky and Maureen Polhemus and earlier, Gail Brooks and Judith Velazquez-Alampi.

As I was finishing the book, I realized I needed an editor, book cover artist and interior layout designer. Wow, was I lucky! Through his website www.authorsupport.com, I met Jerry Dorris, who has created the book cover and is doing the design and layout work, too. Jerry introduced me to the editor of the book, Victoria Wright. Her website is www.bookmarkservices.net. These are two whom I cannot thank enough. If you are working on a book or writing project, whatever you do, hire them right away. You will be happy you did, and your work product will look and read better for it. Paul Facenda took the cover photo that makes me look so young, intelligent, and thin. You can contact him at www.facendaphoto.com

There are many friends who, knowingly or not, have helped me through the years. The most significant is Thomas A. Bergstrom, Esquire. I want to thank you, Tom, for your support and guidance as a mentor (in the law) throughout the years.

Rick Kaytes and Ray Bieg have helped on the technology side of the equation. More recently, John Tucker has entered the scene and is helping to support the project.

Fortunately, I have had the support of many family members and friends. The draft book was reviewed by Mary Jean Boyle, Esquire, and Joseph Longobardi, Esquire, who convinced me that TAXJAMS should be the title. Joseph E. Boyle also reviewed several drafts and had the idea of the index of acronyms and forms. I would also like to thank friends Cliff Farmer, Graham Hook, James DiFilippo, CPA, and James Peterson, CPA, for all their support.

I practiced law in New York City for almost a decade. My clients were Jack and Laura Sommer. I want to thank Jack for the friendship we developed over the years when I represented the Sigmund Sommer Trust, his mother, Viola Sommer, and the Sommer Family. I grew as a lawyer and counselor working on the complex matters that faced the Sommer Empire. Sometimes I miss the excitement of the aggressive New York litigation, but my resignation was required as my then-young boys said they did not know me anymore because I was always at work. I had to rethink my daily office commute (Philadelphia to New York) and those sixteen-hour workdays. This *New York Times* article summarizes the stakes: http://www.nytimes.com/1990/01/20/nyregion/in-a-blaze-of-lawsuits-and-appeals-heirs-battle-judge-and-ex-lawyers.html?pagewanted=all&src=pm

While working for the Sommers and Jack in particular, I had the best experience any young lawyer could have practicing his craft.

During those years, I had the pleasure of "lawyering" with my father Daniel J. McCauley Jr., Esquire, and working with many great New York attorneys and some of the best talent New York City had to offer. They included Randy Mastro, Marvin Gersten, Jay Kaplowitz, Leonard Leads, Steve Morelli and the attorneys who worked for me, including Sam McNulty, Anthony Verwey, M. Kevin Hubbard, Lucas Nardini, Daniel J. DeFranceschi, and Dennis Sheehan.

Robert Zimmerman of Zimmerman Eldelson Public Relations was always one of my favorite New York political celebrities. Then we had ample support through Don Brown, Jackie Bluestein, and Frank DeConta who supported the attorney's discovery regiments.

There are a lot of people at IRS who have taught me a trick or two over the years and many of those tricks are offered herein to help you in your case. I guess I remember those in the nearby jurisdictions and offices because I have dealt with them more frequently than those in Fresno, CA. I have forged relationships of mutual respect with many revenue officers such as James Argir, Nick Aquino, Joe Boylan, Jim Berrett, Julian Davis, Margaret Loftus, Susan Johnston, Steve McCarrick, David Knappenberger, Zachery McNichol, Ed Smith, Tom Houghton (retired), and Jim Dugan. There are simply so many ROs and managers I would also like to thank such as: Kim Paulhill, George Albanese, Larry Eberle, John Amenta, Joe Assalone, Jean Batdorf, Jim Berret, Dan Bramble, Kathleen Brown, Michael Castellano, Norman Chapman, Crystal Cole, Keith Coleman, Deborah Combs, Maria Cordts, Rita Dalton, Linda DeMauro, Linda Derma, Edith Dermody, Sean Dunlevy, Jackie Dunn, Nancy Ellingsworth, Ralph Epstein, Brian Fennel, Richard Gavaghan, Fred Gerland (retired), Deborah Gilson, RO Goldner, Ronnette Green, Kurt Gruminger, Leslie Howard, Shelly Howard, Katherine Hutton, RA, Mark Hendrix, Ursula Jackson, Ruth James, Michael James, Cynthia Jones, RuthAnne Kane, Henry Kline, Lois Klouse, Veronica Lampkin, Madeline Lankford, Appeals Manager

Darryl Lee, Robert Ling, Marvina Lewis, Matt Lopes, Carrie Martin, Sandra Martinez, Dionne McLeod, Francis McNichol, Victoria Morris, Yvonne Muse, James Noone, Jackie Olson, Peter Pavlish, Carol Pugh, Scott Ray, Kevin Reed, Marge Renz, Robert Richards (retired), Sandra Rose, Maria Russo, Ed Sacco, Rasheema Abduls Salaam, Ms. Salmon, Judy Samuels, Yvonne Santiago, Abigail Strauss, Peter Shumsky, Kathy Simione, Barbara Smeck, Michael Stella, Gwen Stewart, Marc Tatmon, Mario Tevis, Linda Thomas, Jalyssa Tinneo, Cynthia Topeleski, Reeder Vaniderstein, Katherine Vasta, James F. Ward, Gloria Washington, Latoya White, Derrick Wilson, and Lisa Wold.

To each of you: I thank you.

PROLOGUE

The primary reason I wrote this book is to help level the playing field between you and the IRS, because they have so much knowledge and experience, and you're new at this nerve-wracking game. Since this is probably the first time you have experienced a taxjam, you probably have no idea what they can and will do, nor what you can and must do to protect yourself, and what steps you can and must take to help you solve your taxjam. If your case is under $50,000 in tax you do not have to hire a representative; you can do it yourself, save the money and apply it to your tax debt.

This book specifically covers tax collection and related issues. There are also chapters that discuss options to settle credit card debt, mortgage foreclosure tax issues, specifically the tax consequences of settling those debts. This book is not intended to be an encyclopedia of tax law but instead a self-help book for IRS issues to be used by individuals who need guidance solving them.

If you owe less than $50,000, this text is sufficient in all respects to guide you through your case. If you owe more than $50,000, however, you must first read this text and try to understand your case. If you encounter a significant problem, you can then seek, or be better informed about, how to assist in your representation.

Throughout the text you will see the logo below. This logo indicates that the section where it is located may involve a complex or problematic tax issue. You can contact us with questions or if you just need help with a particular issue such as preparing very old tax returns. I'm here to help, for a reasonable fee, of course. You can also visit the taxjams.com website for forms or information.

URL: taxjams.com | E-mail: info@taxjams.com

CHAPTER 1

Taxpayers Have Rights

WHEN THE IRS KNOCKS

This is the most important thing you should know when moving forward with your tax case. Congress crafted these rights for you in the Taxpayer Bill of Rights.

Declaration of Taxpayer Rights

I. Protection of your Rights.

IRS employees will explain and protect your rights as a taxpayer throughout your contact with them.

II. Privacy and Confidentiality

The IRS will not disclose to anyone the information you give to them, except as authorized by law. You have the right to know why they are asking you for information, how they will use it, and what happens if you do not provide the requested information.

III. Professional and Courteous Service

If you believe that an IRS employee has not treated you in a professional, fair, and courteous manner, you should tell that employee's supervisor. If the supervisor's response is not satisfactory, you should write to your IRS District Director or Service Center Director.

IV. Representation

You may either represent yourself or, with proper written authorization—a Form 2848: Power of Attorney—have someone else represent you in your place. Your representative must be a person allowed to practice before the IRS, such as an attorney, certified public accountant, or enrolled agent. If you are in an interview and ask to consult with such a person, then the IRS must stop and reschedule the interview in most cases.

You can have someone accompany you at an interview. You may make sound recordings of any meetings with our examination, appeal, or collection personnel, provided you tell the IRS in writing 10 days before the meeting.

V. Payment of Only the Correct Amount of Tax

You are responsible for paying only the correct amount of tax due under the law—no more, no less. If you cannot pay all of your tax when it is due, you may be able to make monthly installment payments.

VI. Help with Unresolved Tax Problems

The National Taxpayer Advocate's Problem Resolution Program can help you if you have tried unsuccessfully to resolve a problem with the IRS. Your local Taxpayer Advocate can offer you special help if you have a significant hardship as a result of a tax problem. For more information, call toll-free 1-877-777-4778 (1-800-829-4059 for users with hearing or speech difficulties) or write to the Taxpayer Advocate at the IRS office that last contacted you.

VII. Appeals and Judicial Review

If you disagree with IRS about the amount of your tax liability or certain collection actions, you have the right to ask the IRS Appeals Office to review your case. You may also ask the court to review your case.

VIII. Relief From Certain Penalties and Interest

The IRS will waive penalties when allowed by law if you can show you acted reasonably and in good faith or relied on the incorrect advice of an IRS employee. IRS will waive interest that is the result of certain errors or delays caused by an IRS employee.

As a taxpayer, you must know and understand the Declaration of Taxpayer's Rights. The IRS, at the first point of contact, gives a copy of these rights to you. They are listed in Publication 1. I have included a copy of Publication 1 at the end in the forms index. After reading Publication 1, take time to learn your options and think out your possible courses of action. Meanwhile, however, here are a few hints that may make one of life's least pleasant experiences a little less stressful and risky.

1. The best scenario is for you to be tax compliant, which means that you have prepared and filed all of your tax returns (See Chapter 2 on Tax Compliance).
2. It is crucial that all communications with the revenue officer (RO) must be truthful. If not, a simple mistake in a question and answer session could become the basis for a criminal case for perjury.
3. It is important to provide all documentation requested by the

RO. If the documents cannot be located quickly, tell the RO so she doesn't jump to sinister conclusions.

4. It is essential to communicate quickly, efficiently, and *on time* with the RO, which will benefit you later when you are negotiating a payment or asking for a penalty to be reduced or abated.

If you are going to owe the IRS money—or what the IRS representatives call a "balance due"—then you will have to fill out a Collection Information Statement which will show your finances. At this point, you may negotiate repayment through an Installment Agreement (See Chapter 9 on Collection Information Statements).

In the Beginning of Your Case

In a typical case, the revenue officer (RO) will hand you Publication 1 and ask if you know your rights. In most cases, people respond "yes" without reading the Taxpayer's Bill of Rights (TBOR). Wrong answer.

Read Publication 1. *These are your rights.* Take time to consider those rights as listed in the TBOR. Know what you are required to do, what you are permitted to do, and have a plan of action. For example, do you know what you can do when there is an IRS representative at the door? I want you to be prepared and know exactly what to do.

If you are nervous, panicking, or feeling intimidated by the IRS, hire a representative. Hiring someone to handle your tax case will remove you from the firing line and reduce the stress until your case is resolved or closed.

In tax matters, a representative is someone with special training to practice before the IRS, such as an attorney, a certified public accountant, or an enrolled agent. Most important, I am talking about a representative who limits his practice to this type of matter. If the issue is an audit, then be sure your representative handles audits *all the time*. If a tax lien has been filed against you, then the representative should handle tax liens *every day*.

Experience is the key to success. Do not be bashful! Ask the following specific questions of the representative to make sure you are hiring the right person for the job:

1. Are you a lawyer, CPA, or enrolled agent? Can you sign a Form 2848?
2. Do you do these kind of cases exclusively and if so for how long?
3. Have you handled a case like mine?
4. What can I expect you to do and what do you expect me to do?
5. I am willing to be there when you need me in phone conferences or meetings; do you want me to be present? I like my clients there, but I prefer to do most of the talking.
6. If tax returns are needed can they prepare the returns quickly?
7. Who in your firm will be my representative and do you guarantee that person will stay on my case?
8. What is the timeframe you estimate my case will take and what do you think the outcome will be?

If you are speaking to a gatekeeper and not your potential representative, ask to speak to him or her. If that is not possible, for whatever reason, that is indicative of future problems. Big red flag. Know who will be assigned to your case. *Be sure your representative(s) will be accessible and responsive.* Otherwise, keep looking. It is imperative that you are comfortable with your representative.

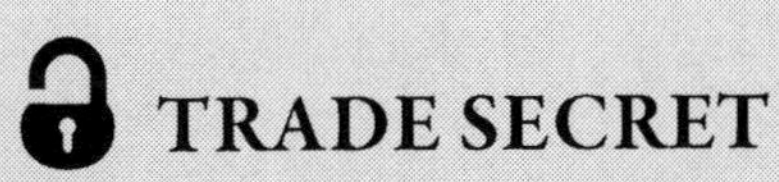

🔓 TRADE SECRET

If the representative answers the questions, you are insulated from making a mistake because you are nervous.

IRS officers are trained to extract information from you not only by listening to the answers you give, but also by observing your tone of voice, your body language, and even the innocuous nervous twitch; everything is being noted. Even aside from the average taxpayer's lack of expertise in the field, this is the best reason to keep the nervous taxpayer off of the firing line.

I prefer my client to be present as a silent observer, while I answer the questions. In this role, the taxpayer helps his case by his willingness to appear, but he doesn't jeopardize his case by sticking his foot in his mouth. His presence helps gain credibility with the RO and eliminates the need to wait for a simple answer or agreement with the schedule to provide more extensive information.

The Power of Attorney

If you decide to hire a representative, you will have to authorize the IRS to speak to him or the IRS will not recognize the individual as your representative. To do this, you must complete an IRS Form 2848. This form is not a durable Power of Attorney. The Power of Attorney is limited and specific, and IRS will only allow the representative to discuss matters specifically identified in the form by you. This is for your privacy and protection. For more information on Power of Attorney, see Chapter 22.

> *Do not answer questions without a chance to review the facts.*

The Pitfalls of Going it Alone

For example, if the RO were to ask: "Have you filed your most recent tax return?" and you say yes, and either you did not do so, or the return is not on record in the services files, this could suggest perjury. Among other potential charges are obstruction of a criminal investigation, obstruction generally, subornation of perjury, false statements, aiding and abetting false statements, obstructing or impeding the administration of Title 26, conspiracy, and aiding and abetting.

On the other hand, if you say, "No, I didn't file those tax returns," that is an admission that could initiate a criminal prosecution for each tax return that is not filed. Federal laws (statutes) can be violated by a simple misstatement, or exaggeration, to any question the RO could ask. You may think you are talking to a revenue officer, but you are really discussing your case with a criminal investigator. Do not lie to, volunteer information to, chat with the CI (criminal investigator).

Rather than answer a direct question off the cuff, ask for time to check your records or *hire a representative to answer for you*. I recommend that if you don't know the answer with specificity you say, "I can't explain that. I need to check my records first," or "I don't have an answer to that right now, but I will get it for you in two weeks," or "I can't answer that question," or "I don't have that information with me."

Let the RO know that while you may not yet fully understand all aspects of your case, you will be responsible and responsive in compiling the documentation needed for the path towards resolution. Don't be afraid to ask the RO what her intentions are and keep open the lines of communication. If you do not have the requested information within the specified timeframe, forward what you do have and let the RO know that it will take you an extended period of time to compile the rest. For example; your accountant may need an additional week to complete a tax return for you. Communication—very important. Do not hide from or ignore a tax issue. Just because IRS mail notifications stop coming or phone calls seem to stop; do not think your case has magically disappeared.

To Recap

1. Listen carefully, and when the RO provides Publication 1, read it carefully and, after consideration, decide what you are going to do, and execute.
2. If you are going to handle your own case, ask for a schedule to provide tax returns, financial records, and any other information requested.
3. When you agree, make sure the timing is realistic because if you miss a date, the penalty is enforced collection, which is a bank levy or a wage garnishment. Enforced collection could also encompass a summons to produce documents for inspection, or audit, or court action.
4. Be clear what you are agreeing to do and be certain of the timeframe.

A Brief Warning

Most tax cases are civil cases to collect tax owed by taxpayers, not criminal cases to put them in jail. If, at any point, the RO or CI reads you the Miranda Warning, *you must immediately stop talking and hire an attorney*. When your Miranda rights enter the picture, you are in a criminal case. There is nothing ambiguous about it. Notify them of your intentions to remain silent until you have a lawyer in the room with you. Then close your mouth.

Below is the Miranda Warning so that you will know the difference between that and Publication 1.

Miranda Warnings

- You have the right to remain silent.
- Anything you say can and will be used against you in a court of law.
- You have the right to speak to an attorney.
- If you cannot afford an attorney, one will be appointed for you.
- Do you understand your rights?

CHAPTER 2

Tax Compliance

com.pli.ance *noun* a: conformity in fulfilling official requirements; b: the act or process of complying with a desire, demand, proposal, or regimen or the coercion. Specifically, with tax compliance, a taxpayer
(1) must file all outstanding tax returns, stop pyramiding or continuing to increase liabilities by paying any balance due/owed for the current tax year and make/pay estimated tax payments for the coming year if required to prevent future tax liabilities;
(2) file all outstanding tax returns and become current in payments for six months before the service will permit entering an installment agreement or other method of resolution.

To win your case you must be tax compliant.

Tax Compliance

The hallmark of the American tax system is voluntary tax compliance. Voluntary compliance means that you obey the law without threat. The object of this book is to teach those of you with a tax liability how to analyze your case, and organize it to become tax compliant. Once you are compliant, the IRS can—and will—work with you.

My definition is: Tax compliance means first that all of your tax returns are prepared *accurately*, filed *on time*, and paid *in full*.

You also must be mindful that you still have to pay tax for future income either through your employer withholding or, if self-employed, through filing timely estimated tax payments.

Generally, tax liabilities are *civil* administrative cases, but the government may also bring *criminal* charges. For example, a non-filer may not have filed income tax returns for the past five years. For each year the taxpayer has an obligation to file but does not do so, he is subject—criminally—to one-year imprisonment plus fines and costs, *and* penalty and interest on the tax. Taxpayers who have failed to file or pay employment taxes (Form 941) are subject to similar criminal sanctions.

The question is: How to resolve the tax case at issue and keep the taxpayer under the radar of the criminal investigation department? This will keep the case in civil collection. Paying the money is better than doing the time, from your perspective and from the IRS's point of view, too.

I will say it again: Tax compliance is critical for the IRS to work with you. If you only learn one thing about tax cases, this is it:

> *Tax compliance is the key to success.*

Non-compliant taxpayers may be faced with enforced collection, which is a very painful, embarrassing, and stressful process. The service prepares and files the missing tax returns, if necessary, then files associated tax liens, provides notice of the lien and a right to a hearing, and then, through enforced collection, can levy accounts or third-party payer income, and/or garnish wages. If the IRS cannot levy enough to pay the tax lien, they can seize personal and real property for auction (see www.irsauction.gov).

In other words, the IRS has what it takes to take what you have.

The point of this book is to help you figure out how to resolve your case and make it "unattractive" to the criminal investigation department, thereby keeping the case in civil collection. A taxpayer does not have an unequivocal right to run up tax debts, owe the government money, and demand an installment agreement, especially when he has the money stashed in an investment account, equity in his house, or hidden in asset sales or transfers. Be careful not to confuse asset protection with a fraudulent transfer of assets. The goal is to protect your assets to the maximum extent permitted by the law, without broaching into tax fraud. If you are concerned about whether your conduct regarding asset protection might be considered tax fraud, see the Asset Protection section in Chapter 4.

Do you owe the service returns or money or both? If you neglect to file returns, the IRS can use information it collects on you to prepare very aggressive tax returns for you. These are referred to as substitutes for returns, or SFRs. The IRS prepares these returns for you if their records indicate that you owe money to them.

Be optimistic; many times when the original returns are prepared by the taxpayer, he has a lower liability, owing significantly less than in the SFRs. You, the taxpayer, can prepare and file original returns. The process of submitting the late but original return is formally called "audit reconsideration." (see Chapter 19 – Audit Reconsideration). Audit reconsideration is a terrific, almost secret, process that can benefit a non-filer allowing him to file old original returns, thereby replacing the high balance owed on the SFR. Don't wait, you can save money with this process and end the jam. I know you simply hear the word "audit" and cringe, but by preparing and filing these past due returns, you are becoming a compliant taxpayer. The IRS looks (comparatively) benevolently upon taxpayers who voluntarily return to the fold. In this arena, the service is exceptionally helpful. Many non-filers are surprised and relieved to learn the process exists. Typically, if the taxpayer comes into compliance on his own accord, the service will not criminally prosecute him for the prior failure to file.

> *REMEMBER—YOU MUST BE TAX COMPLIANT FROM NOW ON!*

Tax compliance is critical to safely avoid criminal prosecution. Moreover, you must be, *and remain,* in compliance to receive any agreement from IRS. Remember, if you are in an installment agreement, for instance, you cannot file an extension on April 15. You must file the original tax return to remain in compliance. The extension to file will/may default your agreement and then we have to do all that work again, and it is harder the second time.

CHAPTER 3

Case Analysis

The Ivy League Blunder: Why You Must Do a Case Analysis

Many years ago, the phone rang. Two Ivy League-educated professionals were calling about our services. I explained that we always started each case the same way—first we filed the Form 2848: Power of Attorney, and then we performed an in-depth case analysis. We would request documents and information from both the IRS and the client. Next, I would review the case to determine the client's options. Moreover, we put the options before the client either in a telephone conference or in writing, so that the client would have an opportunity to think it over.

One of these Ivy Leaguers had a large tax issue: he had not filed tax returns for many, many years. The bulk of his problem and tax liability seemed to stem from the late 1990s, when he was a consultant earning a lot of money. The other Ivy Leaguer was his close friend and attorney. She was trying to help her non-filing friend mend his ways.

The IRS had prepared substitutes for returns (SFRs) for the taxpayer in the late 1990s and there was a liability of approximately $1.5 million dollars, which included tax, penalties, and interest. By 2003 or so, the Ivy Leaguer had gone into semi-retirement, becoming a W-2 employee with adequate withholding. It appeared from our conversations that he had significant assets, both in real estate and in other investments.

The two of them contacted us numerous times to discuss the issues of their case. They had a lot of questions. We insisted they needed a thorough case analysis to determine their best options. They even had us send them a draft power of attorney, a retainer agreement, and other documentation that we required for the formal representation. After a two-week whirlwind of long discussions, during which these Ivy Leaguers collected just enough information to be dangerous, they disappeared.

Nine months later, the attorney half of this team called, extremely excited. She stated that she had prepared *and filed* all of the tax returns that her friend had never filed.

Now, as you will learn in this book, the statute of limitations, ten years in collection cases, was soon to expire and when it did, the liability attached from the IRS-prepared tax returns (1990s) would be forever forgiven. The Ivy Leaguer had trusted his friend, who was not a tax attorney, and as a result, incurred over a million dollars of new tax liability. Neither of these Ivy League-educated professionals understood the statute of limitations and the expiration of the collection statute, an issue covered in my case analysis and book. Nor did they understand that while one might prepare new returns hoping for refunds, it was smarter not to prepare the old returns, which were nearing the expiration of the collection statute. Instead the taxpayer could choose to accept the IRS SFRs and let them expire.

I explained to the attorney what she had done. She had restarted the 10-year collection statute on the high-liability years of the late 1990s, which had been about to expire on the IRS prepared SFRs. She began to stammer. I asked if she had malpractice insurance. She quickly ended the conversation. Neither of these people has been heard from since.

The moral of the story is: Understand Your Case! Make sure you start with a thorough case review and analysis.

The case analysis is the most important aspect of your case.

I know it's painful, but you must read this chapter and complete the case review process. It is crucial that you know the details of your case, such as which tax returns you need to file and which forms you need to complete. Only after you master your case and organize your records can you move forward. In other words, if you hope to resolve your case successfully, and with the lowest possible tax liability, you have to suck it up and organize all of your information—the good, the bad, the ugly. Now.

From now on, you will open all IRS correspondence.

You need to know what the IRS has done already, and what it is going to do next, so that you can respond appropriately. To prevent adverse assessments, penalties, liens, seizures, and levies—and save the most money possible—you must address all communications on time. Therefore, from this day forward, you will

- sign for all certified mail,
- read the mail,
- respond to document requests,
- compile records, and
- answer questions immediately

so your taxjam can be settled as fast as possible.

As you will learn in Chapter 7 (Appeal Rights), the IRS will notify you—via certified mail—that the US Constitution grants you the due process rights to appeal adverse IRS actions all the way to Tax Court.

However, if you miss the appeal deadline set forth in the certified mail, *you forever waive your rights.*

The best practice is to file the appeal, since you can always withdraw it later. Furthermore, during an appeal, the IRS will not levy or seize assets because the statute of limitations is "tolled" or temporarily stopped.

Change of Address

If you are not receiving mail from the IRS you may have changed your address without notifying the IRS. You can call the IRS to change your address in their files or complete Form 8822: Change of Address, and mail it to them (see index of exhibits).

Step One: Organizing Tax Records

1. Gather all of your historical tax information. The best practice is to start with the current year and go back at least seven years.
2. Keep your filed tax returns (and the corresponding backup documentation) in separate files by year in your retention register. The tax retention register can be a simple waterproof plastic box, a safe deposit box, or a digital file where you will retain your important tax return information for future reference. If your tax returns are already prepared, you will keep the tax records organized by year in the retention register for future reference. You will retain all your returns, backup documentation, and relevant correspondence in the retention register in either a physical or digital form.
3. If some or all of your tax returns are not filed, you need to open a file folder for each year and begin to organize your financial information so that you can have the returns accurately prepared. You will then sign, date, and file the tax returns with the IRS and relevant state(s). Each tax return should be mailed in a separate

envelope. Store the copies of the tax returns for future reference in the physical or digital retention register.

4. Open and sort any old IRS or state tax mail you have accumulated. You will sort the mail two ways. First, sort the mail by its relevant tax year. Next, organize the mail by date, with the oldest date on the bottom of the pile for the particular tax year. So, for example, when it is all organized you will have all of the mail about the 2008 tax return in one pile with the oldest letter on the bottom and the most recent letter on the top. Organize and classify all correspondence for each tax year—2009, 2010, 2011—this way too. Keep this correspondence in the same folder as the tax return and backup for the relevant tax year in your retention register. If there is too much mail for one folder you can put it in another file folder and label it 2008 IRS Mail. You are making great progress. Keep up the good work!

5. Go through your tax files, year by year (oldest first), and make a list of which tax returns have been prepared and filed and which ones still need to be prepared. Balances owed can be determined from correspondence in your files. If you are missing some information, don't be concerned; you will be updating your records with information from the IRS next. For now, fill in the list of taxes filed by year and/or the amount owed to the IRS and the relevant state. See Exhibit Index for the Form: Case Analysis Call to the IRS.

IRS Information Master Files

You will now collect valuable information from the IRS so you can determine if your records and history are accurate and complete. This will help you complete the tax history portion of the case review. It is very important that you gather all the information available to prepare any non-filed tax returns or to file an amended return.

The IRS has certain income information that was provided to them by third parties such as banks, brokerage firms, mortgage services, employers, casinos, and such. These parties provide information such as W-2 and Forms 1099 and 1098, which can assist you in preparing accurate tax returns. You will ask the IRS representative to mail you copies of the wage and income files or transcripts that contain this information.

The IRS maintains two primary files on each taxpayer. First, there is an Information Master File (IMF) that contains a record of each tax year. The account transcript, as it is titled, contains the data from the IMF for every year you file, and also has amounts you owe. If it is within the last three years you can ask for a return transcript, which is an account transcript with much more detail. These are only kept for three years; then the system purges the detail and keeps the account transcript. The tax return information is saved by year.

The account transcript contains other basic data: filing status—single, married filing jointly, married filing separately, head of household—the date the return was filed by you or prepared by the IRS, amount of income, taxable income, payments, the dates when notices were sent to you, etc. Other data in the account transcript includes the amount of tax paid, amount of tax owed, penalties for late filing and/or late payment, and the interest due on the tax and penalties, too.

The IRS also maintains a second file on every taxpayer for each tax year, the Information Return Master File (IRMF), which retains wage and income data filed by third parties such as W-2, Forms 1099 and 1098, IRA transaction info, stock account transactions, pension value information, bankruptcy information, and other miscellaneous financial information including, but not limited to, cash transactions over $10,000. These transcripts are called wage and income transcripts. You will request these for

- each year you need to file a tax return,

- each year in which there is an audit, or
- each year for which you intend to amend the original return.

The best practice is to obtain wage and income transcripts for every tax return you file or amend and maintain these in your retention register by tax year.

Congratulations! You are approaching clarity in your tax case history.

1. You have compiled the tax document, transcripts, returns, and IRS correspondence for at least the last seven tax years.
2. You have ascertained whether you filed a tax return in each of those years.
3. You know whether you owe anything to the IRS, or to the state, and the relevant collection statute end date.

In Chapter 15, Statute of Limitations, you will find a detailed explanation of the limitations of collection and the expiration of the tax lien by the passing of time—10 years. This is referred to as the Collection Statute End Date (CSED).

Step Two: Call the IRS and Confirm the Information

The next step in your case analysis is to call the IRS to confirm this information. See Form Case Analysis Call to IRS (below).

When you call the IRS, you want to follow the prompts to order transcripts. We are only calling collections if a levy has already been issued. You may call the IRS at 1-800-829-3903.

TAX JAMS™

Case Analysis: Call to IRS Form

IRS Representative (have rep spell name):

Agent's ID Number (get this number right):

Office Address (city & state):

TAX YEAR	FILED or SFR*	AMOUNT OWED	CSED**
2000			
2001			
2002			
2003			
2004			
2005			
2006			
2007			
2008			
2009			
2010			
2011			
2012			

*SFR – Substitute for Return (prepared by IRS)

**CSED – Collection Statute End Date

Have the form ready and the list of information you have compiled thus far in your case analysis. Remain calm. If you feel nervous when you are speaking with the IRS representative, just tell her that you are too nervous and will call back later. Believe me, it will not be the first time they have heard that.

You must follow the script that is laid out for you.

1. Ask and write down the person's name and ID number so you know and document with whom you are speaking.

2. Give the IRS representative your personal information so they can look you up in the computer and discuss your case history with you.

3. After exchanging basic information, explain that you are attempting to obtain information of your tax history and copies

of transcripts so you can become compliant and know the amount, if any, you owe the IRS.

The representative will know what you need and will try to help you get the information, transcripts or documents you request, such as a CP-2000 letter—ask if any are present and if they are have her send you copies. Ask her to go through your IMF files and determine:

1. if a tax return was filed for each year. If so, get the date and ask whether the tax return was prepared by the IRS (an SFR) or was it an original return;

2. what amount is owed, if any;

3. what is the collection statute end date (CSED), if any money is owed; and

4. again, if there is a CP-2000 filed to any of your tax returns, changing the content on the return you filed; request the rep to print it and fax or mail it to you. This return can be reviewed and amended. Often it is a social security number that was written wrong and it can be adjusted on the phone call, sometimes you need to amend the return.

If you would prefer not to speak with an IRS agent, there is an automated transcript ordering system. Simply call 1-800-908-9946, and follow the instructions.

If this collateral issue exists, a non-filed tax year and a resulting SFR, you need to read Chapter 19, Audit Reconsideration, for instructions on amending your return, how to file an original return even after the IRS has prepared the SFR, how to have the original late filed return accepted and processed as quickly as possible, and where to mail it.

To determine whether a substitute for return (SFR) was filed by the IRS, check your account transcript. If any of the listed transactions, state that the IRS created a SFR, this probably means that the SFR was filed. However, if you subsequently filed your return, call the IRS to determine whether your current tax liability is based on the SFR or the original return you filed. This is an important distiction because SFRs tend to have the taxpayer's income but no business expenses (deductions); thus, the tax is overstated. Therefore, these returns need to be replaced by original returns in order to fix your prior error(s) and save yourself as much money as possible.

A word on substitute for returns (SFRs): The SFR emanates from a notice of deficiency. The IRS sends the notice to you with the expectation that you will prepare an accurate original tax return, sign it, and file it with them. Instead some taxpayers allow the process to continue to the assessment of the tax and eventually the filing of a tax lien. But you *can* file original returns and this process is addressed in Chapter 19, Audit Reconsideration. See also Penalty Abatement (Chapter 12).

The chapter on audit reconsideration is very important to non-filers and covers how you can prepare an original return and file it with the IRS and have the old, normally very large balance reduced to the true and accurate balance. A non-filer is a taxpayer who has not filed two or more tax returns. If this is your situation, you will need the wage and income transcripts mentioned above for the relevant years. These transcripts will have the income information provided to the IRS by third parties required for your tax return. This will support your tax records. Non-filers who are married must consider the asset protection section in Chapter 4 for techniques to protect their joint property or at least half of it.

If you are self-employed, you will need to assemble your business expenses that can be deducted from your income. Your tax preparer will help you identify what expenses you should compile and provide. Start assembling bank statements, copies of checks, and invoices.

When you call the IRS you will be seeking a total of the tax owed and the penalties and interest owed to the IRS. Also ask for a list of tax returns that need to be prepared.

Levy Form 668-A: Wage Garnishments

Now, if you have an emergency—such as a levy or wage garnishment—you must ask for a release of the levy to be sent to the third party. Providing the fax number of the payroll department or bank levy department speeds things up immensely, so be prepared with the right information before calling. Also read Chapter 6, The Taxpayer Advocate, and file Form 911 *immediately*.

If the IRS representative grants the request to release the levy, you'll be lucky. Normally, the IRS representative will require tax compliance and the financials (known as a Collection Information Statement, or CIS) to establish an installment agreement before releasing the levy unless the case is under $50,000 in tax. See the next section, Streamlined Cases.

If the present situation is a hardship turn to Chapter 7, Form 911—The Taxpayer Advocate. File the form, but expect to wait several days before being contacted. After you accurately prepare and file Form 911, begin to prepare Form 433-F: Collection Information Statement, if you owe more than $50,000 in tax. By beginning the collection information statement now you will have the form and backup documentation ready for the advocate when the advocate first contacts you.

In the meantime, you can move forward trying to release the levy and set up an installment agreement and request penalty abatement, too. Be sure to read each relevant chapter and follow the IRS protocol so the request is not summarily rejected without review because it is inadequate. Also, remember to take steps to appeal adverse decisions. In the appeal, you can hire a representative, re-file the paperwork and have a second bite at the apple. If you fail to file your appeal on time, your rights are forever extinguished. *This is a bad day for the taxpayer.* See Chapter 7, Appeal Rights and the Appeals Process.

Streamlined Cases

If your tax liability is under $50,000 in tax and you are tax compliant—that is, your tax returns are current and you have adequate withholding or estimated taxes being made—your case is streamlined. This means that if you can afford to make payments, you can submit an offer to the IRS for a streamlined installment agreement (See Chapter 11, Installment Agreements) based on payments of the amount owed over seventy-two months. However, if you cannot afford this, there are several good options. Start with Chapter 10, Currently not Collectible Status, and also read Chapter 13 on Bankruptcy. Yes, income taxes can be discharged in bankruptcy after meeting specific date sensitive thresholds.

In writing or in a call to IRS collections, or through Form 911, you can ask for penalty abatement, either answering questions over the phone or filing a letter requesting the abatement. If you have a good tax history, usually the agent will grant one or two years penalty abatement. See Chapter 12. This is referred to as the dog bite rule. Dogs can get away with one "free" bite, after which the authorities have strict penalties. Fortunately, as of this writing, the IRS still stops short of actually having recalcitrant taxpayers put to sleep.

Again, before calling collections, read the relevant sections - so you are versed on the legal issues and standards. For example, Chapter 12, Penalty Abatement, will provide an understanding of "reasonable cause," the legal standard the IRS relies upon to grant penalty abatement. In Chapter 17 (Injured Spouse), you will learn why the IRS is withholding refunds from a non-liable spouse and how to request the funds back.

In cases over $50,000, you can call automated collections, with your financial information prepared (See Chapter 9, Collection Information

Statements), and try to negotiate your installment agreement or currently not collectible status. This way, you can prevent a surprise by the enforced collection unit such as levies and seizures. See Chapter 8, Collection Financial Standards, to understand the budget numbers IRS allows.

You will use the collection information statement to perform perhaps the most important function—to resolve your case and lower the tax, penalties, and interest. Remember: You must remain tax compliant to obtain relief from the IRS, so continue to accurately prepare and file your tax returns before April 15 and *without extensions*.

There are actually three parts to your case, the past, the present, and the future. We want to correct the past as best we can, we want to be compliant in the present and we must remain compliant for the IRS to work with us in the future. Once this is accomplished we can try other case resolution methods such as an offer in compromise (Chapter 14) or Chapter 16, Innocent Spouse.

Collecting and Organizing Tax Returns

I want you to complete the Case Analysis Form in the forms index. If you have filed the return and owe nothing, you can put a zero in the column. If you owe money, you should know what how much is owed and insert it across from the year. After putting all the tax debts on the Case Analysis form, you will have a list of the amounts owed. Next to the amount owed, you should request the collection statute end date (CSED) for each year so that you know when the obligation for that particular year will expire. See specifically Chapter 15, Statute of Limitations, for a detailed explanation of CSED and tax debt expiration.

Be careful—you need to know the CSED. If it is about to expire you must consider the ramifications of filing the original return because you will start the 10-year statute of limitations on collection anew. If there will be a balance due by filing the original return, you may choose not to file the original return; the result will be that you will keep the current SFR balance due through to expiration—the CSED. However, if you are considering bankruptcy the SFR cannot be discharged because it is not an original return so you must read about discharging income taxes in Chapter 13, Bankruptcy—and *discuss this issue with bankruptcy counsel.*

On your case analysis list, there may be returns that need to be filed. If you need to prepare returns quickly and cannot prepare the tax returns yourself, you can call us for the limited assignment to help you prepare the returns or immediately go to a local tax return preparer for help. The wage and income transcripts you asked the IRS to print and send to you are important in this regard and should be provided to the tax preparer. The case analysis list may have SFRs prepared by the IRS and amounts owed to the IRS and other years may not be filed yet. First, you should file the years where neither an original return nor an SFR is filed. This way, you become tax compliant and IRS can work with you. You can go back later and file the old original returns to replace the SFRs. Before filing any tax returns, make sure to read the sections of Chapter 4, Tricks of the Trade, regarding asset protection and filing status, payment of tax and extending payment deadlines using Form 1127.

After all returns are filed and you are current with the estimated tax payments or have adequate withholding by your employer, you have met the tax compliance requirement. Now you can move forward to wrap up the case. Chapter 9, Collection Information Statements, is the next step. You must be prepared to negotiate. If you have sufficient income you may be negotiating an installment agreement, so read

Chapter 11 next. Penalty abatement is one of the favorite resolution alternatives of most taxpayers, so also read Chapter 12.

Be mindful in the discussions with a revenue officer or automated collections at the IRS that, if you have significant equity in assets, the IRS will ask you to borrow against it to pay them the amount owed. The IRS is not a credit card company—they do not permit unsecured loans at your discretion. When you borrow at the IRS there are consequences, such as tax liens. If you are intransigent, the IRS will issue levies and seize assets. Thus, if you have savings or retirement accounts, these may be used to pay the IRS. In short, the IRS will search for assets to pay the debt. *Hiding assets is dangerous.* Do not transfer assets to a friend, or that friend may become your cellmate. Read Chapter 5, Liens and Levies, to understand that the IRS has an inchoate "secret" lien when the liability exists—that is when the tax return is filed, even before the lien is filed publicly.

On the other hand, if your Form 433-A: Collection Information Statement (see forms index), shows a paucity of assets or income you can request currently not collectible status and then try an offer in compromise or, if that is rejected, bankruptcy. Your spouse may be considered an innocent spouse or injured spouse if she works and is not liable for the tax debt. So, she must review Chapters 16 and 17.

Non-filers—those who need to file two or more tax returns—may consider what filing status to choose if married filing separately or jointly. If one spouse had withholding and the other did not have adequate withholding the tax returns need to be prepared both ways— married filing jointly and married filing separately—so you can see the consequences. Why should you file jointly and make both spouses responsible for the taxjam of one spouse? See the asset protection discussion in Chapter 4, Tricks of the Trade.

A Word to Tax Protestors

I have one word to say to those of you who protest our tax system: FILE! Those who advocate the tax protestor position and do not file tax returns are criminally prosecuted. The leaders of the movement are charging monthly fees to their followers for letters, subscriptions to their brochures, and books to make money from their followers. They preach lies about the tax code and our Constitution. The Supreme Court has decided the tax protestor arguments and issues.

I will not argue the tax protestor position. When you decide to file accurate tax returns, I will do my best to help you live up to your obligations as a citizen. If your position is that you are not a citizen, then move.

I have seen many ordinary people caught up by the tax protestor organizer who is a very convincing speaker. In reality, he is telling unsubstantiated lies so he can profit. In most cases, the taxpayer is told to file zero income tax returns and this goes on for many years, yet he has substantial income. When the IRS begins filing Substitute for Returns (SFRs) and piling on penalties and interest, the taxpayer is financially devastated. Many of the cases result in a crafty offer in compromise which the IRS rejects because of the case history and ultimately the former tax protestor is reduced to bankruptcy.

CHAPTER 4

Tricks of the Trade

Emergencies

**If you are suffering from a Bank Levy, Asset Seizure, Lien,
or Wage Garnishment:**

If you have just learned the Automated Collections System (ACS) has violated you by seizing your assets, you must immediately file Form 911 for the tax advocate's assistance. Turn now to Chapter 6 on the Taxpayer Advocate. In this section is sample wording for you to include on Form 911. The sooner you file this request for relief of hardship, the higher the probability you will get a release of the levy. After you file the Form 911, proceed to Chapter 3, Case Analysis, because you may need to file tax returns to become compliant or take other proactive measures and begin Form 433-A or 433-F: Collection Information Statement.

How to Make Payments to the IRS to Your Advantage

Cases can be won or lost by properly allocating payments made to the IRS. You will learn right now how to make voluntary payments to the IRS to your advantage. The object in an income tax case is to make voluntary payments to be applied to "tax first." If there is no designation on the check, the IRS can (and will) apply the payment in their favor, to penalty and interest.

In a business tax case, you (the business owner) want to make all voluntary payments to the trust fund portion of the tax first. This minimizes your personal liability. You, the business owner, will be personally assessed by the IRS for the trust fund assessment, that is, the employees' withholding tax which was not paid by the entity; this does not include the matching tax or penalty and interest. So, the sooner you or the business entity start making voluntary payments, the better. Just make certain they are directed to the "trust fund portion of the tax," and keep copies of the cancelled checks.

Making payments is a simple process. Make the payment to the IRS by check and make sure you *keep a copy*. Remember—with certified checks and money orders you will not get the check back, the bank or issuer will. Make the check payable to the Department of Treasury. In the memo section write the end numbers of your social security number and how the check is to be applied. "Tax first" and the year or "trust fund tax first" in a business employment tax case.

If this is a trust fund tax payment from you or the business, make the check payable to the Department of Treasury, and in the memo section write the company tax identification number and "<u>trust fund portion of tax</u>" and the period, if known. It is all right if you do not know which period it is, but be sure to write "trust fund tax" in the memo section.

Keep a copy of every check and store them somewhere sensible so you never have to tear the place apart to look for them in the future, when the IRS knocks.

Lien Payoff & Lien Releases

To obtain the amount you will need to pay off the IRS lien you can call the IRS directly, fax a request (to 1-859-669-3805), or file Form 911 and fax or mail it to the address on the form, requesting assistance from the tax advocate to ascertain the amount needed to pay the lien in full and to obtain a copy of the Release of Lien. The lien payoff department can be reached at 1-800-913-6050.

Lien releases are very important documents, yet most people do not know how to exploit them to their maximum advantage. The obvious first step is to be sure that the IRS has issued a release of lien and filed it with the county courthouse—where the original lien was filed—to mark it satisfied or, better yet, have it removed from the credit bureau records. Second, obtain a copy of this document from the IRS or the local courthouse, make copies of it, and send it to all of the credit reporting bureaus. Request that they remove the lien from your files. Typically they will mark the lien satisfied. This is great because, in our experience, credit scores rise significantly with the satisfaction designation; the credit report now shows an ability to pay more debt, and the debt to credit ratio changes, which is a benefit to the account holder. Even if you don't understand the theory behind it, trust me—the net result of the lien satisfaction provides a huge boost to the credit score.

Now back to the tax advocate: Requesting that the lien be removed from the record is possible if you can demonstrate that the lien being of record (visible for all the world to see) jeopardizes your ability to earn a living. For example, people who work in the world of finance, even people who work with money in stores, are generally not hired because of an existing tax lien, because many employers view tax liens as a security risk. This argument must be made to the advocate who, in turn, will argue it on your behalf to the IRS.

Tax Liens cause havoc for small businesses too. Try to borrow money from a bank or a leasing company when you have tax liens. My view is: Banks should lend money to satisfy a tax lien if the borrower has sufficient assets to borrow against, especially SBA. But, the Small Business Administration does not lend to a person who has a tax lien regardless of the strength of the credit or the assets of the borrower. This just doesn't seem right to me.

Thirty-Day Hold on Account

A 30-day hold is time you request from Automated Collection System (ACS) to compile information for the IRS, during which the IRS agrees not to utilize enforced collection against you. To obtain this hold, all you need to do is ask. It is better to ask for a 30-day hold on your account while you compile information rather than to give off-the-cuff answers that are wrong, and which it will be almost impossible to change later. This brief period buys you time to gather and organize your information to prepare for your next call or meeting; meanwhile, the IRS will not levy or take collection action against you. *Do not waste this valuable time*, because a levy is right around the corner. The service expects you to use this time to take steps towards tax compliance.

While talking to the IRS representative, you must get organized to prepare any outstanding tax returns. Don't forget to ask the representative to fax or mail you copies of your wage and income transcripts for the relevant tax years. These are the Form W-2 and 1099s you received in the years you did not file and which you will need to prepare those old returns. For non-filers who owe several tax returns, this can be overwhelming because of the amount of work ahead. Organizing is critical. Remember, you can mock-up a quick tax return from the wage and income transcripts and amend the return later, so relax. The IRS has the last ten years tax returns on its website.

The problems begin when the taxpayer is not compliant, so if you have any outstanding tax returns, ask for a 30-day hold, as described above, to obtain time to become compliant. If you have outstanding tax returns, you will commonly receive 30 days to accurately prepare, sign, and file the return(s). Expect the representative to give you a call-back date.

> *DO NOT FORGET the call-back date. You must call back or a bank levy or wage garnishment will issue.*

Your case is now in hold status for 30 days. Begin to prepare the Form 433-A (See Chapter 9, Collection Information Statements). Complete Form 433-A and organize your financial documents. There are also important specific techniques for personal financial planning that you can do to make life under the installment agreement more bearable. You must complete Form 433-A: Collection Information Statement, and use budget-planning techniques to negotiate an installment agreement.

In addition to gaining some time to collect your information, you can also ask for an account hold to prepare an appeal, request taxpayer assistance by filing Form 911, an offer in compromise, or other filings. Don't feel obliged to tell ACS what you want to do because the strategy may change. Just ask for the hold and start moving forward.

You also must plan your living expenses so that life during the collection process will be tolerable and comfortable. Representatives of taxpayers commonly call the IRS and request a 30-day hold on the account to get the information together and obtain a balance due. The first hold on the account is to permit the representative time to file tax returns; the second hold (the 120-day hold discussed later in this chapter) is to search for full-payment financing. In the interim, you can prepare any returns and start Form 433-F.

Change of Address

If you are not receiving mail from the IRS you may have changed your address without notifying the IRS. You can call the IRS to change your address in their files or complete Form 8822: Change of Address, and mail it to them.

Appeals

When the ACS issues the enforced collection letter, a CP-504 designated "URGENT" stating, "We intend to levy in thirty days," that is the perfect time to request a hold on the account. The next collection notification letter, form letter 1058: Final Notice of Intent to Levy, arrives in about forty-five days. In the envelope with this letter is an appeal form called a Collection Due Process Hearing Request form.

This is important; you must complete this form and mail it back to the address in the upper left hand corner of the cover letter. By doing this, you are stopping collection action—such as a bank levy or seizure—dead in its tracks, but you are extending the statute of limitations for the time period of the appeal. If you miss this appeal, your rights to move on to Tax Court are waived; the chain of appeals is broken. You can still request an equivalent hearing but you cannot appeal that decision to Tax Court.

WARNING!

If you waste your rights to appeal, the consequences are very bad. When IRS enforced collection resumes, it will not stop. They will start seizing assets.

The appeal right is a bargaining chip, in a sense, and it can keep you out of collection while you work on your case. If you take advantage of your appeal rights, you extend the statute of limitations on collection. Otherwise, you waste this valuable due process right.

Appeals are very important rights. Do not waste the opportunity to settle your case. It normally takes a couple of months to schedule the appeals hearing or settlement conference. This can be done by phone, but the best case is to meet with the appeals officer. After the conference, the appeals officer will issue a written determination letter summarizing your case history, the facts, arguments, and legal conclusions. You can appeal the determination, but there are consequences to that decision—the Tax Court will issue a decision and a judgment has a twenty-year life. Be careful.

So it is in the appeal stage. Now is the time to organize, prepare, and plan your budget and your case strategy. You can do everything to resolve your entire case in this one step. If you want to ask for penalty abatement, innocent spouse relief, an offer in compromise, or an installment agreement, this is the time and place to do it. After filing the appeal you will have about 60 days to get organized before the scheduling letter arrives.

Move fast! You have a great opportunity in the palm of your hand.

The 120-Day Hold

The most useful trick of the trade is to get a hold on the account while you attempt to pay the balance due to the IRS in full. In a typical case, a call is made to Automated Collection Service (1-800-829-1040) to request a hold on the account. The purpose of a 120-day hold is to allow you time to obtain the funds to pay your account balance in full. This hold is granted when the IRS believes you will be able to obtain the money within four months. If you have the ability to get the money to pay your balance, through family, lenders, or any other source, you should request this time to borrow those funds.

Another benefit from utilizing this 120-day hold is that the IRS will not charge you with the installment agreement setup fee.

Form 1127—Extending the Payment Deadline of Tax

There is a little-known secret for extending the deadline by which a tax must be paid. Form 1127: Application for Extension of Time for Payment of Tax Due to Undue Hardship, is a relatively easy form to complete, and may grant you up to an additional six months to pay a tax due to the IRS. If you are requesting an extension to pay tax due on an upcoming return, the IRS must receive Form 1127 either before or on the date the return is due, not including extensions. If, on the other hand, you are requesting an extension to pay an amount the IRS has determined is a tax deficiency, Form 1127 must be received by the IRS before or on the date the payment is due, as indicated on the tax bill.

Generally, the maximum extension the IRS will grant to pay the tax due on an upcoming return is six months, while the maximum extension to pay a tax deficiency is eighteen months. In exceptional circumstances, the IRS will grant a 30-month extension to pay a tax deficiency.

While Form 1127 is a fairly basic form to fill out, you must make sure to successfully convey to the IRS that the extension is necessary to avoid an undue hardship. The explanation of the undue hardship must be written in Part II of the form. You cannot simply make a general statement of undue hardship, but you must explain why the denial of the extension would cause a substantial financial loss.

Part III of the Form 1127 requires you to attach certain documents that support your claim of undue hardship. These supporting documents include a statement of your assets and liabilities at the end of the last month (showing book and market values of assets and whether securities are listed or unlisted) and an itemized list of your income and expenses for each of the three months prior to the due date of the tax.

Asset Protection

The words "asset protection" might make you think of the dark arts of manipulation of asset ownership, midnight transactions, briefcases full of cash being transacted under a bridge, and fraud and criminal conduct. Let me relax your nerve ends; this asset protection has nothing to do with hiding assets or changing title to properties. Changing title to assets involves innocent third parties in a complicated criminal enterprise (and consequences) that they may not fully comprehend. *Do not change title to assets after an inchoate or formal tax lien is against them.*

The tax lien attaches to all of your assets—everything you own or come to own, including income such as wages—before the actual lien is filed in the courthouse and made a public document. The tax lien attaches when the tax return is filed and tax assessed.

Asset protection is deciding whether or not to file married filing jointly or married filing separately. It is the purposeful planning of who will be liable for the tax—one spouse or both. This will also include a discussion of who owns title to stock in a privately held corporation. This planning technique is a preventive measure designed to protect your jointly owned and earned assets from tax liens, levies, or seizures. Why give up both halves when you can sacrifice one half?

If you are married and know you are going to prepare and file old tax returns with large balances due to the IRS, you should *consider* preparing them as married filing separately. The single act of planning to file married filing separately can protect half of the married couples' joint assets from lien and seizure. There is no sound reason for an innocent spouse to forfeit all her equity in her marital assets for the lower rates of married filing joint status. Moreover, this prevents the spouse liable for tax debt from being thrown out of his house by a seizure and forced sale of it as a consequence of the case progressing through enforced collection.

Suffice it to say, the status of filing a tax return can play a very important role in how the case unfolds in enforced collection. Most tax preparers are not forward-thinking in this respect, because they do not concentrate on enforced collection matters, so whether you and your spouse file jointly or separately is not a planning issue you are familiar with using. This is an important case-planning activity for you and must be considered from the perspective of both spouses before the returns are signed and filed. Once a tax return is filed married filing jointly, it cannot be reversed without innocent spouse relief being granted. However, married filing separately returns can be amended to married filing jointly. We look at every case both ways and discuss the options with our clients.

Privately-held companies can be very risky enterprises. Everyone wants to be a stockholder in the family business and an officer in the business, too. But when the business has a tax problem, the company owes a bank debt it cannot pay, or has other creditors suing the entity, it is too late to decide not to be an officer or responsible person. Both spouses should <u>not be officers or check-signers</u> in a single business entity unless they have had their assets protected before the entity came into existence. Face the facts—sooner or later, most businesses fail. So, it is good business judgment to protect at least half of the family assets from creditors. To protect the family assets, do not have both spouses sign personally on the entity's loans, taxes, bank accounts, or other liabilities.

You must direct your family members and professionals that you mutually agree and intend to protect one spouse from business liabilities. Any other decision is reckless.

Tax planning, asset ownership, and worst-case protection are discussions you must have as a married couple, with friends going into business, with an attorney, and with your business's accountant. Meet the business's accountant in the early summer every year to review the business, structure, profit income statement, marketing plans, taxes, and budget. Discuss where the business is going. Are its hard assets in a separate entity from the operating entity? This will be the best investment of time and money you could make.

CHAPTER 5

Enforced Collection: Tax Liens & Levies

Lien For Taxes

If any person liable to pay any tax neglects or refuses to pay the same after demand, the amount (including any interest, additional amount, addition to tax, or assessable penalty, together with any costs that may accrue in addition thereto) shall be a lien in favor of the United States upon all property and rights to property, whether real or personal, belonging to such person.

Internal Revenue Code, Section 6321

Although the language that Congress drafted in Section 6321 sounds very simple and very broad, it is, in fact, very complicated. First, what is a lien? The following are a few of the definitions recognized by the IRS:

1. A claim or charge on property of payment for some debt, obligation, or duty.

- A qualified right to property that a creditor has in and over subject property of his debtor, as security for the debt or charge or performance of some act.

- A right or claim against some interest in property created by law as incident of contract.

- A right to enforce charge upon property of another for payment or satisfaction of a debt or claim.

Property Subject To a Tax Lien

In essence, a lien is a claim, or an encumbrance, placed on property. In the case of a lien for taxes, the Internal Revenue Code creates a lien on all property and rights to property, whether real or personal. This covers not only real property, which is land and buildings on that land, but also personal property, which includes furniture, automobiles, stock in companies, money, cash, gold, coins, equipment, bank accounts, credit card accounts, pensions, IRAs, stocks, bonds, and anything else that isn't real property or land.

The lien for taxes also attaches and encumbers future interests in property or earnings from a taxpayer's job, wages, contractual earnings, or monthly payments or alimony. Congress was very broad in the definition of what a lien can be placed on, to ensure that the United States would be paid for tax debts.

When is a Lien Placed on Property?

The lien arises after the occurrence of three events:

1. assessment of the tax,

2. notice and demand for payment, and

3. nonpayment of the tax due.

This assessment on the tax is upon the filing of the return or the closing of an audit. The IRS will subsequently send a notice to the taxpayer informing him of the tax debt. Once the assessment is made, the taxpayer may choose to pay the tax, thereby circumventing the problem, or not pay the tax and then receive a notice and demand for payment . The notice and demand for payment must be made before the tax lien is filed and a levy issued.

Let's not mince words. The IRS will seize your assets when you refuse to pay or to discuss payment alternatives. Not opening certified mail does not insulate you from the inevitable lien and seizure. Ignoring unpleasant news does not make it go away. Mailing the certified notice and demand letter is the obligation of the IRS, and reading that mail is your obligation. Best practice, *open and read certified mail.* Your due process rights will be in certified mail. If you miss the 30-day filing deadline you will *forever* lose your due process rights. See Chapter 7, Appeal Rights, for more detailed information.

A tax lien cannot be filed if the IRS has failed to give you valid notice of money owed. This failure to provide notice will be evident in your account transcript. However, while this failure complicates the IRS's ability to collect from a taxpayer, it does not fully protect you from collection of tax debt. Even if it failed to make a valid notice and demand for payment, the IRS can still institute a judicial proceeding to collect any tax debts. So again, to protect your rights, *open all IRS correspondence.*

If you have entered into an installment agreement, the IRS is unable to pursue collection activities as long as you comply with the terms of the agreement—monthly payments and tax compliance. Unfortunately, this limitation does not stop the IRS from placing a lien on a your property during the course of such an agreement, in order to protect the IRS's debt collection interest against other creditors and to perfect its claim on your property in the case of bankruptcy.

Statutory (or Secret) Lien vs. Notice of Federal Tax Lien

Now that you know what a lien is, let's distinguish between a statutory or secret lien and a notice of federal tax lien (NFTL). There is a very distinct difference. When you file a tax return and owe the government money, that is a self-determined tax debt; when the IRS determines through its audit processes that an additional amount is owed, that is also a tax debt. Let's say you owe $1,000. If you don't pay it, the IRS will send you a notice and demand for payment. If you still do not pay that debt, the IRS adds penalties and interest to the tax debt.

However, the IRS has not yet filed a tax lien against you, and until that time, this is still a "secret" lien. The public is not yet aware of your obligation to pay the government. In other words, third parties are not on notice of the tax lien; they cannot withhold money from you to pay it over to the government to clear title to your "real" property. Legally, this is referred to as an Inchoate Lien. This is a valid tax lien, but it has not yet been filed in a county courthouse. See Form 668: Notice of Federal Tax Lien, in the index. Keep in mind, though, that the 10-year collection statute has already begun to run.

If a taxpayer does not pay the debt assessed by the IRS within 10 days of being notified, the government can then file Form 668: Notice of Federal Tax Lien. The NFTL puts the public on notice that a tax lien in favor of the government has been placed against Joe Taxpayer on all assets that Joe Taxpayer owns or will own in the future. Thus, buying property from Joe Taxpayer that is encumbered by the tax lien will result in the IRS having a right to seize the property, if the sale proceeds do not satisfy the lien.

The lien is only valid against the person(s) as outlined in Internal

Revenue Code, Section 6323. The tax lien imposed is not valid against any purchaser or holder of a secured interest (a mortgage), mechanics lien, or judgment, until IRS publicly files a notice of federal tax lien.

The IRS must give you notice of the amount of the tax due and make a demand for payment, IRC Section 6303(a). The lien relates back to the assessment date and continues until the liability is marked "satisfied" or is unenforceable due to the expiration of the collection statute or period. The IRS sends this notice to your last address, and if you have not advised the IRS of a change of address, the fact that that you did not receive the actual notice is irrelevant, because the IRS can prove it mailed that notice to your last known address. To change your address, use Form 8827 (see Chapter 4).

The IRS serves each spouse with a notice when you file as married filing jointly, because you are each individually and personally liable for the tax on the joint tax return. Therefore, to collect from you, the IRS must send notice to each of the married filing jointly taxpayers requesting payment in ten (10) days and thereafter file a notice of federal tax lien. After the IRS has made service on your last known address, the IRS may begin enforced collection by garnishment, levy, or asset seizure.

Release of Lien

Generally, a lien will be released by the IRS 10 years after the tax is assessed, unless the IRS has re-filed the lien or issued a certificate of release of the federal tax lien (CRFTL) before that point. A CRFTL will be issued either:

1. Within 30 days of you paying the tax debt;
2. Within 30 days after the IRS accepts a bond you submit guaranteeing payment of the debt; or
3. 14 days after the IRS determines that at the time the NFTL was

filed, you had no outstanding tax debt for the period listed on the NFTL, the assessment was invalid, or the time period for collecting the tax ended.

The amount of tax debt shown on the NFTL is the amount owed at the time the notice was created. However, you must keep in mind that as time progresses, the amount actually owed will change, as a result of interest, penalties, and any payments made to the IRS. To receive an updated lien payoff amount, call the IRS Lien Unit at 1-800-913-6050.

When you receive a release of lien, make sure to circulate a copy of the document to the credit reporting agencies. This CRFTL must be kept in your retention register.

Subordination of a Tax Lien

In certain circumstances, when the IRS has a lien on a taxpayer's property and another creditor has a lien on the same property (usually through a mortgage), the IRS will allow the tax lien to become secondary to the other lien. This means that the taxpayer will be permitted to satisfy the creditor's lien before the tax lien. This generally is permitted when a creditor refuses to extend credit to the taxpayer or allow the taxpayer to refinance the mortgage on his home, unless the IRS will permit the creditor's lien to be satisfied first. This process of having the creditor's lien take priority over the IRS's lien is called subordination. If you wish to apply for subordination, you must file Form 14134: Application for Certificate of Subordination of Federal Tax Lien.

For more information on how to apply for subordination, see Publication 784: Instructions on how to apply for a Certificate of Subordination of Federal Tax Lien.

How To Challenge a NFTL

Once a NFTL is filed, the IRS will give you written notice of your right to a collection due process (CDP) hearing within 5 business days. If you wish to challenge the validity of the NFTL, you must request a CDP hearing by the date shown on the written notice. The address to which you must send the request should also be on the notice.

The following are some common issues that can be argued at a CDP hearing:

1. The validity, sufficiency, and/or timeliness of the notice of CDP rights.
2. Innocent spouse relief.
3. Injured spouse relief.
4. Collection alternatives.
5. Challenges to the appropriateness of collection actions.
6. Challenges to the existence or amount of the liability.

After the CDP hearing, a decision is made regarding the NFTL via a notice of determination. If you disagree with this decision, you have 30 days to seek review by the United States Tax Court.

What is a Levy?

While a lien is only the IRS's right to take possession of your property, a levy is the actual seizure of said property in order to satisfy a tax debt. Not only can property you currently own be levied by the IRS, but the IRS may also take possession of property which belongs to you but is currently held by a third party, such as your wages, retirement account, dividends, bank account, rental income, accounts receivable, the cash value of your life insurance, and commissions.

The IRS can also levy the following federal payments: federal retirement annuity income, Social Security benefits, federal contractor/vendor payments, and federal employee salary and travel payments. Generally, if the IRS electronically levies these federal payments, it will take 15% of each payment.

Once a levy is in place, it continues until the tax debt is fully paid, other arrangements are made to satisfy the debt (such as a payment plan), the statute of limitations for collection has passed, or the levy is successfully appealed. A levy on a bank account attaches only to deposits that have cleared and funds that are available for withdrawal. However, a bank must wait 21 days after receiving a levy, holding the funds in escrow, before it can send any money to the IRS. This allows you time to obtain a release of the funds if you would suffer a financial hardship.

The Levy Process

There are usually three things that must occur before the IRS can levy your property. First, the IRS must determine that there is an outstanding tax debt, and send you a notice and demand for payment. Second, you must fail to pay the money owed for the tax debt. Finally, the IRS must send you a Final Notice of Intent to Levy and Notice of Your Right to a Hearing. This notice must be sent at least 30 days before any property is levied.

How to Appeal a Levy

Once you receive a Final Notice of Intent to Levy and Notice of Your Right to a Hearing, you have 30 days to file a request for a collection due process hearing (CDP). At the end of the CDP, the Office of Appeals will issue a determination. You then have 30 days to request a review of this determination by the United States Tax Court.

If CDP is not available because you missed the 30-day filing period, you may appeal a proposed or actual levy under the collection appeals program. For a more detailed explanation of your appeal rights, see the Chapter 7 on Appeal Rights.

Release of a Levy

The IRS will release a levy if any of the following conditions are present:

1. The tax debt is fully satisfied.
2. The statute of limitations for collection has passed.
3. The IRS failed to send the required notices before the property was levied.
4. The automatic stay of a taxpayer's bankruptcy is in effect.
5. The levy was on property that the IRS was not permitted to levy.
6. Property was levied while the IRS is considering a payment plan request.
7. Property was levied while an offer in compromise or installment agreement is in effect.
8. Anything regarding the tax debt that resulted in the levy is currently being appealed.
9. The levy is creating an economic hardship on the taxpayer.
10. The value of the property exceeds the tax debt, and a release of the levy on part of the property will not affect the IRS's ability to collect enough money to satisfy the tax debt.
11. The expense in selling the property exceeds the IRS's interest in the property.
12. Releasing the levy will help the IRS collect the tax debt.

If the IRS has issued a levy, you can enlist the taxpayer advocate to assist you in releasing the levy. You recall from Chapter 2, Tax

Compliance, that you must be compliant for the IRS to work with you. Begin the processes: prepare your tax return(s) and file Form 911 requesting tax advocate assistance at the same time. The advocate may obtain a temporary release of levy for you to have time to prepare the tax returns. Turn to Chapter 7, The Taxpayer Advocate. You will also need to complete Form 433-F and provide backup documentation. See Chapter 9, Collection Information Statements. If you have not filed tax returns, see Chapter 3, Case Analysis, to organize and obtain the documents you will need to accurately prepare and file the returns. When the returns are prepared, copies may be faxed to the IRS to obtain a release of the levy.

Selling a Taxpayer's Levied Property

Before the IRS sells property that has been levied, it will give a public notice of the pending sale. The IRS must wait at least 10 days after the public notice before it can sell the property. The IRS uses the proceeds first to pay the expenses of the levy and the sale; the remaining money is used to satisfy the tax debt. If a balance due still remains, you are required to pay that. However, if the debt is satisfied by the sale and there is money remaining, the IRS will refund this surplus to you.

You, and anyone else with a legal interest in the sold property, such as a part-owner, have the opportunity to purchase the property within 180 days of the date the IRS sells it. However, the purchaser of the levied property must be paid the amount he paid for the property, plus interest at 20%.

You can bid on assets the IRS has seized and is selling by auction on the IRS website at www.IRSauctions.gov.

CHAPTER 6

The Taxpayer Advocate

Tax Advocate

If you have an emergency, read on. The advocate can help you if you are suffering an imminent asset seizure, levy, garnishment, or if you are just plain scared to death or you cannot afford a representative. If you need help, the tax advocate is a great source for personal assistance.

Taxpayer Advocate Service in Brief

When you have an emergency or a hardship such as a wage garnishment or a bank account levy, your best practice is to file Form 911: Taxpayer Advocate Service (TAS). As you will learn, case advocates have helped many taxpayers resolve their IRS case. This is what you need to know about the process.

To obtain help when you are suffering a hardship, the you must file Form 911 to request assistance from the TAS. There is no relation to September 11, 2001 a/k/a 9/11. This form was in use long before the historic 9/11.

The taxpayer advocate service will appoint a case advocate to assist you with the emergency or hardship you are encountering with the IRS. The TAS case advocate will have the experience to get your problem reso-lved quickly. Not every person qualifies for advocate assistance. TAS can help if you are suffering a seizure or wage garnishment, a financial hardship, or just having a problem getting information or documentation from the IRS.

"The Taxpayer Advocate Service is your voice at the IRS."—Their words. TAS has almost two thousand representatives assisting taxpayers in every state. TAS offers free help to assist taxpayers with the resolution of an imminent or current tax issue that they were not able to resolve with the Service.

When is it Time to File a Form 911 and Ask for TAS Assistance?

If you have not been able to resolve the tax problem or you are intimidated or simply afraid to work alone with the IRS employee, ask for TAS assistance.

TAS can help if:

1. Your problem is causing a financial difficulty for you and your family or business;
2. You or your business are confronted with an immediate threat of adverse action by the IRS; and/or
3. You have tried repeatedly to work with the IRS, but no one has responded or helped you work out your problem.

The TAS will immediately assign a case advocate who will contact you and the IRS and work through the issues with you to resolve the problem. TAS is a government-funded entity that represents taxpayers and has the experience and knowledge to work with the IRS. If you cannot afford a representative, TAS is your best option because they have knowledge and experience that you do not have.

However, the taxpayer advocate will not volunteer a list of resolution actions you could request. They specifically work with you to resolve the problem you list on Form 911. Here is the list; put in the mix all the things you want to accomplish.

Trade Secret

The most important issue to put on Form 911 requesting taxpayer advocate assistance is the specific problem you are experiencing, such as a wage garnishment. You may add the following issues if relevant:

1. Release of the tax lien (so that your credit is better and you can try to borrow money).
2. Release of the wage garnishment or any other levy or garnishment action being taken by IRS.
3. A block in your information master file so that the IRS does not levy again.
4. Assistance in completing Form 433-F or Form 433-A so that you can develop a reasonable installment agreement at the lowest possible amount.
5. Penalty abatement due to the financial hardship you are suffering and due to the fact that you were a good taxpayer before you had tax problems and you need to lower the liability so that it can be paid off.
6. Injured spouse relief and consideration (if applicable).
7. Innocent spouse relief and consideration (if applicable).
8. An explanation of your appeal rights and when you may appeal if you have already missed your appeal period.
9. Wage and income transcripts to assist taxpayer in filing tax returns;

10. Request help filing an appeal to protect your due process rights!

Caveat: Be prepared to complete Form 433-A or 433-F: CIS. Go to Chapter 9, Collection Information Statements, and begin to complete the form and compile the backup documents.

How to Reach the Taxpayer Advocate

You can find the address and phone number for the TAS Office on the IRS website at www.irs.gov/advocate. Or visit our site www.taxjams.com. You can also call the Taxpayer Advocate's toll-free number at 1-877-777-4778. You can ask an IRS person on the phone to help you complete the Form 911 on your behalf. Fax the completed Form 911 to the Taxpayer Advocate for assignment. Add a copy of any levy or final notice of intent to levy.

Form 911 is *Request for Taxpayer Advocate Service Assistance (and Application for Taxpayer Assistance Order)*. This is available by phone at 1-877-777-4778 or online at www.irs.gov.

Background on the Taxpayer Advocate Service

The Taxpayer Advocate Service has been developing for over 30 years. The Internal Revenue Service first formed the Office of Taxpayer Ombudsman in 1979 to serve as a primary advocate for taxpayers within the IRS. That position was codified in the Taxpayer Bill of Rights 1 (TBOR 1) in the Technical and Miscellaneous Revenue Act of 1988. In TBOR 1, Congress added IRC Section 7811 granting the Ombudsman the statutory authority to issue a Taxpayer Assistance Order (TAO) if there was a significant hardship being suffered by the taxpayer. In the Taxpayer Bill of Rights 2 (TBOR 2) in 1996, Congress amended IRC Section 7802 and replaced the Office of Taxpayer Ombudsman with the Office of Taxpayer Advocate. Essentially, the reason for this was that the Taxpayer Ombudsman was selected and working under the IRS Commissioner. Congress wanted the Taxpayer Advocate Service to be independent of the IRS and represent the taxpayers more objectively.

In TBOR 2, there was an amendment made to Section 7811 extending the scope of the TAO, which provided the taxpayer advocate with broader authority in the taxpayer's interest to prevent any significant hardship as a result of the administering of tax laws by the IRS. This was the first time a TAO could be issued by the taxpayer advocate so it could specify a time period within which the revenue officer (RO) for the IRS would have to act on the TAO. Only the advocate, the commissioner, or the deputy commissioner could modify or rescind the TAO. This gave the Taxpayer Advocate's Office its first real authority in protecting the taxpayer from adverse action.

It was at this same time, 1997, that the National Commission on Restructuring the Internal Revenue Service called the taxpayer advocate the "Voice of the Taxpayers."

"Significant hardship" in IRC Section 7811, essentially includes four circumstances:

1.   an immediate threat of adverse action by the IRS;
2.   a delay of more than 30 days in resolving an issue with the taxpayer;
3.   the taxpayer will incur significant costs (professional fees) if relief is not granted; and
4.   the taxpayer will suffer irreparable harm or long-term adverse action.

The report also provides that this list is non-exclusive and if a taxpayer is suffering any significant hardship, the taxpayer advocate has a right to intervene on the taxpayer's behalf.

National Taxpayer Advocate

The National Taxpayer Advocate leads the Taxpayer Advocate Service and is responsible for the case advocates. The National Taxpayer Advocate is Nina Olsen, who serves as an advocate for all taxpayers before the IRS and Congress. She was appointed by the Secretary of the Treasury with consultation with the IRS Commissioner and the IRS Oversight Board. NTA Olsen is an example of someone whose career groomed her for the position of NTA. Ms. Olsen is a graduate of Bryn Mawr College, cum laude, with an AB in fine arts. She received her JD (law degree), cum laude, from North Carolina Central School of Law, and her masters in law and taxation, with distinction, from Georgetown University Law Center. NTA Olsen served as an adjunct professor at Georgetown and other law schools.

Prior to her appointment as NTA in 2001, she maintained a private practice concentrating in tax controversy representation. From 1975 through 1991, she owned and operated an accounting tax practice. NTA Olsen had also served as the Chair of the American Bar Association Section on Taxation for Low Income Taxpayers as well as the *Pro Se Pro Bono* Task Force of the ABA Tax Section. In 1999, she was the recipient of the Virginia Bar Association *Pro Bono* Award and the City of Richmond Bar Association *Pro Bono* Award.

Ms. Olsen has provided strong leadership for the Taxpayer Advocate Service, having assisted millions of taxpayers with tax issues and assisting the IRS in tax collection through the least intrusive means possible.

Recently, Ms. Olsen has been trying to find ways to cut services in TAS due to the exploding demand of taxpayers requesting help. Fortunately, the Advocate has decided not to cut services in the arena of enforced collection cases. She is committed to excellent taxpayer service and assistance. The only area cut to date is assistance in securing refunds more quickly.

CHAPTER 7

Appeal Rights & The Appeals Process

Appeals in Brief

When you file an appeal, you are exercising your Constitutional due process rights. If you want to challenge the decisions of the IRS you must file—on time— the appeal of each decision you want to challenge at each level. Once there is a break in the chain of appeals, you lose the right to continue to challenge the IRS action through to Tax Court.

There are advantages to filing appeals. One advantage of pursuing an appeal is that appeals officers have more latitude to settle a case than revenue officers do. Another advantage is enforced collection—such as levies and wage garnishments—will stop while the appeal is in process to resolve the case. This is a chance to settle your case, and you can address multiple issues at once.

Before levies issue on a tax debt, you will receive two letters. The second letter describes your appeal rights.

First, however, you will receive a letter that makes a demand for payment, or threatens that the IRS will seize assets or issue public notices that they are filing a lien. This letter is designated a CP504, with no appeal rights yet. This letter gives you thirty (30) days to call the IRS and set up full payment or arrange an installment agreement or another collection alternative—Offer in Compromise (Chapter 14), Penalty Abatement (Chapter 12), or Innocent Spouse (Chapter 16). You should start by reading those sections and the Case Analysis (Chapter 3).

The next letter, Letter 1058, Final Notice of Intent to Levy, will advise you that the IRS will seize assets. It will also indicate your appeal rights and includes a copy of the collection due process hearing request form (CDP). The CDP form must be completed and received by the IRS within 30 days of the date on the letter.

The CDP form is to notify the IRS that you are filing an appeal. You must complete the form with your name, Social Security number, address, phone, and the tax periods being appealed. You can handwrite the information on the form or go online to www.irs.gov and type the information into the PDF form on the website, print it out, sign it, and mail it to the IRS with a copy of the final notice so that the appeals office has a copy of the letter you are appealing.

The information you need to complete the form is in that letter (Final Notice of Intent to Levy) that you are appealing. Typically the 1058 letter has the tax periods from the Form 1040 (for example, 2001 and 2002) which are subject to the final notice, levy, and resulting appeal. Check the appropriate box as to whether the letter concerns a levy or a lien, and list those periods on the final notice letter. Remember to sign the appeal. You must file the CDP appeal *on time*.

CAUTION

You must not put your head in the sand after filing your appeal. Get ready!

To prepare for the hearing, list the issues you want to discuss with the appeals officer, such as an installment agreement, offer in compromise, penalty abatement, innocent spouse, and any other relevant issues you've learned about in this book. All of these issues can be raised and discussed during the appeal.

Your job is to bring all of the completed, required, appropriate forms, with all necessary supporting documents, to help you in your discussion with the appeals officer of the background facts of your case. You will have a month or so to put this together before the hearing or settlement conference is scheduled, so *do not waste time*. Start now with the Form 433-A, which the appeals officer will need for the financial analysis of your case. See Chapter 9, Collection Information Statements.

After the hearing and decision, if you do not like the outcome you can appeal to (an independent) Tax Court. If you don't like the Tax Court's decision, you can appeal to the US Court of Appeals and then, finally, to the US Supreme Court. An expensive and time-consuming strategy, but this is a two-way street and the fact that you have these options gives you negotiating power referred to as the threat of litigation. The downside, however, is that during the appeals process the statute of limitations is tolled (or stops ticking/expiring).

These are your the due process rights.

The Initial Stages of Your Appeal

It is common for a taxpayer to disagree with a determination made by the IRS, such as whether or not the taxpayer underpaid for a particular tax year. If you have such a disagreement, you have two options.

First, you may request a meeting or telephone conference with the supervisor of the IRS employee who issued the contested findings. If you still do not agree with the decision made by the supervisor, you may appeal that decision to the (local) appeals office of the IRS ("Appeals").

Appeals functions independently from the departments of the IRS involved in examinations and collections, and it can settle most differences without court trials. Appeals has broader authority to settle cases.

The second option you have is simply to do nothing if you disagree with a determination made by the IRS. If the issue involves an examination of income, estate, gift, and certain excise taxes or penalties, you will receive a notice of deficiency. This notice allows you to go to Tax Court. If the issue involves a trust fund recovery penalty, or certain employment tax liabilities, the IRS will send you a bill for the penalty, which you may then appeal.

During the course of this chapter, your appellate (appeals) rights will be explained. First, there is a basic overview of appeals, followed by a more detailed explanation of the process of seeking appeals within the IRS. Next, there is a rundown of your appellate rights in courts outside of the IRS, namely the Tax Court and federal courts. Finally, there is a warning about the importance of following the deadlines given by the IRS regarding when to seek an appeal.

Checklist of Forms Needed to File Your Appeal

1. CDP Hearing Request Form, if you are seeking a CDP hearing (this MUST be RECEIVED by the IRS within 30 days of the date of the Letter 1058) –or–
2. Collection Appeal Request Form, if you are seeking a CAP hearing
3. Copy of Letter 1058 (or any other IRS letter) being appealed
4. Collection Information Statement

Appeals Jurisdiction

Appeals is able to hear cases regarding the following tax issues:

1. Deficiencies or refunds in income, estate, gift, employment and excise taxes, and penalty cases
2. Abatement of penalty and interest, innocent spouse relief, offer in compromise
3. All collection issues, levies, garnishments, and asset seizures
4. Extensions of time to pay estate taxes

Not all issues fitting into one of the above-listed categories are appropriate for consideration by appeals. Basically, there are two kinds of disputes that may be brought to appeals. First, there are the cases where the IRS and the taxpayer disagree on facts or the law, and both parties have valid claims. Second, there are the cases that present a novel legal issue, meaning the issue has not been ruled on up to that point.

Written Protests

A written protest needs to be filed within 30 days after the IRS sends you a 30-day letter, in order for you to be granted a conference with appeals. A protest may be filed in the following situations:

1. All employee plans and exempt organization cases, without regard to the dollar amount at issue.
2. All partnership and S corporation cases, without regard to the dollar amount at issue.
3. All other cases, unless you qualify for the small case request procedure, or other special appeal procedures, such as requesting appeals consideration of liens, levies, seizures, or installment agreements.

The written protest should be detailed because the more information the taxpayer includes, the more likely he is to succeed on his claims. The protest should contain the following information:

1. Responses to all of the IRS's positions on adjustments to the tax return with which you do not agree
2. Copies of any relevant documents
3. Affidavits and/or appraisals
4. Any computations you made

If the total amount for the tax period is less than $25,000, you may make a small case request instead of filing a formal written protest. Also, if the IRS issues a notice of deficiency (a 90-day letter), a written protest is not used. In that case, you have 90 days to file a petition with the Tax Court.

Representation

At the appeals conference, you have a couple of options regarding representation. You may choose to represent yourself, but a wiser decision is for you to be represented by an attorney, a CPA, or an individual enrolled to practice before the IRS (enrolled agent). Many IRS employees earn the designation of enrolled agent while employed at the IRS. Also, you may choose to allow your representative to appear without you, if you provide Form 2848: Power of Attorney and Declaration of Representative (POA), to the IRS beforehand. You and your representative must execute the POA. See Chapter 22, Power of Attorney.

Appeals Authority

One of the powers unique to Appeals is its ability to make mutual concession settlements based on the hazards of litigation. A mutual concession settlement is reached when a dispute is resolved through compromises by both the taxpayer and the IRS for the purpose of settlement, based on the strength of the opposing positions. There must be genuine uncertainty about the outcome of an issue in order for a mutual concession settlement to be granted. However, appeals will not make concessions unrelated to the merits of the issues solely to eliminate the inconvenience or cost of further negotiations or litigation.

Generally, appeals cannot raise new issues against you unless the grounds for such actions are strong and the potential effects on tax liability have real importance and great consequence. You may always raise new issues, though.

Procedures For Appealing IRS Collection Actions

There are two procedures a taxpayer may follow for appealing IRS collection actions to Appeals: Collection Due Process or Collection Appeals Program. The majority of appeals are collection due process appeals.

Collection Due Process

The taxpayer has a right to a collection due process (CDP) hearing by Appeals for the following collection actions:

1. The first time a notice of federal tax lien is filed for a tax and period.
2. Before the first levy is placed on the taxpayer's property for a tax and period.
3. After a levy is placed on a taxpayer's state refund.
4. After a levy is placed when collection is in jeopardy.

Once the IRS mails a notice of federal tax lien or a final notice of intent to levy (Letter 1058), the taxpayer has 30 days to request a hearing with Appeals. The IRS cannot levy or seize the taxpayer's property within 30 days from the date the notice is mailed. If the taxpayer's request for a CDP hearing is not timely, the law does not require a suspension of collection action by the IRS, and the taxpayer cannot go to court if he disagrees with the IRS's decision.

In order to request a CDP hearing, first complete Form 12153: Request for a Collection Due Process or Equivalent Hearing. This form will be included in the package containing the Letter 1058 sent by the IRS. Then, Appeals will contact you to schedule a conference. If the request is timely, the 10-year period that the IRS has to collect your taxes will be suspended until the date the determination becomes final or when you withdraw your request for a hearing. At the conclusion of the CDP hearing, Appeals will issue a determination letter. If you do not agree with the determination, you may request a judicial review of the determination by petitioning Tax Court within 30 days of the determination. In this appeal to Tax Court, you will be contacted by IRS Appeals yet again to try to settle the issues in the appeal.

If you miss the 30-day filing period, the IRS Appeals office will conduct an appeal of sorts, which they call an equivalency hearing. This appeal has no due process appeal rights meaning you cannot appeal the decision and go to Tax Court. This is described in more detail below, in the ***Equivalency Hearing*** section. *Be careful!* If you filed your CDP on time, but the IRS claims you did not do so, you *must* appeal that issue or lose your due process appeals rights. So, proof of mailing or faxing is very important to you.

The best practice is to file the appeal and ask the revenue officer to hold it while you negotiate the case. If you do not feel you are being treated fairly, tell the RO you cannot reach an agreement and to process the appeal. If you must go over her head to achieve the end result, so be it. But remember—while in appeals draft your wish list and start preparing the documents to request the desired relief.

Filing the CDP Appeal

The procedure to file the appeal is simple. Complete the form by neatly printing the information from the 1058 letter onto the appeal form. The form requires the taxpayer's name, address, Social Security number, and the tax periods being appealed. Typically the 1058 letter has the tax periods from the Form 1040, for example, 2001 and 2002, which are subject to the final notice, levy, and resulting appeal. In short, place that information from the collection letter onto the CDP form. Also attach a copy of the notice being appealed.

Collection Appeals Program

The following IRS collection actions may be appealed under the Collection Appeals Program ("CAP"):

1. Notice of federal tax lien. The taxpayer may appeal a proposed filing of this notice or the actual filing.
2. Notice of levy. The taxpayer may pursue an appeal before or after the IRS places a levy on his wages, bank account, or other property.
3. Seizure of property. The taxpayer may pursue an appeal before or after the IRS makes a seizure.
4. Rejection or termination of an installment agreement.

If the taxpayer appeals a lien, levy, or seizure, normally the IRS will stop any collection action on the tax periods involved in the appeal. If the taxpayer appeals an installment agreement issue, the IRS cannot place a levy until 30 days after the rejection or termination of the agreement. If the taxpayer appeals within the 30-day period, the IRS is prohibited from levying until the appeal is complete. Once Appeals makes a decision, that decision is binding on both the taxpayer and the

IRS. The taxpayer cannot subsequently obtain a judicial review of an Appeals decision following a CAP hearing.

Process for Filing a CAP Hearing

Scenario 1: Your only contact has been an IRS notice or via telephone:

- Call the IRS on the number shown on the notice
- Describe why you disagree and that you want to challenge the decision
- Be prepared to discuss your case analysis and path to resolution (see Chapter 3)
- Before you can come to Appeals you will need to first discuss your case with a collections manager and have a valid reason why you are unable to work with a revenue officer. For example, the RO has been intransigent and unwilling to explore collection alternatives.

Scenario 2: You have been contacted by a revenue officer:

- Call the revenue officer whom you have previously contacted
- Describe why you disagree and that you want to challenge the decision
- Be prepared to discuss your case analysis and path to resolution (see Chapter 3)
- Before you can come to Appeals you will need to first discuss your case with a Collections manager and have a valid reason why you are unable to work with a revenue officer. For example, the RO has been intransigent and unwilling to explore collection alternatives.
- Complete Form 9423: Collection Appeals Request. You only

have 2 days from the conference with the collections manager to submit Form 9423 to the RO.

- You will immediately be contacted by Appeals. Your case will be decided within 3 days of being contacted. Be prepared to offer solutions.

Appealing to the Courts Outside of the IRS

If you and Appeals cannot agree on the issues, or if you skipped the IRS appeals system outright, you can take your case to court, outside of the IRS. Based on the nature of the issues, you may pursue your case in either Tax Court or a federal court (either a United States District Court or the Court of Federal Claims).

If the disagreement is over whether you owe income tax, estate tax, gift tax, or certain excise taxes—or penalties relating to those liabilities—you can go to Tax Court. You have 90 days after a Notice of Deficiency is mailed to you to file a petition with Tax Court. If you discuss the case with the IRS during the 90-day period, this discussion **DOES NOT** extend the deadline.

If your claim is for a refund of any type, you may take the case to a district court or to the court of federal claims. Those courts also have jurisdiction over cases involving some employment tax or manufacturer's excise tax issues. If you file a formal refund claim with the IRS, and the IRS does not respond in 6 months, you may file suit immediately in either of those courts.

If the IRS sends you a letter disallowing a refund claim, you have two options. You may request an appeals review of the disallowance, or you may file a refund suit. A refund suit must be filed no later than two years from the date the IRS Notice of Claim Disallowance letter is mailed. An appeals review of a disallowed claim does not extend the two-year period for filing suit.

Importance of Meeting Deadlines

Every notice sent by the IRS regarding money you owe or the IRS's collection plans against you must be appealed by a specific deadline if there is a dispute (generally, 30 or 90 days, depending on the nature of the notice). The notice should clearly state any relevant deadlines. It is of the utmost importance that you appeal *before* the deadline has passed. The consequences of missing a deadline are very detrimental. Generally, if you disagree with a decision made by the IRS but you fail to appeal that decision within the set timeframe, you lose your appellate rights and are legally obligated to follow the IRS's determination, regardless of the merit of your dispute. Therefore, it is crucial that you know the appropriate deadlines and meet them.

Many clients insist that they have not received any notices of levy, garnishments, lien filings, etc. However, we always find them within the piles of envelopes they bring us for review.

It is your responsibility to be sure the IRS has your correct mailing address. Not receiving—or not opening and reading—an IRS notice **will not** extend any deadlines. Hiding your head in the sand will not serve you well. If you want to resolve your tax problems, *you must read your mail.*

Equivalency Hearing

If the 30-day period to file the collection due process hearing request has expired, you may still file the CDP forms and request an equivalency hearing. Be forewarned, however, that although the IRS does not normally pursue enforced collection during or leading up to an equivalency hearing, it still may levy or garnish during the period. You cannot appeal to court from an equivalency hearing because the 30-day period to file the appeal expired. The consequences of not filing an appeal are very severe; you forever lose your Constitutional due process rights—that is, your right to a trial. You should always err on the side of filing the appeal within that 30-day period, because you can always withdraw the appeal later.

There are three methods to stop enforced collection during an equivalency hearing.

1. Call the appeals officer and request a release of the levy or garnishment.
2. File a cap appeal, a collection appeal form, which can be obtained from the IRS website at irs.gov.
3. File Form 911 and request a release of the levy or garnishment from the taxpayer advocates' office.

The specific reason for the removal of the levy is that you are making an attempt through the equivalency hearing to develop a collection alternative such as an installment agreement, offer in compromise, or placement in CNC status. You can argue that this cannot be done without a completed Form 433-A and that you need time to complete the forms and compile the requested backup documentation, and the levy is preventing you from paying necessary living expenses. See Chapters 8 and 9.

The submission of the collection information statement is an important part of the collection negotiation and is not to be taken lightly. This process is highly detailed and requires your *attention to every detail*. You are required to complete the form under penalty of perjury and submit proof of expenses. The proof comes in the form of supporting documentation, such as three months' bank statements, proof of housing and utilities—copies of the monthly invoices from the electric company and gas supplier, food, household and clothing expenses, transportation expenses such as the car payment, insurance, maintenance, and gas. If you have life insurance, health insurance, or monthly medical bills, these should be provided as necessary living expenses.

You may also claim life insurance on the collection information statement so it is advisable to provide proof of this before submitting the forms. If you do not have life insurance, consider purchasing it. Also, secured payments such as court-ordered child support, a judgment, or state tax lien can be claimed on Form 433-A. The IRS usually wants proof of the order/judgment or lien and the monthly payment. A copy of the court order is satisfactory, and evidence of withdrawal on the payroll statement or through the checking account will usually suffice. In completing the CIS you should now move to Chapter 9 for more detail on completing the specific forms and the required backup documentation. There are planning tips in that section, too.

CHAPTER 8

Collection Financial Standards

Collection Financial Standards in Brief

Collection financial standards, also referred to as the national and local standards, are the maximum costs the IRS deems necessary for certain living expenses. The IRS uses this information to determine a taxpayer's ability to pay an overdue tax debt. Allowable living expenses are based on national standards and can include expenses that meet the necessary expense test. An expense meets this test if it is *necessary to provide for a taxpayer's (and his family's) health and welfare and/or production of income.* "National standard" is the amount a taxpayer is

Necessary expenses are the monthly amount equal to all expenses necessary to provide for the taxpayer and his family for health, welfare, and production of income.

allowed for their family size, and the amount actually spent is not questioned (assuming that less than the standard is spent).

Generally, the total number of people the IRS allows for necessary living expenses are the same as the number of exemptions on the taxpayer's most recent income tax return. So, if a taxpayer claims an exemption for himself and one additional person (such as his spouse), then the IRS will consider the collection financial standards for a household of two people (the taxpayer and the exempted person) when determining that taxpayer's maximum cost of living. In most tax cases, the most heated arguments surround the application of the national standards.[1]

If the IRS determines that the facts and circumstances of a taxpayer's situation suggest that using the national standards would not allow the taxpayer to afford basic living expenses, the IRS may deviate from the national standards and allow higher actual expenses. However, taxpayers must provide proof that supports a claim that using the collection national standards does not leave them enough money to provide for basic living expenses. For example, you can argue the higher expenses are necessary to generate income or you will need time to lower them—one year is the maximum amount of time granted for the taxpayer to adjust his expenses.

Understanding the collection financial standards is necessary for successfully working out deals with the IRS regarding the repayment or compromise of tax debts, such as obtaining an installment agreement or entering into currently not collectible status (CNC). The IRS makes deals based on the taxpayer's lack of income or higher-than-average expenses. The IRS compares a taxpayer's actual living expenses—submitted on Forms 433-A and 433-F, both of which are collection information statement forms (CIS)—to the national standards. This review is performed before negotiating a deal with a taxpayer. If the taxpayer's expenses fall within the standards, and the taxpayer is still unable

---

1   Revised October 11, 2011

to pay off a tax debt, the IRS may then consider a deal such as an offer in compromise. Therefore, failing to understand the national standards could jeopardize your ability to settle with the IRS or to achieve the best result. Conversely, if you have assets and /or income sufficient to repay the IRS, under existing law it cannot settle the debt for less.

Financial standards are broken up into national and local standards. National standards apply nationwide, while local standards vary by county in most cases. These different standards will be discussed thoroughly during the course of this explanation of collection financial standards. The tables contained in this guide are from the IRS website www.irs.gov. Other information is cited accordingly.

National Standards: The Five Necessary Expenses

National standards[2] have been established for the following necessary expenses:

1. Food
2. Housekeeping supplies
3. Apparel and services
4. Personal care products and services
5. Miscellaneous

Food includes food at home and away from home. Food at home is the amount of money spent for food at food stores. It does not include nonfood items. Food away from home is all meals and snacks, including tips, at fast food, take-out, delivery, and full-service restaurants.

Housekeeping supplies include laundry and cleaning supplies, statio-

---

2   The standards are derived from the Bureau of Labor Statistics Consumer Expenditure Survey.

nery supplies, postage and delivery services, miscellaneous household products, and lawn and garden supplies.

Apparel and services include clothing, footwear, material for making clothes, alterations and repairs, clothing rental, clothing storage, dry cleaning and sent-out laundry, watches, jewelry, and repairs to watches and jewelry.

Personal care products and services include products for hair, oral hygiene products, shaving needs, cosmetics and bath products, electric personal care appliances, and other personal care products.

Taxpayers are allowed the total monthly national standards amount for their family size, without questioning the amount they actually spend. If the amount claimed by the taxpayer is more than the total allowed by the national standards, he must provide documentation to substantiate that those expenses are necessary living expenses.

The following chart shows the monthly costs the national standards allow for different-size households. A breakdown of costs per category is given for households of up to four people.

Expense	1 person	2 people	3 people	4 people
Food	$300	$537	$639	$757
Housekeeping supplies	$29	$66	$65	$74
Apparel & services	$86	$162	$209	$244
Personal care products & services	$32	$55	$61	$67
Miscellaneous	$87	$165	$197	$235
Total	$534	$985	$1171	$1377

For more than four people,
*add an additional **$262** per person to the 4-person allowance*

National Standards: Out-of-Pocket Health Care

The health care expense standards have been established for minimum allowances for out-of-pocket health care expenses[3] (see table below). Out-of-pocket health care expenses include the following:

1. Medical services
2. Prescription drugs
3. Medical supplies (such as eyeglasses).

Elective procedures, such as plastic surgery or elective dental work, are generally not allowed.

Taxpayers and their dependents are allowed the standard amount monthly on a per-person basis, without questioning the amount they actually spend. If the amount claimed is more than the total allowed by the standards, the taxpayer must provide proof to substantiate that those expenses are necessary living expenses. The number of people in the household is generally the same as the allowed exemptions on the taxpayer's most recent year income tax return. *The out-of-pocket health care standard amount is allowed in addition to the amount taxpayers pay for health insurance.*

If you incur medical expenses that exceed the out-of-pocket allowance, you will need receipts to prove the expense, such as a pharmacy printout, doctor co-pays, etc.

Out-of-Pocket Costs

Under 65	$60
65 and Older	$144

---

3   The out-of-pocket health care standard is based on Medical Expenditure Panel Survey data.

Local Standards: Housing and Utilities

The housing and utilities standards[4] are local standards that are broken down to the state and county level (see table below). The standard for a particular county and family size includes both housing and utilities allowed for a taxpayer's primary place of residence. Again, family size is determined to be the same as the allowed exemptions on the taxpayer's most recent year income tax return.

Housing and utilities standards include the following:

1. Mortgage or rent
2. Property taxes
3. Interest
4. Insurance
5. Maintenance and repairs
6. Gas
7. Electric
8. Water
9. Heating oil
10. Garbage collection
11. Telephone and cell phone

You are allowed the standard amount, or the amount actually spent on housing and utilities, *whichever is less*. If the amount you claim is more than the amount allowed by the housing and utilities standards, you must provide documentation to substantiate that those expenses are *necessary living expenses*. We often argue that a larger house is necessary because it provides a home office space.

---

4   The local standards for housing and utilities are derived from U.S. Census Bureau and Bureau of Labor Statistics data.

The following table is an example of the local standards for housing and utilities for one state (Pennsylvania):

Pennsylvania - Local Standards: Housing and Utilities

Maximum Monthly Allowance (for all States: http://www. irs.gov/businesses/small/article/0,,id=104696,00.html)

County	Housing and Utilities for Families of:				
	1	2	3	4	5+
Adams	1373	1613	1700	1895	1926
Allegheny	1219	1432	1508	1682	1709
Armstrong	1010	1186	1250	1393	1416
Beaver	1147	1348	1420	1583	1609
Bedford	1028	1207	1272	1418	1441
Berks	1356	1593	1678	1871	1901
Blair	1017	1195	1259	1404	1426
Bradford	1066	1252	1319	1471	1494
Bucks	1836	2156	2272	2533	2574
Butler	1291	1516	1598	1782	1810
Cambria	969	1139	1200	1338	1359
Cameron	960	1127	1188	1324	1346
Carbon	1171	1376	1450	1616	1642
Centre	1309	1537	1620	1806	1835
Chester	1939	2277	2399	2675	2718
Clarion	986	1158	1220	1360	1382
Clearfield	976	1146	1208	1346	1368
Clinton	1034	1215	1280	1428	1451

County	Housing and Utilities for Families of:				
	1	2	3	4	5+
Columbia	1082	1271	1339	1493	1518
Crawford	1045	1228	1294	1442	1466
Cumberland	1344	1579	1664	1855	1885
Dauphin	1297	1523	1605	1789	1818
Delaware	1607	1888	1989	2218	2254
Elk	1025	1204	1268	1414	1437
Erie	1121	1316	1387	1546	1571
Fayette	946	1111	1170	1305	1326
Forest	923	1084	1143	1274	1295
Franklin	1227	1441	1519	1694	1721
Fulton	1139	1338	1410	1572	1597
Greene	975	1145	1207	1346	1367
Huntingdon	994	1167	1230	1371	1394
Indiana	1028	1207	1272	1418	1441
Jefferson	928	1090	1148	1280	1301
Juniata	1114	1308	1378	1537	1562
Lackawanna	1234	1449	1527	1703	1730
Lancaster	1351	1587	1672	1864	1894
Lawrence	1063	1249	1316	1467	1491
Lebanon	1226	1440	1517	1691	1719
Lehigh	1424	1673	1763	1965	1997
Luzerne	1144	1344	1416	1579	1604
Lycoming	1121	1317	1387	1547	1572
McKean	930	1092	1151	1283	1304
Mercer	1072	1260	1327	1480	1504

County	Housing and Utilities for Families of:				
	1	2	3	4	5+
Mifflin	997	1171	1234	1376	1398
Monroe	1477	1735	1828	2038	2071
Montgomery	1803	2117	2231	2487	2528
Montour	1164	1367	1440	1606	1632
Northampton	1512	1775	1871	2086	2120
Northumberland	1005	1180	1244	1387	1409
Perry	1201	1410	1486	1657	1683
Philadelphia	1157	1359	1432	1597	1623
Pike	1430	1680	1770	1973	2005
Potter	1002	1176	1239	1382	1404
Schuylkill	1044	1227	1293	1441	1464
Snyder	1103	1295	1365	1522	1546
Somerset	981	1152	1214	1354	1375
Sullivan	982	1153	1215	1355	1377
Susquehanna	1126	1322	1394	1554	1579
Tioga	1081	1270	1338	1492	1516
Union	1166	1370	1443	1609	1635
Venango	944	1109	1168	1302	1323
Warren	970	1140	1201	1339	1361
Washington	1168	1372	1446	1612	1638
Wayne	1206	1416	1492	1664	1691
Westmoreland	1152	1353	1425	1589	1615
Wyoming	1184	1390	1465	1633	1660
York	1351	1587	1672	1864	1894

Transportation

The transportation standards for taxpayers with a vehicle consist of both nationwide figures for monthly loan or lease payments (ownership costs), and additional amounts for monthly operating costs, which are local standards. The operating costs generally average $236/month and include the following:

1. Maintenance and repairs
2. Insurance
3. Fuel
4. Registrations and licenses
5. Inspections
6. Parking
7. Tolls

1. Ownership Costs (National Standards)

The ownership costs (see table below) provide the monthly allowances for the lease or purchase of up to two automobiles. A single taxpayer is normally allowed one automobile.

A problem may arise if you own an old car and do not have any remaining car payments at the time you enter into a payment plan with the IRS. The IRS will not factor any unexpected car payments when calculating the payment plan. Yet, if your car breaks down and you need a large-dollar repair you will not have the excess cash to repair it. Typically, older cars have much higher repair costs than newer models. We recommend to our clients that they carefully consider selling the old car and leasing or purchasing a newer car before entering into a payment plan so they do not have to worry about the old car dying after a payment plan is in effect, at which point they would most likely lack the finances to replace it.

For each automobile you will be allowed the lesser of:

- the monthly payment on the lease or car loan, or
- the ownership costs shown in the table below.

If you have no lease or car loan payment the amount you will be permitted for ownership costs will be $0.

	One Car	Two Cars
National	$496	$992

2. Operating Costs (Local Standards)

In addition to ownership costs, you are also allowed a budget for operating costs that is adjusted by regional and metropolitan area. For each automobile, taxpayers will be allowed the lesser of:

- the amount actually spent monthly for operating costs, or
- the operating costs shown in the table below.

	One Car	Two Cars
Northeast Region	$278	$556
Boston	$277	$554
New York	$342	$684
Philadelphia	$299	$598
Midwest Region	$212	$424
Chicago	$262	$524
Cleveland	$226	$452
Detroit	$295	$590
Minneapolis -St. Paul	$216	$432
South Region	$244	$488
Atlanta	$256	$512
Baltimore	$250	$500

	One Car	**Two Cars**
Dallas-Ft. Worth	$277	$554
Houston	$312	$624
Miami	$346	$692
Washington, D.C.	$270	$540
West Region	$236	$472
Los Angeles	$295	$590
Phoenix	$291	$582
San Diego	$301	$602
San Francisco	$306	$612
Seattle	$192	$384

Public Transportation

There is a single nationwide allowance for public transportation[5] for mass transit fares for a train, bus, taxi, ferry, etc. This amount is $182. Taxpayers with no vehicle are allowed the standard amount monthly per household without questioning the amount actually spent.

If you own a vehicle and use public transportation, expenses may be allowed for both, if they are needed for the health and welfare of you or your family or for the production of income. However, the expenses allowed would be the actual expenses incurred for ownership costs, operating costs, and public transportation, or the standard amount, *whichever is less.*

If the amount claimed for ownership costs, operating costs, or public transportation is more than the total allowed by the transportation standards, you must provide proof that those expenses are necessary living expenses.

---

5   Based on Bureau of Labor Statistics expenditure data

CHAPTER 9

Collection Information Statements

Collection Information Statements (CIS) in Brief

If you owe the IRS less than $50,000 in tax (or if you can pay your debt down to that) you can avoid completing the CIS form and disclosing assets, income, and expenses. If your case is $50,000 or under, it is classified as streamlined. In this situation you can set up an Installment Agreement (IA) either by phone or at the www.irs.gov web site.

🔓 TRADE SECRET

The standard payment deal for a streamlined case is a simple formula: the payment equals the tax divided by seventy-two months and is paid monthly on the date of your choice.

The IRS charges a small fee for IA setup. We prefer to have automatic deductions come straight from the checking account so the payment is not late resulting in a default of the IA.

Cases above the streamline tax threshold, and those who cannot pay down to the limit, must begin completing a CIS, Form 433-F for Automated Collection System or Form 433-A for a revenue officer. In this chapter, there are detailed planning options and techniques discussed. Be sure to focus on these planning ideas and to implement those appropriate to your personal situation and budget. For instance, do you have term life insurance? It is an allowed expense.

 **BEST PRACTICE TIP:** The CIS forms are completed and signed *under penalty of perjury*. I have not had a client prosecuted for this offense, but I represent a client now who was prosecuted for perjury and was sentenced to jail and fined by a Federal Court judge for hiding assets. Joe Taxpayer said, "I am paying you to keep me straight. What I did was stupid. I never want to go to prison again. I thought I was buried alive in there!" Joe's tumultuous enforced collection experience is stark so be careful and disclose all your assets.

Preparing a Collection Information Statement (Form 433)

Form 433-A

Form 433-A: Collection Information Statement for Wage Earners and Self-Employed Individuals (CIS), is used to determine how much money a taxpayer is capable of paying to the IRS in order to satisfy tax liabilities. The IRS uses the CIS information when deciding whether or not to accept an offer in compromise (OIC), installment agreement

(IA), or a taxpayer's request to enter into currently not collectible (CNC) status.

Form 433-A (CIS) basically compares your monthly income to necessary living expenses to determine your ability to pay the IRS. Since this form is somewhat lengthy and complex, this chapter will first establish which information you need to fill it out, and then break the form down, section by section, explaining how to complete it appropriately.

Who Should File Form 433-A

Form 433-A should only be filled out by wage earners and self-employed individuals.[1]

The following people may need to complete Form 433-A:

- An individual who owes income tax on Form 1040.
- An individual who may be a responsible person for a Trust Fund Recovery Penalty.
- An individual who may be personally responsible for a partnership liability.
- An individual owner of a limited liability company that is a disregarded entity.
- An individual who is self-employed. According to the IRS, a taxpayer is self-employed if he is in business for himself, or carries on a trade or business as a sole proprietor or an independent contractor.

Sections to Complete on Form 433-A

If you are self-employed, you must fill out every section of the form. If you are a wage earner, you must fill out sections 1 through 4. *Caveat: you cannot ignore any parts of a section that you are required to fill out.*

---

1   See generally, IRS Publication 1854: How to prepare a Collection Information Statement.

So, if there is a certain line that does not apply to you, just write "N/A" to fill in the blank. When there is not enough space for you to fill in a response, or more lines are needed, additional sheets of paper may be added. If additional sheets are added, you should note on the appropriate line that they have been added, and those sheets should clearly indicate which section they apply to.

Sections 1 Through 3

Sections 1 through 3 of Form 433-A are fairly straightforward. Write in your name, social security number, and employer identification number (this number is the taxpayer's business tax identification number, if self-employed) at the top of page 1 of the form.

- **Section 1** (Personal Information) is simply demographic information about you and your spouse.
- **Section 2** (Employment Information) asks for information about your current employer and your spouse's employer or, if you are self-employed, information about your business.
- **Section 3** (Other Financial Information) is looking for some additional background information about your finances. Keep in mind that Section 3 asks for copies of applicable documentation, meaning that if you answer yes on any of the lines, proof should be attached to the form, if possible, when it is filed.

Section 4: Personal Asset Information

The purpose of Section 4 is to calculate value of all of your current personal assets. Since this section is very important, this guide will break it down line by line, to ensure that you fill it out appropriately.

Line 11: Cash on Hand

The taxpayer must simply add up all of the cash he currently has on hand.

Line 12: Personal Bank Accounts

You must describe each personal bank account, and then total the amount of money in all of the accounts. These accounts include all checking accounts, online bank accounts, money market accounts, savings accounts, stored value cards (such as a payroll card from an employer, an electronic benefit card from a government agency, or a child support payment card), and safe deposit boxes. Even if an account has no money in it, it must be included. Bank loans should not be included in this section.

Line 13: Investments

You must describe each current investment or interest in a business. For each investment, you must deduct any loan balance from the current value to determine equity. Then, the equity of each investment must be added together. This section should include the following: stocks, bonds, mutual funds, stock options, certificates of deposit, retirement assets (such as IRAs, Keogh, and 401(k) plans), and all corporations, partnerships, limited liability companies or other business entities in which you are an officer, director, owner, member, or otherwise have a financial interest.

Line 14: Available Credit

You must describe the amount of available credit on each of your credit cards, and add all of the available credit together. You should only include credit cards issued by a bank, credit union, or savings and loan.

Line 15: Life Insurance

If you have a life insurance policy with a cash value you must provide the total amount of available cash in the life insurance policy or policies. If you do not have life insurance with a cash value, answer no for 15a and the line is complete.

If you answer yes, then you must describe each policy that has a cash value. For each policy, deduct the outstanding loan balance from the current cash value. Once the numbers are determined for each policy, add them together to calculate the total available cash from life insurance.

You can have a term life insurance policy and deduct the amount paid as an allowable expense in the expense column. As there is no cash value you do not have to complete the section but may want to disclose the policy as a backup document.

Line 16: Transferred Assets

This section is only relevant if you have transferred any assets in the past 10 years for less than full value. If not, you answer no and move on to 17a. If you answered yes, then you must list each asset involved in such a transfer, and describe the nature of each transfer.

Line 17: Real Property

Two notes about Lines 17 through 19. First, in each of these sections, you are required to determine fair market value of properties you own. Fair market value is simply the amount you could sell the asset for today. Second, each section requires you to state the date of the final payment of certain loans. This is the date that the loan or lease will be fully paid.

 **BEST PRACTICE TIP:** The IRS will verify real estate asset values at websites such as www.zillow.com. If the property has a substantially lower value, due to its condition, this should be explained as a note and supplemented with photos and other relevant evidence.

For <u>Line 17</u>, you must determine the equity in all of real property that you own, rent, and lease.

List the location of each property you lease, own, or are about to purchase. If you are leasing or renting, the lessor or landlord must be listed. If you are purchasing a property, the lender must be listed. The equity in each property is calculated by deducting its current loan balance from its current fair market value. The total equity of all properties is calculated by adding together the equity of each property.

Line 18: Personal Vehicles

This line is very similar to Line 17, except that instead of real property, the taxpayer must determine the equity he has in all of his leased and purchased personal vehicles, such as cars, boats, RVs, etc. Describe each vehicle (year, make, model, and mileage). If you are leasing, list the lessor. If you are purchasing a vehicle, list the lender. Use Kelly Blue Book or any similar source for value and submit a copy as backup. As with real property, the equity in each vehicle is calculated by deducting its current loan balance from its current fair market value. The total equity of all vehicles is calculated by adding together the equity of each vehicle.

Line 19: Personal Assets

This line is similar to lines 17 and 18, except that you must determine the equity in all leased and purchased personal assets not included in previous sections, such as all furniture, personal effects, artwork, jewelry, collections (coins, guns, etc.), and antiques. Do not include assets of minimal value, such as pillows or kitchen chairs. Again, equity in each asset is calculated by deducting its current loan balance from its current fair market value. The total equity of all assets is calculated by adding together the equity of each asset. The IRS allows $3,500 for personal assets.

Describe each asset and list its location. If you are leasing the asset, identify the lessor. If you are purchasing the asset, identify the lender.

Monthly Income/Expense Statement: Lines 20 Through 45

If you are a wage earner, you can go to this section (Lines 20 through

45) next. However, if you are self-employed, you must first complete Sections 5 and 6 (see below).

This section is broken down into two parts: Total Income (Lines 20 through 32) and Total Living Expenses (Lines 33 through 45).

Total Income

Each line in this section is for a different source of income. Determine total income by adding them all together. The sources of income that require no explanation are interests, dividends, pension/social security (for you and your spouse), child support, alimony, and other.

The following categories of income listed in this section are not as obvious, though, so further explanation is included.

Wages (Lines 20 and 21)

You must list both the gross wages and/or salaries for you and your spouse (any deductions are not considered here, but are instead part of the calculations for the Total Living Expenses section).

If you are paid weekly, multiply that amount by 4.3 (because some months have 4 weeks, but others have 5). If you are paid every two weeks, multiply that amount 2.17. If you are paid twice a month, multiply the amount by two. Where is line 22?

Net Business Income (Line 23)

Use the number calculated in line 82 of Section 6. If the net business income determined in line 82 is a loss, you should enter "0" here. If the amount is more or less than previous years, attach an explanation.

Net Rental Income (Line 24)

List the amount earned on any rental properties, after ordinary and necessary monthly businesses expenses are paid. Do not include deductions for depreciation or depletion. If the net rental income is actually a loss, you should simply write "0." If your rental property is losing money, the IRS will insist that you simply sell it to cut your losses.

Distributions (Line 25)

Enter the monthly average of total distributions from partnerships, subchapter S corporations, or limited liability companies.

Total Income (Line 32)

Calculate total monthly income by adding Lines 20 through 31.

Total Living Expenses (Lines 33 through 45)

Each line in this section is for a different type of expense. Determine your total monthly living expenses by adding them all together. You can only include necessary expenses, meaning those that provide for the health and welfare of you and your family and/or provide for the production of income, and must be reasonable in amount. The following types of expenses generally cannot be included: tuition for private schools, public or private college expenses, charitable contributions, voluntary retirement contributions, payments on unsecured debts such as credit card bills, cable television and other similar expenses.

The types of expenses that require no explanation are child/dependent care, life insurance, and taxes (income and FICA). The following categories of income listed in this section are not as obvious, though, so further explanation is included.

Food, Clothing, and Miscellaneous (Line 33)

Determine how much you are spending on clothing, food, housekeeping supplies, and personal care products for one month. If the amount you claim is higher for one of the specific expenses listed than the national standard for food, clothing, and miscellaneous (these standards are explained in detail in the Collection Financial

Standards chapter of this book), you must verify and substantiate that amount.

Housing and Utilities (Line 34)

Enter the monthly rent or mortgage payment for your principal residence. If the following expenses are not included in the rent or mortgage payments, their average monthly cost must be added as well: property taxes, homeowner's or renter's insurance, necessary maintenance and repair, homeowner dues, condominium fees, and utilities. Utilities that must be added include gas, electricity, water, fuel, oil, other fuels, trash collection, telephone, and cell phone.

Vehicle Ownership Costs (Line 35)

Enter the total monthly lease, purchase or loan payments for your vehicle(s).

Vehicle Operating Costs (Line 36)

Enter your average monthly costs for insurance, licenses, registration fees, inspections, normal repairs and maintenance, fuel, parking, and tolls.

Public Transportation (Line 37)

Enter your average monthly public transportation expenses for bus, train, and taxi fares, as well as any other mass transit fares.

Health Insurance (Line 38)

Enter monthly expense for health insurance.

Out of Pocket Health Care Costs (Line 39)

Enter the monthly total of medical services, prescription drugs, and medical supplies, such as eyeglasses and hearing aids. If this amount is higher than the national standard for out-of-pocket health care costs (see table below), the taxpayer must verify and substantiate that amount.

The following table shows the monthly standard amount allowed for out-of-pocket costs based on a person's age:

Out-of-Pocket Costs

Under 65	$60
65 and Older	$144

Court Ordered Payments (Line 40)

Enter all court-ordered payments. Child support and alimony are two common types of court-ordered payments. You will need copies of the court order as backup documents.

Other Secured Debts (Line 44)

Enter the average monthly payments for any other secured debts not already included.

Total Living Expenses (Line 45)

Calculate total monthly living expenses by adding Lines 33 through 44.

Section 5: Business Information

If you are self-employed and your business is a sole proprietorship (i.e., you file Schedule C), answer yes to line 46, and continue with Sections 5 and 6. If the business is *not* a sole proprietorship, answer no, and skip Sections 5 and 6. Instead, you will complete Form 433-B for the business.

Lines 47 Through 53

These are straightforward lines requesting basic information about the business.

Line 54: Payment Processor

List and describe all third-party processors used for the business to accept credit card payment (such as PayPal, Authorize.net, Google Checkout, etc.).

Line 55: Credit Cards Accepted by Business

List all credit cards accepted by the business.

Line 56: Business Cash on Hand

List all cash the business currently has on hand. Cash that is in a bank should not be included.

Line 57: Business Bank Accounts

List all of the business's bank accounts, and calculate the total amount of cash in all of the accounts. Include checking accounts, online bank accounts, money market accounts, savings accounts, and stored value cards (such as payroll cards, government benefit cards, telephone cards, and prepaid debit cards for expenses). Even if a bank account for the business has a zero balance, it still must be included.

No personal account information should be included here (personal accounts are listed in Section 4). Also, do not include bank loans.

Line 58: Accounts/Notes Receivable

You must determine the business's total outstanding balance for all accounts/notes receivable. An account receivable is money owed to a business by its clients and shown on its balance sheet as an asset. A note receivable is a claim for which formal instruments of credit are issued as evidence of debt, such as a promissory note. The total outstanding balance is calculated by adding the amount due for each account/note receivable together.

You must include e-payment accounts receivable and factoring companies, and any bartering or online auction accounts. All contracts must be listed separately, including any contracts awarded, but not yet started—this includes federal government contracts.

Line 59: Business Assets

This line is similar to Sections 17 through 19, in that you must calculate the total equity your business has in its assets. The equity for each asset is determined by deducting its current loan balance from its current fair market value, and then, the equity from all of the assets must be added together.

You should list all assets used in the trade or business that were not included in previous sections. Examples of these assets include all tools, machinery, equipment, and inventory. Also, Uniform Commercial Code filings must be included. Finally, you must include vehicles and real property owned/leased/rented by the business, if not previously included in Section 4.

Section 6: Sole Proprietorship Information

Two notes about Section 6. First, you should only filled it out if you are self-employed. Second, lines 60 through 81 should reconcile with the business's Profit and Loss Statement.

The first step for filling out this section is checking off whether you use the cash or accrual accounting method. Under the cash method, income is not counted until cash (or a check) is actually received, and expenses are not counted until they are actually paid. Under the accrual method, transactions are counted when the order is made, the item is delivered, or the services occur, regardless of when the money for them (receivables) is actually received or paid. After selecting your method of accounting, list the starting and ending dates for which the income and expenses described in this section apply.

Lines 60 through 81 are broken into two parts: Total Monthly

Business Income (Lines 60 through 69) and Total Monthly Business Expenses (Lines 70 through 81).

Total Monthly Business Income

This section is fairly straightforward. Determine your business's total monthly income by adding all of the following: gross receipts, gross rental income, interest, dividends, cash, and any other income (which must be specified).

Total Monthly Business Expenses

Determine your total monthly business expenses. Each line in this section is for a different type of business expense. Some of the categories are straightforward, including gross wages and salaries, rent, vehicle gasoline and oil, repairs and maintenance, insurance, and other expenses.

Other expenses that must be listed in this section require a little additional explanation. Materials purchased (Line 70) are items directly related to the creation of a product or provision of a service. Inventory purchased (Line 71) includes goods bought for resale. Supplies (Line 74) are items used in the business that are used up within one year, such as books, office supplies, and professional equipment. Utilities (Line 75) include gas, electricity, water, oil, other fuels, trash collection, telephone, and cell phone. Finally, current taxes (Line 79) include real estate, excise, franchise, occupational, personal property, sales, and employer's portion of employment taxes.

Net Business Income (Line 82)

Once the total monthly business expenses are calculated, they are deducted from the total monthly business income, resulting in the net business income. This number is also used on Line 23 of Section 4. If the amount is a loss, the taxpayer must enter "0" on Line 23.

Attachments

You must include copies of the following documents when filing your Form 433-A:

1. Three months of pay stubs, reflecting deductions from all employers for each person listed on Form 433-A.
2. Three months of receipts for living expenses, including all utilities (electric, oil, gas, etc.), telephone, water, sewer, groceries, and property taxes.
3. Three months of transportation expenses, to include all vehicle repairs and maintenance, automobile insurance premiums, and automobile loan payments. (including the value and mileage of vehicles).
4. Three months of healthcare expenses, including a pharmacy-generated printout of your prescription amount, insurance premiums, co-payments, and out-of-pocket costs.
5. Three months of bank statements (both sides of each page), to include checking, savings, IRA and brokerage accounts, pension earnings, and/or income received from other sources, current mortgage payment, and/or rental payment and lease agreement.
6. Automobile leases, if any.
7. Any child support and/or alimony received, if any.
8. Court-ordered payments, received or paid, if any.
9. Any life insurance policy that has a cash value. If there is a loan against the policy, provide proof of the loan.
10. Any real estate, other than his primary residence, that you own, to include the most recent statement from your lender, the current market value of the property, and the settlement sheet.
11. Proof of rental income, if any.

Signature(s)

You must include your signature on page 4 of Form 433-A. If there is joint income tax liability, both the husband and wife must sign page 4.

Form 433-F

Generally, if you owe a small amount of money, the IRS may request that Form 433-F be filed, instead of Form 433-A. Form 433-F is a short version of 433-A (two pages instead of six). Since Form 433-A asks for all of the information in Form 433-F, the IRS will generally accept that form, even if Form 433-F is requested. It is in your best interest to file Form 433-A, if you have the time to do so because it is more thorough, thereby giving more weight and merit to your claims. If you are submitting this information by phone or online, you can use Form 433-F; however, if this is being submitted in-person to a revenue officer, she will require Form 433-A.

Since Form 433-F generally asks for the same information as Form 433-A, the following explanation will refer to sections of Form 433-A (which have been thoroughly explained earlier in this chapter). Any differences between the two forms will be clarified.

Preliminary Information

You cannot ignore any parts of a section that is required to be filled out. So, if there is a certain section or question that does not apply to you, simply write "N/A" to fill in the blank. Also, if there is not enough space for you to complete your response, you may add additional sheets of paper. If you do so, however, be sure to indicate— on the actual form in the appropriate section—that you have been added them, and the sheets themselves should clearly indicate which section they apply to.

The top of the first page asks for basic information about you and your spouse. This section is very straightforward.

A. Accounts/Lines of Credit

This section asks for the same information as the personal bank accounts and investments portions (Lines 12 and 13) of Section 4 of Form 433-A. You should follow the same rules and restrictions for filling out lines 12 and 13 of Form 433-A.

The end of this section requires you to fill out the number of dependents that will be claimed on next year's return and the number of dependents claimed on last year's return. Also, you must indicate whether the dependents are under or over the age of 65.

B. Real Estate

This section asks for the same information as the real property owned, rented, and leased portion (Line 17) of Section 4 of Form 433-A. You should follow the rules and restrictions for filling out Lines 12 and 13 of Form 433-A. This section differs from Line 17 of Form 433-A, in that you must check off which property is your primary residence, include the year each the property was purchased or refinanced, and the purchase price or refinance amount.

C. Other Assets

This section asks for the same information as the personal vehicles leased and purchased and personal assets portions (Lines 18 and 19) of Section 4 of Form 433-A. Follow the rules and restrictions for filling out Lines 18 and 19 of Form 433-A. For each asset you must include a description, the monthly payment, the year purchased, the final payment date, the current value, the balance owed, and the equity.

D. Credit Cards

This section asks for information similar to the available credit portion (Line 14) of Section 4 of Form 433-A: type of credit card, credit limit, balance owed, and minimum monthly payment. Follow the rules and restrictions for filling out Line 14 of Form 433-A.

E. Wage Information

This section asks for information similar to Section 2 of Form 433-A. Follow the rules and restrictions for filling out Section 2 of Form 433-A. However, this section also asks for the following information for you and your spouse: the amount of money grossed per pay period, taxes per pay period (federal, state, and local), date of birth, and total income from the last year's 1040 Tax Return.

F. Non-Wage Household Income

This section asks for the same information as the total income portion of Section 4 of Form 433-A. You should follow the rules and restrictions for filling out the Total Income portion of Form 433-A. Below is a table of which 433-A line matches up with the information requested in 433-F.

A few notes about filling out this section. First, unlike the total income portion of 433-A, there is a section for you to include any unemployment income. Also, Form 433-F requires that you differentiate pension and social security income. Finally, Form 433-F combines all other sources of income into a single category (as opposed to two "Other" categories in Form 433-A).

Form 433-F, Section F	Form 433-A, Section 4
Alimony income	Line 29
Child support income	Line 28
Net self-employment income	Line 23
Net rental income	Line 24
Unemployment income	N/A
Pension income	Lines 26 and 27
Interest income	Line 22
Social Security income	Lines 26 and 27
Other	Lines 30 and 31

G. Monthly Necessary Living Expenses

This section asks for the same information as the total living expenses portion of Section 4 of Form 433-A. Follow the rules and restrictions for filling out the total living expenses portion of Form 433-A. Below is a table in which each 433-A line matches up with the information requested in 433-F.

Form 433-F, Section G	Form 433-A, Section 4
Food / Personal Care	
Food	Line 33
Housekeeping supplies	Line 33
Clothing and clothing services	Line 33
Personal care products and services	Line 33
Miscellaneous (cable, Internet, etc.)	Line 33
Transportation	
Gas/insurance/licenses/parking/ maintenance/etc.	Line 36
Public transportation	Line 37
Housing and Utilities	
Rent	Line 34
Electric, oil/gas, water, trash	Line 34
Telephone and/or cell phone	Line 34
Real estate taxes and insurance	Line 34
Medical	
Health insurance	Line 38
Out-of-pocket healthcare expenses	Line 39
Other	
Court-ordered payments	Line 40

Child/dependent care	Line 41
Estimated tax payments	Line 43
Term life insurance	Line 42
Retirement (employer-mandated)	N/A
Retirement (voluntary)	N/A
Profit and loss statment	N/A
Other (left blank on form)	Line 44

A few notes about filling out this section. First, while Form 433-A combines all food/personal care costs and housing and utilities costs, Form 433-F requires you to break those costs down into their sub-parts. Second, unlike in Form 433-A, there is a space for you to include retirement costs (both employer-mandated and voluntary) and costs from your profit and loss statement. Finally, any documents to prove costs that are required in filing Form 433-A, must also be included when filing Form 433-F.

H. Additional Information

This final section is for you to negotiate an installment agreement with the IRS. You suggest a monthly payment amount, the day of the month each payment will be made, and the maximum down payment that you are able to pay to lower the balance due. Your payment proposal should not span longer than 60 months (five years). However, if you cannot afford a payment plan that fully pays the balance in five years, the IRS may accept an installment agreement for less but over a longer time.

Finally, all unfiled tax returns must be signed and attached in order for the IRS to consider a payment plan.

Signature(s)

You must include your signature on page 2. If there is joint income tax liability, both spouses must sign page 2.

 **BEST PRACTICE TIP:** The IRS only has 10 years to collect on each year's assessment. They will extend payment plans longer than 60 months (five years) if your income shows that you cannot full pay the account in those 60 months. Sometimes they will even allow balances to expire. You should consult the collection statute expiration dates (CSED), which you should have gotten during the case review step. If you do not know the CSED for each year, contact the IRS and request that information. For example, if your CSED is within five years, the IRS is going to push for a higher payment plan. This will pay more of the balance off before the CSED is reached. If you have a considerable amount of time before the CSED, then the IRS can set up a lower installment agreement because they have longer to collect from you. Knowing the CSED is extremely important when setting up an installment agreement!

CHAPTER 10

Currently Not Collectible Status

Currently Not Collectible Status in Brief

This chapter on Currently Not Collectible (CNC) status begins with an explanation of the most important factor in determining whether the IRS will grant you CNC status —if it is an undue hardship to pay the taxes owed. Next, the process of achieving CNC status will be described. Then, the 10-year tax collection rule will be explained. The chapter ends with a brief warning about the dangers of avoiding payment through CNC status.

Usually, a taxpayer fails to pay the taxes within 10 days after notice and demand by the IRS because he doesn't have funds available. The IRS can then collect the tax through a levy on all property. Once the IRS processes a levy (e.g., takes money from a bank account) the taxpayer has certain legal rights as explained in Chapter 5, Enforced Collection, and Chapter 7, Appeal Rights.

You may owe money to the IRS with no means of paying that debt. You might be unemployed or only earning enough to cover your necessary living expenses, and if you paid anything toward old tax liabilities, it would cause you a financial hardship. In this event, you should negotiate to be placed in currently not collectible status. This is sometimes the best option because you do not have to pay anything on the tax debt while your account remains in CNC status. You will only be placed in CNC status if collection would cause undue hardship. CNC status suspends all collection activity but does not forgive or compromise the tax debt. Interest and penalties continue to accrue during the CNC period. Please note that CNC does NOT extend the statute.

If you owe the IRS and cannot afford to pay them any amount after paying your reasonable living expenses, you need to focus on this step in order to be placed in CNC status. If you have a financial hardship and cannot make payments on the past due tax liabilities, CNC status allows you to not make any payments to the IRS on old tax liabilities as long as you remain tax compliant going forward.

> *If you are compliant the IRS can and will work with you. Tax compliance is the accurate preparation, timely filing, and payment of any tax due.*

You will need to compile your financial information on a Form 433-A: Collection Information Statement (CIS), or 433-F (See Chapter 9). You can convey the information to the IRS by Internet, phone, mail, or in person to a revenue officer, or in an appeal. Be prepared to complete the form or request time to do so, and *do not give financial data off the cuff.* If you are wrong or low in your estimated expenses, it is hard to convince them to raise your necessary living expenses later. Review Chapters 8 (Collection Standards) and 9 (Collection Information Statements) for more detailed information on completing the forms and backup data.

If by a preponderance of the evidence (meaning it is more likely than not), the CIS demonstrates your inability to make a payment agreement with the IRS, CNC status can be a temporary state of relief while you try to increase your income. You may want to consider or file an offer in compromise or wait to become eligible to discharge your income tax liability in bankruptcy.

CNC status basically means that you, the taxpayer, cannot pay tax debts at this time. Before the IRS assigns this status to you, it first must confirm that you are tax compliant. In other words, you must have all of your taxes filed. Second, the IRS must receive the evidence that you have no ability to pay (proof of unemployment compensation, Social Security, or a pay stub are good examples). This backup evidence is usually provided through an IRS form, which can be obtained by going to the IRS website at www.IRS.gov and then searching for Form 433-A.

You may use Form 433-A: Collection Information Statement. This form will allow you to inform the government of your complete financial condition. All assets, bank accounts, mortgages, loans, insurance, credit cards, household, and living expenses must be listed on this form. The form must be signed by you under penalty of perjury and forwarded to the revenue officer along with the supporting documents such as proof of unemployment compensation, pay stubs, and copies of bank account statements.

Once the IRS reviews the CIS and determines your financial situation and approves your CNC status, it must stop all collection activities, including levies and garnishments on wages. The IRS must also send you an annual statement stating the amount of tax still owed. No payments are required as long as you remain in CNC status. If your wealth dramatically increases the IRS will default the CNC status and request payments, because you may now have the ability. However, if this increase in wealth diminishes you may re-qualify for CNC status if you can prove once again that any collection would be an undue hardship.

What is Undue Hardship?

Before you may be granted CNC status, the IRS must first determine that paying any tax debts would cause an undue hardship. Undue hardship does not simply mean that it would be difficult or annoying for you to pay off your debts. The IRS will only find that an undue hardship exists if paying your tax debt will result in you being unable to pay your reasonable basic living expenses. Generally, CNC status is granted to taxpayers with no income or assets, no equity in assets, or insufficient income to make any payment without causing hardship. If an undue hardship does exist, any levy must be released by the IRS for as long as you remain in CNC status.

As you have learned in Chapter 9 (Collection Information Statements) the IRS considers national standards, local standards, and other expenses to calculate your reasonable living expenses. National standards are used for clothing, food, housekeeping, and personal care expenses. If you claim more than the national standards, you must substantiate and justify each separate expense above the total national standard. For housing and transportation, you are allowed the local standards or the amount actually paid, *whichever is less*. Other expenses that may be considered are those that provide for the health and welfare of you and your family, or are for the production of income.

For purposes of determining a specific taxpayer's reasonable amount of living expenses, any information that is provided to the IRS by the taxpayer is considered (with reference to the previously mentioned standards), including the following:

- The taxpayer's age, employment status and history, ability to earn, number of dependents, and status as a dependent of someone else;
- The amount reasonably necessary for food, clothing, housing, medical expenses, transportation, current tax payments,

alimony, child support, or other court-ordered payments, and expenses necessary to the taxpayer's production of income;

- The cost of living in the geographic area in which the taxpayer resides;
- The amount of property exempt from levy which is available to pay the taxpayer's expenses;
- Any extraordinary circumstances such as special education expenses, a medical catastrophe, or natural disaster; and
- Any other factor that the taxpayer claims bears on economic hardship and brings to the attention of the IRS.

The Process of Getting Placed in CNC Status

The process of being placed in CNC status begins when you are found to be liable for taxes and do not have the financial means to pay and/or are suffering an ecomonic hardship. You may wish to pursue CNC status through the IRS. To do so, you may follow one of many avenues. You can:

1. Call ACS (This method is for the most proactive taxpayers);
2. If a revenue officer has contacted you, you may provide financial information to her;
3. Send to ACS a CIS and request CNC in writing. This is sent to the correspondence desk.
4. You may, within the time frame stated in the correspondence, request a hearing with the IRS Office of Appeals (Appeals Office) in front of an impartial settlement officer.

In any case, you must compile and submit a CIS with backup financial information to demonstrate your circumstances. This is generally done with Form 433-A: Collection Information Statement for Wage Earners and Self-Employed Individuals, or 433-F: Collection Information Statement. If the taxpayer is using the Automated

> # DO YOUR HOMEWORK
> # AND BE PREPARED.
>
> *Before you call ACS, complete your CIS. They will ask you detailed questions about your necessary living expenses. If you give low monthly costs for food and clothing it will be hard to adjust the number higher in a subsequent call. The IRS has a long memory.*

Collection System, Form 433-F must be used. The collection information statement should indicate that if the taxpayer's wages were levied, he would be unable to pay reasonable living expenses.

The next step is the IRS decision regarding whether an undue hardship would exist if you were required to pay the tax debts in an installment agreement. If the IRS rules in your favor then you do not have to make monthly payments or worry about levies, wage garnishments, or asset seizures during CNC status. Also, any existing levy must be released until the CNC status is revoked. The good news is that the statute of limitations on collection—the ten-year statute—continues to run towards its expiration. The corresponding bad news is that interest and penalties continue to accrue (grow) during CNC status.

10-Year Limit for Collection; the Risk
of Rolling the Dice With CNC

The IRS has 10 years to complete collection action on each year's tax debt. The clock starts once the tax liability is assessed (i.e., filing a return). That clock does not stop while you are in CNC status. If the ten-year statute expires while you are in CNC status, the total tax liability expires—including all interest and penalties that have accrued during the course of the CNC period. The IRS can no longer collect these debts. However, the longer you are in CNC status, the higher the risk of having to pay the IRS a very large amount of money. Consider this worst-case scenario.

Suppose Joe Taxpayer is granted CNC status, and remains in CNC status for nine years. During that ninth year, Joe turns his life around and is now able to start paying his tax debts. Remember, CNC status has merely suspended collection—it does not forgive or compromise the tax, interest, and penalties that accrue during CNC period. Joe is now going to owe nearly a decade worth of back-taxes, interest, and penalties. This sum would be exponentially higher than the original amount owed nine years earlier. Therefore, it is important to keep in mind that while seeking CNC status might be tempting, avoiding payment while under CNC status is not without its risks.

Once the case is assigned CNC status, it is a good time to consider an offer in compromise or any other collection alternative (e.g., penalty abatement, bankruptcy, or innocent spouse relief). Read Chapters 11 to 17 for an explanation of these options.

For a more detailed explanation of the statute of limitations for IRS collection actions, see Chapter 15.

CHAPTER 11

Installment Agreements

Installment Agreements in Brief

Sometimes a taxpayer simply does not have access to the amount of money owed to the IRS at the time the payment is due. If this is the case, an option may be to set up an installment agreement[1] with the IRS. An installment agreement is a plan agreed upon by both the IRS and the taxpayer, where the taxpayer is given a certain amount of time (usually no more than 60 months) to pay money owed to the IRS in set monthly increments. During the course of this chapter on installment agreements, the process of creating such an agreement will first be explained, followed by a discussion of the benefits versus the downside of paying in this manner, in order to determine whether it is the best option for a taxpayer. Finally, the possibility of taking out a loan from a third party lender, family member, or friend in lieu of setting up an installment agreement will be examined.

---

1   Also referred to as a payment plan, payment agreement, and payment option.

1. A taxpayer does not have a right to an installment agreement when he can fully pay the balance due the IRS.
2. An installment agreement for a balance due to the IRS of less than $50,000 is called a *streamlined agreement*:
   a. Balance due or amount of tax owed to the IRS divided by 72 months = Installment Payment (e.g., $50,000 divided by 72 = $694.44 per month).
   b. Streamlined agreements can be set-up one of several ways: over the internet at www.irs.gov; in writing by filing Form 9465-FS to request an installment agreement; or by telephone to the Automated Collection System. In a streamlined agreement you should not have to provide financial information on Form 433-F.
3. Non-streamlined agreements: Agreements for tax liabilities over $50,000.
   a. As above, but not online and IRS will require financial disclosures. Agreements become more complicated in that the IRS requires proof of income (3 months of both pay stubs and bank statements to determine if there is extra W-2 or other income). IRS also requires proof of expenses that exceed the national standards such as court ordered payments, alimony and/or child support, and medical expenses. See also, Chapters 8 and 9 on Collection Information Standards and Collection Information Statements.

Setting Up an Installment Agreement

There are a few ways to set up an installment agreement with the IRS. The options available to you vary depending upon the amount of money owed to the IRS. If you owe $50,000 or less in combined tax, penalties, and interest there are three options. First, you can use the online payment agreement available on the Internet at https://sa2.www4.irs.gov/irfof/lang/en/eiaTPstatus.jsp. Second, you may call the number on the tax bill or notice and try to set up an agreement on the phone with an IRS agent. Finally, you may fill out Form 9465-FS: Installment Agreement Request, and mail it to the address on the tax bill.

It is more difficult to qualify for an installment agreement if you owe more than $50,000 in combined tax, penalties, and interest. You may not use the online payment method; however, you still have the option of calling the number on the tax bill in order to try and work out an installment agreement. A second option is to fill out and mail both Form 9465: Installment Agreement Request, and Form 433-F: Collection Information Statement, to the address on the tax bill.

After you have submitted a request for an installment agreement, the IRS will decide whether or not to accept the terms you have requested. A written response will be sent notifying you that the IRS either accepts the terms you requested or requires a modification of those terms.

There are certain fees involved in setting up an installment agreement. First, there is a $105 user fee for new installment agreements. There are a couple of ways to reduce this fee, though. First, the fee is reduced to $52 for agreements where the payments are deducted directly from the taxpayer's bank account. Also, if the taxpayer's income is low enough, based on poverty levels established by the Department of Health and Human Services, the taxpayer may be eligible for a reduced user fee of $43. There is also a $45 fee for reinstating defaulted agreements or restructuring an existing agreement.

The Benefits

There are a couple of benefits to establishing an installment agreement with the IRS. First and foremost, an installment agreement gives you a feasible way of paying money owed to the IRS, if the total amount owed is not currently at your disposal.

Another reason you might consider entering into an installment agreement is that IRS enforced collection actions, such as levies against your personal or real property, are generally not made during the following times:

- While an installment agreement is being considered
- While an installment agreement is in effect
- For 30 days after a request for an installment agreement has been rejected
- For any period while a timely appeal of the rejection or termination of an installment agreement is being evaluated by the IRS

Basically, entering into an installment agreement, or requesting to do so, at the very least might buy you some more time before the IRS begins to pursue collection actions.

The Downside

It is important that you keep in mind that while setting up an installment agreement may make paying money to the IRS more manageable, the use of such an agreement results in paying more than the original amount owed. Based on the terms of the agreement, these additional payments might be quite substantial. The following simplified example proves this point:

Suppose Joe Taxpayer owes $15,000 in taxes. An installment agreement is then entered into with the IRS, where Joe has 36 months to pay off the money owed, at an interest rate of 5% and a failure-to-pay penalty of 1% each month. Based on those numbers, the payments could be around $508.50 per month. At that rate, Joe would end up paying $18,306 over the course of the 36 months; $3,306 more than was originally owed.

Also, there are the previously discussed fees associated with setting up an installment agreement that can range from $43 to $105.

Taking Out a Loan as an Alternative to an Installment Agreement

There are certain situations where taking out a loan in order to pay off money owed to the IRS in a single payment might be a cheaper option than entering into an installment agreement with the IRS. Based on the example given in the previous section (**The Downside**), Joe Taxpayer owed $15,000 to the IRS but ended up paying $18,306 over the course of a 36-month installment agreement. However, based upon the availability of favorable interest rates with third-party lenders, taking out a loan could have resulted in ultimately paying less and removing the tax lien earlier. The following chart shows how this is possible:

Interest Rate	Monthly Payment	Number of Months	Total Paid to Lender	Savings to Taxpayer
7%	$463	36	$16,674	$1,632
9%	$477	36	$17,172	$1,134
11%	$491	36	$17,679	$627
13%	$505	36	$18,195	$111

This chart is based on a $15,000 loan to be repaid over 36 months with different interest rates, compared to the installment agreement set up by Joe Taxpayer. Notice that even with an interest rate of 13%, you end up paying $18,195, which is $111 less than would be paid under Joe's installment agreement. If you were able to find a loan with a 7% interest rate, you would pay $1,632 less than Joe. Therefore, given favorable interest rates, taking out a loan with a third-party lender could be a better alternative than entering into an installment agreement with the IRS.

In larger tax cases, the revenue officer (RO) may require you to apply for a loan with a bank or mortgage lender to try to borrow against the equity in a home or other asset. Many people do not understand the mathematics shown on the chart above. In actuality, the RO is trying to save you money and have the debt paid sooner. The penalties imposed by the system are admittedly high but are an integral part of the self-assessing tax system. In some cases, the penalties can be abated. See Chapter 12 (Penalty Abatement). If you are an innocent spouse you can request relief, see Chapter 16.

The point is, that even after an installment agreement has been entered, other relief can be requested to lower the tax, penalty or interest.

CHAPTER 12

Penalty Abatement

Penalty Abatement in Brief

When a taxpayer fails to file or pay his taxes on time, the Internal Revenue Service may impose a financial penalty and interest on the tax. The longer the taxpayer takes to pay the penalty, the more it increases—to a maximum of 25%. Therefore, over a period of a few months, a relatively minor penalty for failure to file on time, or failure to pay the tax on time, or both, can become substantial.

The good news is that the penalties may be abated (reduced or terminated). There are many reasons why the IRS may abate a penalty. Generally, if the taxpayer's conduct that caused the penalty was reasonable, then the penalty will be abated. In addition, there are specific reasons why a number of penalties may be abated.

In this chapter I will explain the legal standard for penalty abatement, reasonable cause, then I will describe a number of common penalties and how to abate them, and finally, I will discuss the basics of challenging the interest on those penalties.

The IRS requires a good reason for late filing and/or late payment of the tax due. The abatement request must show *reasonable cause* to obtain relief. You can ask for the first year penalty to be removed because of a good tax history, but if you are a habitual non-filer, it is rarely granted unless you send a letter in with the return(s) explaining your reasons for not filing. Try to nip the assessment of the penalty in the bud by addressing it up front. If your request is denied, be prepared to appeal. You must appeal because the appeals office has broader authority than do first level reviewers.

THE GOLDEN RULE

Always appeal your request, if denied,
to protect your Constitutional due process rights.

The Abatement Process

To file for penalty abatement you will complete Form 843. You may use this form to claim a refund or request an abatement of certain taxes, interest, penalties, fees, and additions to tax assessed by IRS. You must file a separate form requesting abatement for each year or period (if quarterly), or type of tax or fee. Of course, there are exceptions listed in the form's directions on line 5.

The best source of information if you are filing Form 843: Claim for Refund and Request for (Penalty) Abatement, is www.irs.gov.

Search Internal Revenue Manual in the search bar on the upper left side of the page. Once you find the IRM— the IRS manual, go to Chapter 20 on penalty and interest. Part 20.1 is the Penalty Handbook. This is the source most practitioners use to model their penalty abatement arguments. Attorneys might add some case law to the argument, but in the first filing outlining the facts and the background, and making a compelling story, is all that is necessary. The significance of this section is that it gives you a basic understanding of the reasonable cause standard and what the IRS will consider as a basis for penalty abatement in more detail than the outline format provided.

Reasonable Cause

The general rule is that a penalty will be abated if your failure is due to reasonable cause. This is the legal standard: Was your conduct in not filing or paying your tax on time reasonable under the circumstances? If it was reasonable, then the IRS can abate the penalty; if not, then the penalty will not be abated. Reasonable cause means that you exercised ordinary business care and prudence in your affairs, but you were still unable to comply with the requirements of the law.

You must submit to the IRS a written request for penalty abatement due to reasonable cause. The request must include all relevant facts that support your claim. You can make your initial request for abatement after an examination by the IRS but before a penalty has even been assessed, or with a return that either is filed late or indicates taxes that will be paid late. If the IRS denies the initial request, you may make additional requests for penalty abatement based on new information.

TRADE SECRET: I have found over the years that the best practice for the taxpayer is to send a letter with the late return requesting that a penalty for failure to file on time not be assessed. Taxpayers achieve a much higher success rate preventing the assessment of that penalty by explaining the reasonable cause at the time of filing, which also saves the time and expense of requesting abatement after the assessment. Send a short letter explaining the problem. Specifically request that the penalty for failure to file not be assessed because of the circumstances described in the letter. More often than not, the letter will prevent the penalty for failure to file the tax return on time from ever being assessed. Remember to send each late tax return (together with the explanatory letter) in separate envelopes.

This is a list of scenarios that may or may not constitute reasonable cause:

1. A death, serious illness, or unavoidable absence of the taxpayer, or a death or serious illness in his immediate family may constitute reasonable cause.

2. A fire, natural disaster, or other disturbance that destroyed tax records or prevented compliance in some way may be reasonable cause.

3. The inability of the taxpayer to get hold of records needed to comply with a tax obligation may constitute reasonable cause.

4. If the failure to satisfy a tax debt was a result of a recent change in either tax law or a tax form, and the taxpayer could not reasonably be expected to be aware of the change, this may constitute reasonable cause.

5. Generally, a lack of funds will *not* constitute reasonable cause, yet undue hardship due to lack of funds may be cause for penalty abatement.

6. Ignorance of the law typically does not constitute reasonable cause. However, ignorance of the law supplemented with factors such as limited education or a lack of previous tax experience, may support reasonable cause.

7. Claiming that the taxpayer (or his subordinate) made a mistake or forgot to satisfy a tax requirement *does not* establish reasonable cause. However, such acts may be considered by the IRS if the taxpayer establishes that he exercised ordinary business care and prudence and the other facts support reasonable cause.

Likewise, relying on another person to pay a tax debt is generally not sufficient to establish reasonable cause.

8. Reliance on the false advice of a competent tax advisor or preparer may constitute reasonable cause.

9. Reasonable cause can be established where the taxpayer relied on erroneous written or oral IRS advice. However, a taxpayer can only rely on this advice until he is informed that the advice is no longer valid.

10. Any unreasonable error or delay by the IRS in performing a ministerial act may be reasonable cause. A ministerial act is a procedural or mechanical act that does not involve the exercise of judgment or discretion (such as filing or data input).

When determining whether reasonable cause exists, the IRS reviews the two previous tax years and other open periods to check for payment patterns and penalty history. The IRS also considers the length of time between the event cited as the reason for non-compliance and ensuing compliance and whether the taxpayer could have anticipated the event that caused the non-compliance.

10 Common Tax Penalties and How to Abate Them

1. Filing a Return After its Due Date

A taxpayer who fails to file a tax return by the due date (including any extensions) is subject to a penalty of 5% of the amount of tax due for each month the return is not filed, up to a maximum of 25%. A minimum penalty of $135 or the net amount of tax owed, whichever is less, is imposed where a taxpayer fails to file a return within 60 days of the due date (with extensions). If a taxpayer requests an extension and is denied, the IRS will typically give the taxpayer 10 more days to file, before imposing penalties.

Below is a partial list of scenarios that may or may not constitute reasonable cause for failure to file a return on time:

1. Reliance on an attorney or accountant to file a return or obtain an extension of time is not reasonable cause

2. A child's reliance on his parents to file his returns does not establish reasonable cause even if the parents are legally obligated to file the returns.

3. A taxpayer cannot rely on his spouse to file a return. Yet, reasonable cause may be found where one spouse has all the income and records and refuses to discuss financial matters with his spouse.

4. A taxpayer's reliance on an advisor may be reasonable cause where he is not capable of meeting the ordinary business care and prudence requirement due to illness, senility, incompetence, or mental retardation.

5. Reliance on the advice of counsel that a taxpayer does not need to file a reutrn may be reasonable cause.

6. Depending on the jurisdiction, reasonable cause may or may not exist where the taxpayer's advisor provides false information about a filing deadline.

7. A taxpayer's belief that a return, but no tax, is due is not reasonable cause

8. Reasonable caused may be established by a taxpayer's inability to file an correct return.

9. Neither a large workload nor preoccupation with business affairs is reasonable cause.

10. Fifth Amendment concerns (ie. the privilege against self-incrimination) do not establish reasonable cause.

2. Paying Less than the Tax Shown on the Return

A taxpayer who fails to pay the amount of tax shown on a tax return by the due date is subject to a penalty of 0.5% of the amount of tax owed for each month that amount remains unpaid, up to a maximum of 25% (50 months).

There is reasonable cause for failure to pay if the taxpayer can show that he exercised ordinary business care in providing for payment of his tax liability, but was unable to pay or would suffer an undue hardship if he paid by the due date. A lack of funds due to changed circumstances alone is not reasonable cause for a failure to pay. All the facts and circumstances of the taxpayer's financial situation are considered by the IRS, including the amount and nature of his expenditures in light of the income expected prior to the due date of the tax. Therefore, if you go to Las Vegas and blow all your money before your taxes are paid, the IRS will not consider your lack of funds as a reasonable cause not to pay. However, if your child becomes ill and unexpected medical expenses arise shortly before tax payments are due, you are far more likely to have failure to pay penalties abated for reasonable cause.

The taxpayer cannot rely on facts or events occurring after the due date when attempting to establish reasonable cause. However, the IRS can present post-due-date evidence to prove that the taxpayer was unreasonable in failing to pay taxes on time.

3. Underpaying Tax Owed Due to Negligence

If any portion of an underpayment of tax is due to negligence or disregard of the tax laws, a 20% penalty of this portion is imposed. Negligence is a failure to make a reasonable attempt to comply with the tax laws or to exercise reasonable care in preparing your tax return. Disregard of the tax code is carelessly, recklessly, or intentionally ignoring those rules. A taxpayer has not acted negligently when he reasonably relied upon the advice of a tax professional or lawyer.

If a taxpayer is negligent is keeping his records, and he does not make a reasonable attempt to present a fair and accurate accounting of his tax status to the IRS, he will probably be charged with the negligence penalty. However, if the taxpayer did not keep adequate records for reasons other than negligence, there will be no negligence penalty. The adequacy of a taxpayer's records is determined on a case-by-case basis (factors include the type and size of his business).

The negligence penalty may be abated if the taxpayer can prove that there was reasonable cause for the underpayment of tax, as long as the taxpayer acted in good faith.

Finally, if an underpayment is due to disregarding a tax rule, and this disregard was the result of the taxpayer having a legitimate disagreement with the legal validity of the rule, there will be no penalty if the disagreement is disclosed to the IRS, the challenge to the rule's validity is made in good faith, and there is a reasonable legal basis to the challenge.

4. Committing Fraud

If a tax underpayment of tax is due to fraud, a 75% penalty is imposed. The IRS defines fraud as the intentional wrongdoing of a taxpayer for the purpose of tax evasion.

The failure to file a tax return does not alone establish fraud; there must be some indication of fraud, including the following:

1. Consistently failing to report large amounts of income over a period of years.
2. Deliberately failuring to maintain adequate financial records, or including false information in those records.
3. Lying to IRS investigators.

If there was reasonable cause for an underpayment, and the taxpayer acted in good faith, no fraud penalty is imposed. The IRS typically will not impose fraud penalties where the taxpayer, in good faith, allows a tax professional to prepare his return.

Finally, when a husband and wife file a joint return, and one spouse is charged with the fraud penalty, the fraud penalty is not also automatically charged to the other spouse, without the IRS determining that spouse had also committed fraud.

5. Penalties Related to Tax Deposits

Employers must periodically collect and deposit certain taxes with authorized financial institutions. A penalty is imposed if the taxpayer fails to deposit the amount of tax owed by the depositing deadline. A deposit will not be considered late if it is mailed at least two days before the deadline.

A deposit-related penalty may be removed by the IRS if there was reasonable cause for the failure to deposit. The following situations constitute reasonable cause:

1. Death/serious illness or unavoidable absence of the person who was responsible for making the deposit.
2. The loss of financial records by fire or other disaster.
3. The taxpayer cannot determine the correct amount of a deposit for reasons that he has no control over, such as a complete loss of records due to a flood.
4. The taxpayer lacked the funds to make the deposit, if the lack of funds was not due to his negligence.

Finally, if a *first-time depositor* mistakenly sends the deposit to the IRS, instead of the correct depository, the penalty may be waived.

6. Substantially Misstating the Value of Assets

If an underpayment of tax is due to a substantial valuation misstatement, 20% penalty is charged to the taxpayer. A substantial valuation misstatement will be found if the value of any property claimed on a tax return is undervalued by 150% or more, as determined by the IRS;

1. The penalty increases to 40% if the underpayment is the result of the taxpayer undervaluing the property by 200% or more.
2. If there was a reasonable basis for the substantial valuation misstatement, and it was made in good faith, the penalty will not apply.

7. Underpaying Estate and Gift Taxes Due to Understating the Value of Property

A 20% penalty is charged to the underpayment of estate and gift taxes that are the result of valuation understatements of property that was transferred either by will or gift. The penalty applies if the taxpayer undervalues the property on his return by 35% or more. If the property is undervalued by 60% or more, the penalty increases to 40%.

There are two circumstances where the penalty will not apply. First, there is no penalty if the underpayment is less than $5,000. Second, if the taxpayer had reasonable cause for undervaluing the property on his return, and it was claimed as such in good faith, there will be no penalty.

8. Substantially Understating Income Tax

A 20% penalty is charged on underpayments of tax due to a substantial understatement of income tax. A substantial understatement exists if the amount of income tax the taxpayer did not pay due to the understatement exceeds the greater of 10% of the tax required to be shown on the return or $5,000. For example, assume Joe Taxpayer claimed $60,000 for his income tax, and the actual income tax should have been $70,000. The understatement would be $10,000 ($70,000 owed minus $60,000 claimed). Since $10,000 exceeds the greater of 10% of $70,000 ($7,000) or $5,000, the IRS would consider this to be a substantial understatement, so the 20% penalty would be imposed.

The penalty will not be imposed if there was reasonable cause for the underpayment, assuming it was made in good faith. When determining whether reasonable cause existed, the IRS will focus on the degree of the taxpayer's effort to assess his correct income tax liability.

If a taxpayer relies on the advice of a tax professional, the IRS will typically consider that reliance as reasonable cause and good faith, thereby not imposing the penalty.

Also, a taxpayer's reliance on false information reported on certain forms (Form W-2, Form 1099, or other information returns) is proof of reasonable cause, only if he did not know, or have reason to know, that the document contained bad information.

9. Paying Tax with a Bad Check (or Other Form of Payment)

The IRS charges a penalty if a bad check (or other form of payment) is submitted to the IRS for the payment of tax. The penalty is 2% of the amount of the check, if the check is for $1,250 or more. If the check is less than $1,250, the penalty is either $25 or the amount of the check, whichever is less.

The IRS will abate this penalty if the taxpayer can prove he submitted the check in good faith, with reasonable cause to believe that it was a valid check.

10. Submitting a Frivolous Tax Return

A $5,000 penalty—regardless of whether any tax is due—may be imposed on any taxpayer who files a frivolous tax return. A return is considered frivolous by the IRS if it lacks sufficient information on which the IRS can determine the taxpayer's actual tax liability. The penalty will also be imposed if the return is based on a position that the IRS has previously identified as frivolous, or it reflects the taxpayer's intention to delay the IRS's ability to enforce the tax laws.

The following are examples what may constitute a frivolous tax return:

- It contains skewed descriptions of line items.
- Many or all of the lines are left blank.
- It asserts bogus constitutional objections, such as the government does not have the right to collect taxes. This excuse is often used by tax protestors to no avail.
- It contains clearly inconsistent information.
- It contains clearly unallowable deductions.

Intentionally failing to sign a tax return may result in the IRS imposing the frivolous submission penalty, regardless of the accuracy of the return.

If the taxpayer withdraws a return within 30 days of being notified by the IRS that it has deemed the return frivolous, then the penalty will be abated.

Challenging The IRS's Denial of a Request For Abatement of Tax Penalty Interest

A taxpayer may challenge the IRS's denial of his request for tax penalty and interest abatement in Tax Court, if he files a petition within 180 after the date a final determination not to abate is mailed by the IRS. If the following three requirements are met, the Tax Court may overrule the IRS's decision not to abate the interest.

1. The taxpayer must bring the action, by filing a petition for review with the Tax Court, within 180 days from the date the final determination letter is mailed. If the taxpayer misses this deadline, he loses his opportunity to contest the penalty.

2. A final determination must be made by the IRS regarding a taxpayer's request for abatement before the Tax Court will accept a taxpayer's petition for review. If there is any disagreement as to whether a communication made by the IRS to the taxpayer

was actually a final determination, the Tax Court will base its decision on whether the IRS intended for that communication to constitute a final determination.

3. The IRS's failure to abate interest must be an abuse of discretion. The Tax Court will generally find an abuse of discretion is evident and overturn the IRS's decision if the failure to abate interest would be widely perceived as grossly unfair.

CHAPTER 13

Tax and Bankruptcy

Bankruptcy in Brief

Can certain income taxes be forgiven in bankruptcy? YES! The general rule is that income taxes cannot be discharged (or forgiven) in a bankruptcy proceeding. Most of us would assume income taxes could not be forgiven in bankruptcy. In fact, most attorneys and accountants do not know the specific treatment of tax debt in a bankruptcy. As with every rule, there are exceptions to the general rule that income taxes cannot be discharged. The secret is that specific income taxes can actually be discharged or forgiven in bankruptcy. Taxpayers who want to consider bankruptcy must discuss with their bankruptcy attorney his knowledge of tax discharge. If this is an option for you, read on to learn the specific rules that apply.

Income taxes can be forgiven or eliminated in bankruptcy if they meet certain rules.

- The taxes had to be filed by the taxpayer at least two years ago if these were filed late (or not at all) and three years ago if filed on time,

- The IRS had to have assessed them over 240 days ago,
- The taxpayer cannot have been involved in fraud or evasion in the relevant years,
- A taxpayer filing a case under chapter 13 of the Bankruptcy Code must have filed any tax returns that were required to be filed for tax years ending in the four years before the date of the filing of his petition by the creditor's meeting, BUT
- Trust taxes such as employer withholding *cannot* be discharged.

A person can discharge certain income taxes, but one must apply specific bankruptcy code provisions to determine which, if any, taxes can be erased or discharged in bankruptcy. In bankruptcy jargon, there are basically two types of taxes: non-priority taxes and priority taxes.

Taxes that can be discharged in bankruptcy are called non-priority taxes. Taxes that cannot be discharged in bankruptcy are called priority taxes, which an employer holds in trust for the government from either the employee's check, or the sales transaction in the case of sales tax. The taxpayer is held to be personally liable for priority taxes, such as businesses taxes.

Bankruptcy is not a panacea, or total solution, but it is an opportunity that should be considered by taxpayers who have overwhelming income tax debt or are suffering from enforced collection, such as wage garnishments, bank levies, or seizures that are making life impossible.

A significant benefit of bankruptcy is the automatic stay provision in the bankruptcy code. With the exception of criminal proceedings, actions for a family support order or the modification of such an order, actions to collect support from property that is not property of the bankruptcy estate, tax audits, demands for tax returns and/or assessments, the automatic stay provides that once the debtor's attorney files the bankruptcy case, the IRS (and, in fact, all creditors) must stop all actions in furtherance of attempting to collect a debt, and the debtor can, in certain cases, request a release of the assets by the court. This benefit is more expansive than just taxes; all creditors must stop calling, collecting on judgments, or suing the debtor. Bankruptcy provides benefits that other collection alternatives, such as installment agreements and offers in compromise, can never provide to the debtor.

You now know that there *are* exceptions to the general rule that income taxes cannot be discharged or erased in a bankruptcy proceeding. The next step is determining which income taxes can be extinguished in bankruptcy.

Most individuals who voluntarily commence a bankruptcy case do so under either Chapter 7 or Chapter 13. The two primary exceptions are individuals who wish to reorganize (as opposed to liquidate, which is only accomplished under Chapter 7 of the Bankruptcy Code), but have unsecured debt that exceeds $360,525 or secured debt which exceeds $1,081,500, and fishermen and farmers. If an individual's debt exceeds either of the two limits, he/she will be ineligible to file a case under Chapter 13. If the individual is either a fisherman or farmer, he/she may be eligible to file a case under Chapter 12 of the Bankruptcy Code. Chapter 12 has increased debt limits which permit fishermen and farmers to reorganize their financial affairs and still continue to operate their business.

A Chapter 7 bankruptcy is referred to as liquidation. An individual who is trying to discharge all of his debts files a Chapter 7 bankruptcy and certain income taxes can be included. In a Chapter 7, the Bankruptcy Code provides for a full discharge of allowable debts. Certain non-priority income taxes fall within the definition of allowable debt. In a Chapter 13 bankruptcy, an individual is required to have sufficient income to establish a payment plan to repay any arrearages on secured debts and sometimes a portion of any unsecured debt over a period of time of not less than 3 years and not to exceed 5 years. Most unsecured debt, such as credit cards, which remains unsatisfied at the completion of the Chapter 13 plan period is discharged. In a Chapter 13 bankruptcy, a portion of the debtor's income is paid to the court-appointed trustee who makes monthly payments to the creditors.

It is critical to be able to distinguish between a priority and non-priority tax claims. This determination is especially important because priority tax claims must be paid in full in Chapter 13; they are non-dischargeable in Chapter 7 and sometimes in Chapter 13. Income tax that is not secured by equity in assets can be discharged if it meets the requirements outlined below.

Notice of Federal Tax Lien

Whether or not the IRS filed a notice of federal tax lien (NFTL) can be found in your account transcripts. This determines if the IRS is a secured creditor in the bankruptcy or an unsecured creditor. If the IRS filed a notice of federal tax lien, the claim is secured; if you have any assets to which this lien can attach, then the IRS is a secured creditor. The filing of the NFTL is important to the IRS in securing its position as one of your creditors. This is one important reason why the IRS is so quick to file a NFTL against you. The NFTL secures the government's interest against the your assets and prevents the discharge of the debt that has attached to a hard asset, such as real estate.[1]

For an income tax to be dischargeable in the bankruptcy proceeding, it must be a non-priority tax. To determine if income tax from a particular year is dischargeable there are specific requirements established in the Bankruptcy Code. They are as follows:

1. The original return was due to be filed, with extensions, more than three (3) years before the bankruptcy petition (Petition) was filed.[2]
2. The tax return was filed at least two (2) years before the petition.[3]

---

1   Bankruptcy Code § 506.
2   Bankruptcy Code § 507(a)(8)(A)(i).
3   Bankruptcy Code § 523(a)(1)(B).

3. The tax assessment is at least 240 days old.[4]
4. The tax return was not fraudulent.[5]
5. You are not guilty of tax evasion.

Essentially, the tax debt must come from a tax return that was due to be filed at least three years before you file your petition for bankruptcy.[6] Therefore, we must review your IRS account transcript to see if an extension to file the return was received and accepted by IRS. If you did file for the extension to file that particular year's tax return, it would extend the three-year period from April to October.

The due date of the tax return will include any extensions. This is a common problem area in calculating the three-year period. Many taxpayers do not recall that they filed for an extension from April 15th to October 15th, extending the three-year period by six months. This is the specific reason why account transcripts need to be obtained for each tax year that a taxpayer has a liability, so that the exact date that he filed his tax return can be determined. Failing to consider extensions is a common mistake. Even a seasoned attorney could be negligent and improperly file within the three-year period by not reviewing the IRS account transcripts to determine if an extension to file the return was filed by the taxpayer and extended the three-year period.

The tax debt must originate from a tax return that *actually was filed* at least two years before you file your petition in bankruptcy, but which *was due to be filed* more than three years ago.[7] This time period is measured from the actual date that the tax return was filed, not its due date. In this instance, a tax return can be filed late. The tax return for the year 2000 could be filed in 2005, as long as two years

---

4   Bankruptcy Code § 507(a)(8)(A)(ii).
5   Bankruptcy Code § 523(a)(C).
6   Bankruptcy Code §507(a)(8)(A)(i).
7   Bankruptcy Code §507(a)(8)(A)(ii).

have expired (from filing) before you file the petition in bankruptcy to discharge the liability.

The tax assessment must be at least 240 days old.[8] This is known as the assessment requirement. Thus, if the IRS audits the return, you must allow an IRS final determination in the audit or an IRS proposed assessment to become final and then count 240 days. If the IRS has not audited or challenged the self-reported balance due, the assessment is final. This information is in the IRS account transcript, and it must be reviewed carefully before filing the petition.

When you are preparing to file for bankruptcy, you can order all of the account transcripts from the IRS and provide them to the bankruptcy attorney for his review. Make sure the bankruptcy attorney knows the significance of the account transcripts, the timing rules to discharge income taxes, and that the income taxes can be discharged by filing an Adversary Proceeding.

The rules that the tax was not fraudulent, nor was the taxpayer guilty in court of tax evasion are self-explanatory.[9] However, there are Chapter 13 exceptions when fraud could be discharged in bankruptcy. This issue is explained later in this section.

Proving Prior Years' Taxes Were Filed

Chapter 13 debtors are required to file with the appropriate taxing authorities, by the day before the first scheduled meeting of creditors, all tax returns that the debtor was required to file for all taxable periods ending in the four years before the petition. Be prepared to bring copies of the returns to the first creditor's meeting. Creditors may also request a copy, and if the latest tax return is requested, it must be provided to them.

---

8   Bankruptcy Code section 523(a)(1)(B).

9   Bankruptcy Code section 523(a)(C).

Substitute For Return (SFR)

A substitute for return (SFR) is a tax return prepared by the IRS and filed because the taxpayer did not file an original return. The IRS uses wage and income information provided by third parties, such as employers' Form W-2 and Form 1099 to create the SFR. If the IRS filed an SFR, it cannot be discharged in bankruptcy. Moreover, since all tax returns have to be filed, be prepared to file original returns before the meeting of the creditors.

Releasing Tax Liens and Liens
That Can Survive The Bankruptcy

A caveat respecting the tax lien and the release of it with respect to your real estate: as you learned in the section about tax liens, the Notice of Federal Tax Lien (NFTL) attaches to all of your assets when the tax is assessed or it becomes your debt. In bankruptcy, you can receive a release of the tax lien by showing there is no value or equity in the property to be released. The IRS gives consideration to other liens that were filed before the NFTL; in other words, liens filed before the NFTL such as a mortgage or judgment, take priority to the NFTL.[10] Thus, if there is equity in the real property, the tax lien attaches to the equity and remains a valid lien after you are discharged from the bankruptcy.

In the tax lien section (Chapter 5), we discussed the fact that a tax lien can be discharged or removed through another process—subordination or discharge of the tax lien. In this process, you can pay the IRS an amount equal to the equity in the property to transfer it to an unrelated third party in a real estate sale or to remove a lien from

---

10   26 U.S.C. §6325(b)(2)(B) Discharge of property.

equipment or other assets. See Chapter 5's section on subordination for a more extensive explanation.

Non-Dischargeable Taxes

A taxpayer cannot discharge trust fund taxes in bankruptcy.[11] Specifically, these are withholding taxes that are withheld from an employee's paycheck or sales taxes collected in a business transaction. Trust fund taxes, also referred to as civil penalties, are priority taxes and cannot be discharged. However, there is a 10-year statute of limitations respecting the collection of trust fund taxes by the IRS. This is generally 10 years from the date of assessment, not the filing of the businesses tax return. The IRS has three years to assess the trust fund tax to the responsible persons, usually the businesses owner/operator.

Bankruptcy Code section 523(a)(1)(C) prevents the discharge of debts, specifically tax debts, where the taxpayer attempted to evade the payment or committed fraud in the filing of the return. Although we are not going to delve into the specifics of the fraud cases where the code and courts have permitted discharge of tax debt associated with fraud, suffice it to say there are Chapter 13 bankruptcy cases in which the court has allowed discharge. However, there are many cases where the court has dismissed the taxpayer's case for bad faith, as well. There are also cases where the IRS has accepted an offer in compromise in these circumstances.

The courts look at these cases on a case-by-case basis, but the judges seem to stop tax protesters from discharging tax debt where the service has charged them with fraud penalties. The courts view a taxpayer who came to court with unclean hands as manipulating the system for his

---

11   Bankruptcy Code section 507 (a)(8)(C) prevents the discharge of a "tax required to be collected or withheld and for which the debtor is liable in any capacity."

own purposes. The case law is clear that the courts will not allow this, as it is within the discretion of the judge to permit discharge. So if charged with fraud, bankruptcy can be attempted, but the adversary proceeding will no doubt consist of a thorough review of intent and how the taxpayer used his money.

Tolling/Reach Backs

It is critical that you and your bankruptcy attorney review the IRS account transcripts to determine if there is tolling. Tolling is a legal term that means the countdown for a certain time period—for example, the 240-day assessment period—is stopped, thereby extending the deadline. This is similar to a time-out in a sports event. A team, the IRS, calls a time-out if an offer in compromise (OIC) is filed. During the time-out, the IRS huddles and decides what the strategy will be after the OIC is over because the OIC prevented the IRS from collecting tax from the taxpayer during the period after the OIC was filed.

In tax cases, taxpayers can stop the IRS from collection by filing an appeal, a collection due process hearing request, or an offer in compromise. It is important to be able to review the IRS account transcripts to determine if there was tolling of the three-year period, the two-year period, or the 240-day period. For instance, the 240-day period after an assessment is extended by any time during which an offer in compromise is pending or in effect during the 240 days, plus 30 days. Further, additional time periods during which any collection action is stayed as a result of an appeal of a collection action will have an additional 90 days added. If this is the case, have a tax attorney confer with your bankruptcy attorney to make sure that you don't file the bankruptcy prematurely. If that is done, it is possible that none of the taxes will be dischargeable. I saw a bankruptcy case where the attorney did not know of the tolling; the case was filed 11 days before the taxes would be dischargeable and thus the taxpayer could not discharge the taxes. The object is to discharge the income tax in bankruptcy; in order to do this successfully, you must follow the rules outlined above and consider the tolling exception to the rules.

Bankruptcy Timeline Example

Suppose Joe Taxpayer has filed his petition for bankruptcy on January 1, 2010, and now wishes to discharge income tax debt through the bankruptcy proceeding. There are three deadlines that must be considered when determining whether a certain income tax debt is dischargeable.

First, for an income tax return filed on time, the original return must have been due to be filed, with extensions, more than three years before the bankruptcy petition was filed. Three years before January 1, 2010 (the date the bankruptcy petition was filed) is January 1, 2007. Therefore, in order for an income tax to be dischargeable, the return from which it arose must have been due to be filed before January 1, 2007.

If any extensions were granted, they must be included in the calculation. Suppose Joe was granted a 6-month extension to file his return. So, if the original deadline for filing the return was December 1, 2006, but a 6-month extension was granted, the new date the return was due to be filed was June 1, 2007. Because June 1, 2007 is less than three years earlier than the date the bankruptcy petition was filed, Joe would be unable to discharge the income taxes arising from that return.

Second, for an untimely-filed income tax return, the tax return must have been filed at least 2 years before the petition. Two years before January 1, 2010 is January 1, 2008. Joe must have filed the return from which the income tax he is attempting to discharge arose before January 1, 2008.

Finally, the tax assessment must be at least 240 days old. Assume that the current date is January 1, 2010 (the date Joe filed his petition for bankruptcy); 240 days before January 1, 2010 is May 6, 2009. This means that the IRS must have made a final determination about the relevant return (including any audits) no later than May 6, 2009.

Based on those dates, Joe would be able to file his petition for bankruptcy on January 1, 2010, if the return from which the income tax in question arose was due to be filed before January 1, 2007, the return was actually filed before January 1, 2008, and the IRS made a final determination of the return before May 6, 2009. If any of those events occurred after those dates, then January 1, 2010 would be too early to file for bankruptcy, and the income tax could not be discharged.

Now, suppose that on March 1, 2008, Joe filed an offer in compromise for the tax owed for the return we have been using in the example. From that date, until the IRS makes a decision about the offer in compromise, all of the countdowns for the three previously discussed deadlines stop, if the countdown is actually occurring at that time. Once the IRS makes a decision, either granting or rejecting the offer, the countdowns continue, with the addition of 90 days.

Suppose it takes 6 months for the IRS to make a decision on the offer in compromise. This means that any of the pending countdowns occurring from March 1, 2008 to September 1, 2008 must be stopped during that timeframe, because of tolling.

In order to determine how tolling would affect Joe, we must choose a date by which the return was due to be filed, a date when it was actually filed, and a date when the IRS made its final determination. Suppose that the return was due to be filed December 1, 2006, the return was actually filed on December 1, 2007, and the final determination was made on May 1, 2009. Based on these dates, tolling, resulting from the offer in compromise, would affect Joe in the following ways:

1. The return was due to be filed on December 1, 2006, so the 3-year deadline was met on December 1, 2009. Since the offer in compromise was filed in 2008, before December 1, 2009,

tolling applies to this deadline, pushing it forward an additional 6 months plus 90 days. The new earliest date on which the bankruptcy petition could be filed—with the possibility of discharging any income tax obligation for this tax period—is August 30, 2010.

2. The return was filed on December 1, 2007, so the 2-year deadline for an untimely filed income tax return was met on December 1, 2009. Since the offer in compromise was filed in 2008, before December 1, 2009, tolling applies to this deadline, pushing it forward an additional 6 months plus 90 days. The new earliest date on which the bankruptcy petition could be filed, with a possibility of discharging any income tax obligation for this tax period, is August 30, 2010.

3. The IRS made its final determination on May 1, 2009, which occurred after the tolling event had already completed (the IRS made its decision on the offer in compromise of September 1, 2008). Therefore, the tolling event has no impact on this determination date, and the earliest date the bankruptcy petition could be filed, with a possibility of discharging any income tax obligation for this tax period, is determined by adding 240 days. The date that this deadline is met is December 27, 2009.

The effect tolling has on Joe is clear. *Without* a toll-inducing event (filing an offer in compromise), Joe would have met all three deadlines by filing on January 1, 2010, based on the dates of the three event listed above. However, *with* tolling, the first two deadlines are pushed forward to August 30, 2010. That date would then become the earliest date on which Joe could file his petition for bankruptcy. So, if Joe did not understand the concept of tolling and filed the petition on January 1, 2010, the income tax for the return in question would not be dischargeable through the bankruptcy proceeding.

Bankruptcy Estate Taxes

When a taxpayer files a bankruptcy, he is referred to as a debtor. The bankruptcy case creates what is called an estate, which generally includes all legal and equitable interest in property of the debtor. There are certain exceptions, such as exempt property and abandoned property. Abandoned property is part of the estate when it is filed, and then abandoned or subsequently removed from the estate. Exempt property, on the other hand, is never part of the bankruptcy estate.

In a Chapter 7 or 11 filed by an individual, the bankruptcy estate is treated as a separate taxable entity from the debtor and the bankruptcy estate may be required to file a separate tax return and pay taxes separately from the debtor. The trustee of the bankruptcy estate or the debtor-in-possession will file tax returns using a separate tax I.D. number from the taxpayer. The debtor is responsible for filing his own return and paying income taxes on income earned during the year that was not part of the bankruptcy estate.

In a Chapter 7 or 11 bankruptcy, *where the Court dismissed the case* for failure to cooperate (e.g., file schedules or make payments), the estate is no longer treated as a separate taxable entity from the individual. The debtor is treated as if the bankruptcy petition was never filed. In this circumstance, the debtor must file amended returns on Form 1040X to replace the return previously filed for the bankruptcy estate. If the debtor is an individual in a Chapter 7 or 11 bankruptcy, all income, deductions, or credits that belong to the bankruptcy estate should not be included on the debtor's tax return. Also, any debts cancelled in the bankruptcy should not be included as income on the debtor's return. However, the bankruptcy estate must reduce certain losses, credits, and the basis of property by the amount of cancelled debt.

Bankruptcy law determines which of the debtor's assets become part of the bankruptcy estate. A transfer of an asset from the debtor to the bankruptcy estate is not treated as a disposition for income tax purposes.

As a result, the transfer does not result in a taxable event to the debtor. At a point in time when the bankruptcy estate is dismissed or terminated, the transfer back to the debtor of the estate's assets does not result in a taxable event either. Also, the abandonment of property by the estate to the debtor is a non-taxable disposition of property. In the event that the debtor received abandoned property from the estate, the debtor retains the same basis as he had at the time he filed the bankruptcy.

Bankruptcy Tax Attributes

In an average Chapter 7 bankruptcy, the taxpayer does not have tax attribute issues. When a taxpayer has one of the following issues he will need to complete Form 908:

1. Net operating loss carryovers.
2. Carryovers of excess charitable contributions.
3. Recovery of tax benefit items.
4. Credit carryovers.
5. Capital loss carryovers.
6. Basis, holding period, and character of assets.
7. Method of accounting.
8. Passive activity loss and credit carryovers.
9. Unused at-risk deductions.
10. Other tax attributes as provided in the regulations.

The bankruptcy estate receives the debtor's assets and his tax attributes, meaning the basis of assets, capital losses, passive losses, loss carry forwards, and refund claims. The attributes are reduced in the bankruptcy. The debtor can plan the issues by first reviewing IRS Publication 908: The Bankruptcy Tax Guide, and IRC 1328 and 108. The taxpayer must file Form 982: Reduction of Tax Attributes Due to Discharge of Indebtedness (and Section 1082 Basis Adjustment), to show his reduction in attributes with his return in the year of his discharge. The filing of Form 982 will prove the attributes that remain for the taxpayer for the next tax year.

The tax attributes of the estate are to be reduced by any excluded income from the cancellation of debt that occur during the bankruptcy. When the bankruptcy estate is terminated, the debtor assumes any remaining tax attributes that were taken over by the estate and any of the listed attributes that arise during the administration of the estate. If, after the bankruptcy, the debtor receives Form 1099-C for cancellation of debt during the bankruptcy, the debtor may not have to report the entire amount of cancelled debt as income, as exceptions apply to the general rule. Generally, debt that is cancelled or forgiven in a bankruptcy must be included in gross income for tax purposes, such as credit card debt. However, debt that is discharged in a bankruptcy is not included as income for tax purposes. The debt includes any indebtedness for which the taxpayer is liable or which attaches to the taxpayer's property.

If the taxpayer excludes cancelled debt from income because it is cancelled in the bankruptcy case, he must use the excluded amount to reduce certain tax attributes, such as the basis of assets, losses, and credits.

Summary

Specific income taxes can be erased or wiped out in bankruptcy. The rules are very tricky and detailed so the taxpayer must find a knowledgeable bankruptcy attorney. The IRS can be a secured creditor by filing a NFTL. The NFTL attaches to the taxpayers equity in real property or other assets. The liens can be paid off, avoided, or removed, in the bankruptcy.

Discharging income taxes in bankruptcy can be done if the tax is non-priority and fits within the specific rules. Generally, the taxes have to have been filed three years and assessed more than 240 days ago and there can be no issue of tax evasion or a conviction for fraud. This is a very basic outline, but if you are considering bankruptcy you will know to discuss all tax issues with bankruptcy counsel.

Make sure the bankruptcy attorney agrees to file an adversary proceeding, if necessary, and to review the IRS account transcripts for the filing dates and any filing extensions that extended the relevant dates.

CHAPTER 14

Offer in Compromise

Offers in Compromise in Brief

This is the concept behind those pennies-on-the-dollar promotions you have seen on TV. Many tax firms use this come-on to seduce taxpayers who owe money to the IRS to sign up with them. These firms hype the offer in compromise (OIC) program as an easy out, suggesting that with their help, the IRS will settle your tax liabilities for a mere fraction of what you owe. They twist the truth about as far as they can. Think about it for a moment: Does it sound too good to be true? It is.

However, there is an "offer in compromise" program, and the government will settle for less when there is no way in the world the taxpayer could ever pay his debt in full.

During the course of this chapter on offers in compromise, first I will explain the importance of understanding a taxpayer's reasonable collection potential and how to calculate that number. Then, I will describe in detail the process of submitting an offer in compromise to the IRS.

Finally, I will touch on how to appeal the IRS's decision, if an offer in compromise is rejected.

In an OIC, you need to account for your equity in your assets and your excess income truthfully. The IRS valuation unit will independently value your assets. The IRS's valuation unit is highly skilled and experienced. Do not underestimate them.

CAUTION: Do not hide assets or "forget" to list the real value of properties on the Form 433-A (and the supporting documents you submit), because they are signed *under penalty of perjury*. The Department of Justice criminally convicted (for the IRS) a former tax preparer for not listing assets on his own OIC and submitting the OIC based on fraudulent documents. He served two years at Fort Dix Prison. Subsequent to the OIC filing, he was audited and the IRS found income that he had not reported on his tax returns. They found tax evasion to add to the criminal case. Joe Taxpayer told me, "What I did was stupid. I want you to represent me and never let me do anything like that again. I never want to go to prison again!"

The IRS also calculates your disposable income and multiplies it to determine your ability to pay.

The fact that you do not have a job does not zero out your income and ability to pay the IRS. The IRS will average your past income or take the industry average for a person of your trade or education level and calculate your potential earnings.

So, pennies on the dollar this is not. But if you have a financial hardship or are disabled, this is a path you must consider. Remember—

you must be fully compliant; all tax returns must be filed. If you start the OIC process you must be prepared to supplement your filings and to appeal if your OIC is rejected. On appeal, you can use the bankruptcy argument as a negotiating position. During the process, remember to call and speak to the examiner. Be forthright with your circumstances. Do not hide. They will find you.

The Offer in Compromise Program

When a taxpayer is unable to pay off a tax debt, he has a few options to resolve that problem with the IRS, depending on his ability to pay. An offer in compromise is an agreement between a taxpayer and the IRS, where a taxpayer satisfies a tax debt by only paying off a certain portion of it. Basically, an offer in compromise is somewhere between an installment agreement, in that the taxes are paid off over an extended period of time, and currently not collectible status, in that less than the full amount of money owed to the IRS is ultimately paid. Submitting an offer in compromise is the appropriate option when it is in both the best interest of the taxpayer and the IRS to accept such a settlement.

There are three reasons why the IRS will accept an offer in compromise: doubt about collectibility, exceptional circumstances, and doubt about liability. First, doubt about collectibility means that the IRS doubts that the taxpayer would be able to pay off all of the money owed in the amount of time the IRS has to collect a certain debt. Second, the IRS may grant an offer in compromise given exceptional circumstances, even if the taxpayer has the money to fully pay all taxes owed. These circumstances generally arise when a taxpayer anticipates future costs that will consume a large amount of his assets, such as when the taxpayer has a child who was recently diagnosed with a disease that is very expensive to treat. Finally, doubt about liability means that there is a legitimate doubt that the tax liability assessed by the IRS is correct.

In that case, an offer in compromise might be accepted if a taxpayer is willing to pay an amount that both he and the IRS agree is owed. An example of this scenario is when a taxpayer is an innocent spouse, and makes this claim to the IRS during the OIC. If this claim results in the IRS having a legitimate doubt as to the taxpayer's liability, the OIC may be accepted.

Reasonable Collection Potential

A taxpayer's reasonable collection potential ("RCP") is the highest amount of money the IRS determines that it can collect from a taxpayer. Generally, in order for a taxpayer's offer in compromise to be approved by the IRS, the offer must be greater than or at least equal to the taxpayer's RCP.

The IRS calculates a taxpayer's RCP using a formula found on Form 433 (OIC): Collection Information Statement. The formula for an individual is as follows:

> **Total Available Assets +**
> **[(Total Household Income – Household Expenses)**
> **x (48 or 60)]**
> **= RCP**

While this equation may seem a little complex, it actually is not too difficult to follow. First, the taxpayer needs to determine his total household monthly income and, from that, deduct all of the household's monthly expenses. Then, this number is multiplied by 48 (if the taxpayer plans to pay the offer in five months or less) or 60 (if the taxpayer plans on paying the offer in more than five months). This number is then added to the taxpayer's total available assets. This sum is the RCP, and generally, the IRS will not accept an offer in compromise for any less.

The following is an excellent example of how to calculate a taxpayer's RCP (for an individual wage-earner):

Joe Taxpayer is single and owes the IRS $70,000.00 in back taxes, penalties and interest. Below is Joe's relevant financial information:

Primary Residence:

1. Fair Market Value $195,000
2. Mortgage $170,000

Car:

1. Fair Market Value $25,000
2. Debt $30,000

Other Valuable Assets: Fair Market Value $2,000

1. Income – $5,100 per month
2. Living Expenses – $4,850 per month

Based on this scenario, Joe's RCP can be determined using the formula, through these four steps.

1. Determine monthly income minus costs: $5,100-$4,850 = $250
2. Assuming Joe will repay the debt within 5 months, multiply the number calculated in (1) by 48: $250 X 48 = $12,000
3. Determine Joe's total assets: equity in his home + equity in his car + value of his other assets = (fair market value of his home – mortgage) + (fair market value of his car – debt) + value of

his other assets = ($195,000-$170,000) + ($25,000-$30,000)[1] + ($2,000) = $25,000 + $0 + $2,000 = $27,000

4. Add the numbers calculated in (2) and (3) to determine Joe's RCP (minimum offer amount): $39,000

Given Joe's current assets, income, and expenses, his RCP is $39,000, and he owes $70,000 to the IRS. Therefore, if the IRS agrees to an offer in compromise for $39,000, Joe would save $31,000 ($70,000 – $39,000). Suppose Joe was not familiar with the RCP formula, and he thought a reasonable offer would be for $60,000. If the IRS accepted such an offer, Joe could lose up to $21,000 in savings ($60,000 – $39,000). This is why it is crucial for a taxpayer to understand his RCP before submitting an offer in compromise to the IRS.

Submitting an Offer in Compromise to the IRS

Form 656 Booklet: Offer in Compromise, is the IRS's publication on pursuing an offer in compromise. The booklet breaks down the offer in compromise process to seven steps. The following is an explanation of those steps:

Step 1. Gather financial information

In order to successfully submit an offer in compromise, you must be certain about your current financial situation. It is crucial that you have proof of all of your cash, investments, available credit, assets, income, debt, and household costs. The household income and expenses include yours, those of your spouse or significant other, your children, and any other people that

---

1   For purposes of determining an individual's assets for calculating his RCP, a person's equity in his property cannot be negative, because a negative number simply means that the person has no equity in the property. Since Joe's car debt is higher than the car's value, he has no equity in his car, so the car is not included in the calculation of his assets.

reside in the household. Once all of this information, including all available documents proving this information, is collected, you may move to step 2.

Step 2. Form 433-A (OIC): Collection Information Statement for Wage Earners and Self-Employed Individuals

This form should be filled out by an individual wager earner and/or a self-employed individual. The IRS uses this form to calculate your RCP, in order to determine the minimum offer in compromise that should be permitted. However, you have an opportunity on the form to explain any exceptional circumstances (as discussed in the first section of this chapter) that affect your financial situation and may make you eligible for an offer in compromise that is less than your RCP.

Step 3. 433-B (OIC): Collection Information Statement for Businesses

This form should be filled out if your business is a corporation, partnership, limited liability company (LLC) classified as a corporation, single member LLC, or other multi-owner/multi-member LLC. This form is similar to 433-A, but instead of calculating an individual's RCP, it is used to determine a business's RCP.

Step 4. Attach required documents

Based on whether you filled out Form 433-A and/or B, certain documents need to be included in the offer in compromise application packet. Only send copies of those documents, *not originals*.

Documents to be attached with Form 433-A:[2]

- Copies of most recent pay stub, earnings statement, etc., from each employer (of the taxpayer and his spouse/significant other)

---

2   See page 7 of Form 433-A (OIC)

- Copies of bank statements for the three most recent months
- Copies of the most recent statement, etc., from all other sources of income such as pensions, Social Security, rental income, interest and dividends, court order for child support, alimony, and rent subsidies
- Copies of the most recent statement for each investment and retirement account
- Copies of the most recent statement for lender(s) on loans such as mortgages, second mortgages, and vehicles, showing monthly payments, loan payoffs, and amounts owed
- List of notes receivable, if applicable
- Accountant's depreciation schedules, if applicable
- Documentation to support any special circumstances described in the "Explain special circumstances" section on page 2 of Form 656, if applicable
- Form 2848: Power of Attorney, if the taxpayer wants his attorney, CPA, or enrolled agent to represent him, and he does not have a current form on file with the IRS

Documents to be attached with Form 433-B:[3]

- A current profit and loss statement covering at least the most recent 6–12 month period, if appropriate,
- Copies of the most recent statement for each bank, investment, and retirement account,
- If an asset is used as collateral on a loan, include copies of the most recent statement from lender(s) on loans, monthly payments, loan payoffs, and balances,

---

3   See page 6 of Form 433-B (OIC)

- Copies of the most recent statement(s) for outstanding note(s) receivable,
- Copies of the most recent statements from lender(s) on loans, mortgages (including second mortgages), monthly payments, loan payoffs, and balances,
- Copies of accountant's depreciation schedules, if applicable,
- Copies of relevant supporting documentation of the special circumstances described in the "Explain special circumstances" section on page 2 of Form 656, if applicable,
- Form 2848: Power of Attorney, if the taxpayer wants his attorney, CPA, or enrolled agent to represent him, and he does not have a current form on file with the IRS.

Step 5. Form 656: Offer in Compromise

This form is your actual offer in compromise. The form identifies the tax years and type of tax on which the taxpayer is looking to compromise. More importantly, it contains the offer amount and the payment terms.

The payment terms are submitted in Section 5 of Form 656. The taxpayer must decide how long he plans on taking to repay the debt when completing this section. If the taxpayer can pay the full amount offered in 5 months or less, he should choose payment option 1, and include the amount of each payment and the proposed date of payment. Choosing option 1 also requires 20% of the total offer amount to be paid up front (this payment should be included in the application packet).

If the taxpayer cannot pay off the tax debt in less than 5 months, he should choose payment option 2. Selecting this option requires the taxpayer to decide the amount he will pay each month and the total amount of time it will take to fully pay the offer. The taxpayer must also include payment for one month of the offer with the application packet.

If possible, a taxpayer should choose option 1. The IRS has a slightly different formula for calculating a taxpayer's RCP based on whether the taxpayer chooses option 1 or option 2. Recall the example given in the RCP section of this guide with Joe. In that example, Joe could pay in 5 months or less, so the difference between his monthly income and costs was multiplied by 48, and his RCP was $52,200. If Joe planned on paying the offer in over 5 months, the difference between his income and costs would be multiplied by 60, and his RCP would be $54,000. Therefore, by choosing option 2, while Joe would have more time to pay, he would be required to pay an additional $1,800 ($54,000 – $52,200).

Step 6. Include initial payment & $150 application fee

The following payments must be included with the application packet in the form of a check, cashier's check, or money order. First, if you chose payment option 1, include 20% of the offer. If you chose payment option 2, include the first month's installment. Second, you also need to include a separate check for $150 for the application fee.

However, if you meet the Low Income Certification guidelines,[4] then the initial payment and the application fee are not required. There are two requirements for a taxpayer to be eligible for Low Income Certification. First, he must be filing as an individual (as opposed to a business). Second, his gross monthly household income must be lower than the number assigned by the Low Income Certification chart (Section 4 of Form 656), based on the size of his family and state of residency.

Step 7. Mail application package

Once the application packet is completed, it must be mailed to the appropriate IRS facility. The mailing location varies based on the state in which you reside and can be found at the end of the Application Checklist on page 23 of Form 656 Booklet. *Keep a copy of the complete application package, including all supplemental documents.*

---

4   Explained in Section 4 of Form 656

Appealing a Rejected Offer in Compromise

If the IRS denies your offer in compromise, then file Form 13711: Request for Appeal of Offer in Compromise. This form gives you the opportunity to discuss any reasons you disagree with the IRS's rejection of your offer in compromise. If you have any such disagreements, you should include any and all documents supporting your claims.

You should *always* appeal the denial of an offer in compromise. Most offers are declined at the initial stage to help weed out frivolous claims. When you appeal, your case goes to a settlement officer. An officer has more discretion to settle cases than a person at the initial level. For one, they can consider things such as bankruptcy. If your tax debts qualify for bankruptcy (see Chapter 13 on Bankruptcy), the IRS would be better off settling for a discount payment from you rather than get nothing in a bankruptcy proceeding. This is not considered at the initial stage, which is just a dollar-and-cents determination based on the RCP. In an appeal, many more issues are considered. Always file an appeal if your offer in compromise is denied. You have already paid the filing fee so you should get your case considered to the fullest extent.

CHAPTER 15

Statute of Limitations

Statute of Limitations: a statute prescribing limitations to the right of action on certain described causes of action or criminal prosecutions; that is, declaring that no suit shall be maintained on such causes of action, nor any criminal charge be made, unless brought within a specified period of time after the right accrued. Statutes of Limitation are Statutes of Repose, and are legislative enactments as prescribed the periods within which actions may be brought upon certain claims or within which certain rights may be enforced. In criminal cases, however, the Statute of Limitations is an act of grace, a surrendering by the sovereignty of its right to prosecute.

Statute of Limitations in Brief

S tatutes of limitations set a date after which no one can bring an action. For our purposes, statutes of limitations protect you from the government collecting on the balance due, tax lien, or even tax judgment after what is called a "date certain." The typical limitation is ten years from the date of assessment but there are different collection statute end dates for other tax matters. You must always know the collection statute end date (CSED). In every case analysis, you must look to the CSED as a factor in making the best decisions for your case. If you do not know the collection statute end date, in this chapter you will master how to get it and understand its consequence in your case. This is very important information, especially in older cases.

The statute of limitations sets forth the maximum period of time during which legal proceedings can be initiated against a party. From the taxpayer's point of view, the statute of limitations prevents or is a legal bar that allows the taxpayer to escape liability for the tax debt. Thus, the statute of limitations provides a time period after which the government's right to collect is forever surrendered. Generally, the IRS has ten (10) years in which to collect tax, either through administrative collection procedures or by initiating a judicial collection suit.

For example, the administrative collection process is initiated by filing a lien and collecting from the taxpayer either voluntarily or through enforced collection, levy, and seizure. The IRS may initiate a judicial suit against the taxpayer to convert the tax lien to a judgment. If the IRS initiates a suit during the ten-year collection period, the judgment can extend that statute indefinitely. The ten-year collection period may be extended by consent of the taxpayer or suspended (tolled) during an appeal, judicial action, offer in compromise, or other means recognized by statute. We never recommend agreeing to such an extension.

It is important to understand how the ten-year statute of limitations is calculated. The statute begins to run the day after a tax return is filed. This is known as the assessment date. The tax is assessed and penalties and interest begin to accrue if the tax is not paid in full. The IRS must (administratively) collect the tax within the ten (10) year period following the assessment.

Once assessed, a collection statute end date is established. The

CSED can be suspended or extended by action taken by the taxpayer or the government. It is important to obtain the CSED when you are analyzing a case because this information may influence or determine the taxpayer's decision with respect to resolving the case.

For example, if the collection statute end date is two years away it is a wise decision to enter into a partial payment installment agreement for the remaining two years and let the rest of the tax liability expire under the statute of limitations.

On the other hand, if we learn that the tax liability and assessment is over three years old, bankruptcy may be an option to consider because at this point you meet the legally required deadline to consider it (see Chapter 13 Bankruptcy). Filing an offer in compromise is another possibility (see Chapter 14), but again, all missing tax returns must be filed. The IRS may accept an offer in compromise for a lesser amount than the tax liability or for the amount they could collect in an installment agreement for remaining period of the collection statute and the

THE CSED IS IMPORTANT.

It tells you the last day the IRS can collect the tax you owe to them. It is especially important in older cases, but the case review is even more important because, by doing the manual review of your tax records year by year, all of the issues can be considered together and become part of a global solution. So, if you still haven't done your case review, go back to Chapter 3 right now, remove your head from the sand, and get to know all the details of your case.

amount of equity in assets the taxpayer has. An installment agreement will expire with the statute unless the taxpayer agrees to extend the statute. As a general rule, I do not agree to extend collection statutes.

To reiterate, the general rule is the ten-year collection statute. This is provided for in IRC, Internal Revenue Code, and Section 6502. The best practice is to know the CSED because if applicable, it will end your case and you will no longer owe the tax. When the statute expires, you may request a lien release and file it with the local court to remove the lien from the public record. You can also forward a copy of the release of lien to the credit reporting agencies to have the file marked satisfied.

See Internal Revenue Code, Section 6502 in the Tax Lien Section (Chapter 5) of this book.

Voluntary Extension of The Statute of Limitations

If you are requested to extend the statute of limitations by signing Form 872, the general rule would be to *refuse*. In collection cases, as a general rule I refuse to extend the statute of limitations on collection. However, in audits we are often asked to extend the statute and more often than not, we do. Extending the statute is a wise choice in audit situations because it gives you more time to pursue your appeal rights.

There are two circumstances in which the IRS may request an extension of the statute of limitations in collection:

1. The IRS has authority to request it when obtaining an installment agreement that will only partially pay the liability within the collection statute of limitations. I refuse to extend the collection statute in these requests, too.

2. The IRS can also seek an extension in connection with releasing a tax lien after the ten-year period has expired. Once

an extension is issued, the IRS may collect through levy or a judicial proceeding.

Thus, the best practice is for you *not* to extend the statute, because the IRS can then initiate a judicial proceeding to make the lien a judgment. You must be informed of your right to refuse to extend the statute.

An example of a statutory extension to the statute of limitations is the filing by the taxpayer of an offer in compromise or an appeal. While an offer in compromise is pending, the IRS is generally prohibited from enforced collection. In this situation, the ten-year collection statute is suspended from the time the IRS receives the offer plus 60 days. With respect to an appeal or a collection due process (CDP) hearing request (IRC, Section 6320 and 6330), if the taxpayer files the request on time, the statute of limitations on collection is suspended for the period of a year. So, the IRS gives up its right to levy during the CDP hearing, but the statute is suspended—and thereby extended on the back end—for the period from the filing of the CDP and the time it takes to issue the determination letter from the appeals office.

Can a taxpayer terminate an extension of the statute of limitations? YES! If the taxpayer has executed an agreement to extend the statute of limitations, Form 872, he can terminate or cancel the extension by filing Form 872-T.

Trade Secret

Form 872-T: Joe Taxpayer, who had not filed a tax return in 2000, had a large tax liability leveled against him from an IRS-prepared SFR (Substitute for Return), which is the tax return the IRS prepares if the taxpayer fails to file a return. The IRS receives payment information from third-party sources such as employers, banks, third-party payers (Form 1099), mortgage companies, brokerage firms, and casinos. This information indicates the taxpayer would owe tax on the income. This particular taxpayer was a daytrader and had hundreds of stock transactions in one year. Joe, figuring he lost money and didn't owe taxes, never filed a return.

The IRS prepared a SFR return from the enormous list of Form 1099 stock sale information. The IRS meticulously counted each sale as income. The IRS did not have information on the cost of the stock or the sales commission, which would be deducted from Joe Taxpayer's sales profit or income. This return showed the taxpayer owed about $980,000.00.

The CSED on 2000 was to expire in July 2011. A revenue officer asked the taxpayer sign a twenty-year extension of the statute. He did. The IRS would have twenty (20) more years to collect the tax owed from the taxpayer. OUCH!

In my review of the case transcripts, I found the extension of the statute of limitations to collect the tax coded in his file. There was a code on the transcript. We have Form 872-T and it was printed and sent to the taxpayer for signature and filing. The installment agreement payments will continue to pay the more recent tax years after the CSED runs on the oldest year. The oldest year had a very large tax liability. So, resetting the statute to run has saved the client a great deal of money and will allow him to pay his remaining taxes over the CSED relevant to those liabilities. Needless to say, the client is relieved in more than one sense.

Case Study CSED—Collection Statute End Date

A taxpayer called me during the Christmas holidays with a New Year's Resolution he was working on and wanted to keep. Joe Taxpayer wanted to solve his old tax problem once and for all. He explained he had an employment tax problem that arose from his small business. Many years ago he had a few employees building decks and garages. Joe was able to pay the employees but he could not make the payroll tax deposits. He could just make payroll and pay his operating expenses, but he wasn't even paying himself, and he never had enough money to pay those taxes. As he was digging this large financial pit, he did not know he was personally liable for the businesses taxes.

The IRS assessed him about $50,000 in tax penalty and interest because his records were a mess and he couldn't prove the taxes were less. The IRS just made up numbers—referred to as substitutes for returns (SFRs)—and told Joe that if he could ever figure out how to complete the tax return he could file them. The debt has been owed for what seemed like most of his life and he wanted to file his offer in compromise for New Years. Joe, like many good taxpayers, ran into a business slump and couldn't pay the taxes and stay in business at the same time. Joe wanted to get a new start and have his old life back.

Joe continued telling me about his case history. He had hired a national firm seen frequently on TV to prepare an offer in compromise (OIC) in an attempt to make IRS an offer to settle the debt. Joe wanted me to look the OIC over and give him an opinion of the likelihood of success or to determine if the paperwork needed a change or two.

Joe had a new girlfriend and really wanted to marry her. To support the two of them he would be buying old houses, using his skills to fix them up, and reselling them. As things stood, he would've had to have a family member as a partner to provide the financing. He wanted to end his tax issues so he could obtain his own financing and do the deals on his own. After all, it was his craftsmanship that provided the improvements to the property. With the liens removed, Joe could obtain lower-interest financing and make a higher profit.

Joe Taxpayer faxed the OIC to us for review and came in for our meeting on December 30. I asked the first question: "When did you file these old taxes?"

Joe said, "When they were due, almost ten years ago."

I hope by now you know where this is going. We were scheduled to call the representative that had worked with Joe to prepare the OIC. We were supposed to look it over and bless it for filing or recommend any changes.

Joe and I initiated the call to his representative at the tax mill. He listened in as I asked his representative the key questions: "Did you get Joe Taxpayer's transcripts from the IRS? What is the CSED?"

When he replied, "What's that?" I knew, as you are probably thinking, too, that we had to investigate the CSED. So, I told the tax representative we would call him back later that day.

Next the taxpayer and I called the IRS to ask for the CSED. The CSED was March 31 of the next year. The collection statute expired in a short *three months* and Joe would owe IRS *nothing*. The IRS rep told us the case was not in a queue to receive a revenue officer and there were no indications of a levy. I advised Joe not to file the OIC, simply let the statute expire and obtain a release of lien. The OIC would toll or suspend the collection statute of limitations and extend the CSED. There was no benefit to his filing an OIC. Joe Taxpayer decided not to file the OIC.

We called his representative back and explained the CSED to him. We faxed him a copy of the transcripts we received from IRS. Joe asked the national tax firm for a refund. The national firm returned half of the $6,000.00 in fees they charged Joe.

CHAPTER 16

Innocent Spouse

Innocent Spouse Relief in Brief

Spouses have the option of jointly filing a single tax return, instead of each spouse filing an individual return. The main reason spouses choose to file jointly is because in doing so, they receive better tax rates than if they file individually. However, this benefit is not without its risks. When spouses file a joint return, this results in joint liability, meaning both spouses are individually responsible for all payments on the return. Therefore, if conduct by the filing spouse

In order to successfully obtain innocent spouse relief, you must file Forms 8857, 12507: Innocent Spouse Statement, 12508: Questionnaire for Non-Requesting Spouse, and 12509: Statement of Disagreement.

("guilty spouse") results in penalties, the other spouse ("innocent spouse") may be responsible for those payments.

Luckily for the innocent spouse, she may obtain a limited release from joint liability for tax (including interest), penalties, and other amounts, if she is eligible for innocent spouse relief. There are three different avenues by which an innocent spouse may seek relief. One rule offers relief if an innocent spouse does not have knowledge about an understatement on a return. Another rule offers extra protection to an innocent spouse when the spouses are separated. Finally, there is a catch-all rule, to ensure that the innocent spouse will not unfairly be denied relief.

During the course of this chapter, the innocent spouse relief law will be discussed. Then, the process of seeking innocent spouse relief will be explained. Finally, a warning will be given about the consequences of attempting to abuse innocent spouse relief.

Innocent Spouse Lacking Knowledge of an Understatement

An innocent spouse who has signed a joint return will be released from liability for tax, interest, penalties, and other amounts, if she can establish all of the following:

1. A joint return has been made for the taxable year.
2. On the joint return, there was an understatement of tax attributable to erroneous items of the guilty spouse.
3. The innocent spouse establishes that in signing the return, she did not know and had no reason to know, that there was such understatement. (This requirement is explained in more detail in the "Knowledge" section).
4. Taking into account all the facts and circumstances, it is unfair to hold the innocent spouse liable for the tax liability for the year

in question. (This requirement is explained in more detail in the "Equitable Relief: A Catch-All Provision" section. Even though that section applies to a different avenue for gaining relief, the equity (fairness) principles described are equally applicable to this requirement.).

5. The innocent spouse requests relief no later than two years after the date on which the IRS has begun collection activities. (This requirement is explained in more detail in the "Procedure for Requesting Innocent Spouse Relief" section.).

The third element of the rule requires that the innocent spouse either lacked "actual knowledge" of an erroneous item of an understatement or had no reason to know about it. Actual knowledge generally exists where the spouse had knowledge of an understatement on a return. However, the following are a few situations where the spouse lacked such knowledge, yet for the purposes of innocent spouse relief, actual knowledge is determined to exist:

1. Knowing that the spouses received an item might constitute actual knowledge, even if there is no knowledge that it was not fully included on the return.
2. Regarding an erroneous deduction or credit, actual knowledge of the item includes knowledge of the facts making the item not allowable as a deduction or credit.
3. Regarding a fictitious or inflated deduction, actual knowledge by the innocent spouse is established only if she knew the expenditure was not incurred or not incurred to the extent depicted.

However, mere knowledge of the source of an erroneous item does not establish actual knowledge of that item. For example, if an innocent spouse knew the guilty spouse owned certain stocks, but was unaware those stocks were paying dividends, and then the innocent spouse did not have actual knowledge of those dividends. On the other hand, a spouse does not need to know of the source of an item in order to establish actual knowledge. Therefore, if an innocent spouse knew the guilty spouse received a certain amount of money, but was unaware of its source, the innocent spouse still had actual knowledge of any understatement of that money.

Even if the innocent spouse lacks actual knowledge, innocent spouse relief will not be available if she had a "reason to know" about the understatement. The following facts and circumstances are relevant in determining whether a spouse had reason to know of an understatement:

1. the nature of the erroneous item and the amount of the erroneous item relative to other items,
2. the spouses' financial situation,
3. the innocent spouse's educational background and business experience,
4. the extent of the innocent spouse's participation in the activity resulting in the erroneous item,
5. whether the innocent spouse failed to inquire about items on the return or omitted from the return that a reasonable person would question, and
6. whether the erroneous item represented a departure from a recurring pattern reflected in prior years' returns.

An innocent spouse's claim that her cultural upbringing caused her to refrain from questioning the guilty spouse about financial matters is not likely to succeed. Also, the innocent spouse cannot deliberately avoid learning about an item in order to shield herself from liability. In both of these situations, the knowledge requirement will automatically be satisfied. However, if the innocent spouse was physically abused or had reasonable fear of abuse, which prevented her from questioning the guilty spouse, then she will be deemed to not know about the relevant finances (see Extra Protection for Separated Spouses and Equitable Relief sections below).

In determining whether an innocent spouse has actual knowledge or reason to know of an understatement of tax attributable to an erroneous item, courts have used different approaches. In cases involving omitted income, courts have asked whether the spouse had actual knowledge of (or reason to know of) the underlying transaction that produced the income (the "knowledge of the transaction test"). In cases involving erroneous deductions, the courts have used either the knowledge of the transaction test or an alternative test that asks whether a reasonably prudent taxpayer at the time of signing the return could be expected to know that it contained the erroneous item.

Equitable Relief: A Catch-All Provision

The IRS has the authority to relieve a spouse or former spouse from joint return liability when (1) taking into account all the facts and circumstances, it is inequitable (unfair) to hold the innocent spouse liable for any unpaid tax or deficiency in tax, and (2) relief is not available to the innocent spouse under the previous two relief rules. Equitable relief is granted at the discretion of the IRS. This authority to treat a taxpayer equitably permits the IRS not only to grant relief to the innocent spouse for the guilty spouse's understatement of tax but also to grant relief for the nonpayment of a reported tax.

The following factors are considered when determining whether to grant equitable relief:

1. The innocent spouse is divorced or separated (legally separated or merely living apart) from the guilty spouse.
2. The innocent spouse would suffer economic hardship if the IRS does not grant relief.

3. The innocent spouse did not know and had no reason to know of the item giving rise to a deficiency. The following factors are considered:

    a. the innocent spouse's level of education,

    b. deceit or evasiveness of the guilty spouse,

    c. the innocent spouse's level of involvement in the activity giving rise to the liability,

    d. the innocent spouse's involvement in business and household financial matters,

    e. the innocent spouse's business or financial expertise, and

    f. any lavish or unusual expenditures compared with past spending patterns.

4. The guilty spouse had a legal obligation to pay the outstanding income tax liability under a divorce decree or similar decree or agreement..

5. The innocent spouse received a significant benefit, beyond normal support, from the unpaid income tax liability or from an item giving rise to the deficiency.

6. The innocent spouse made a good faith effort to comply with income tax laws in the years following the taxable year(s) to which the request for relief relates.

7. Abuse of the innocent spouse by the guilty spouse weighs in favor of the grant of relief to the requesting spouse.

8. Poor mental or physical health of the innocent spouse at the time she signed the return or at the time she requested relief may weigh in favor of the grant of relief to the innocent spouse.

Procedure For Requesting Innocent Spouse Relief

An innocent spouse must file Form 8857: Request for Innocent Spouse Relief, to obtain full or partial relief from joint return liability, to obtain separate return relief, or to request equitable relief. In the alternative, a written statement signed under penalties of perjury that contains the information required by Form 8857 may be submitted. The innocent spouse must submit Form 8857 (or the alternative, a written statement) no later than two years from the date of the first collection activity concerning the joint tax liability against the innocent spouse.

An innocent spouse should assert all possible grounds for relief from joint liability in one timely filed claim. She may elect full or partial relief from liability on the basis of lack of knowledge of the erroneous item, she may elect to allocate the deficiency on a separate return basis, and she may request equitable relief in one claim. If multiple types of relief are requested, the IRS will determine which relief is available. However, the IRS will not consider any type of relief not requested. Luckily for the innocent spouse, a failure to assert alternative grounds for relief is not fatal, because the IRS will offer the innocent spouse an opportunity to amend the claim to elect relief on other grounds.

The earliest time to file a request for relief is upon receipt of a notification of an audit or a letter or notice from the IRS indicating the possibility of an outstanding liability for the year in question. Any request for relief filed before then is a premature claim that will not be considered by the IRS.

CHAPTER 17

Injured Spouse

Injured Spouse Relief in Brief

Generally, when spouses jointly file a tax return, they are both equally and individually responsible for making sure that all of the taxes are paid, regardless of which spouse is the source of any money owed to the IRS. However, even if the spouses choose to file jointly, both still have the right to receive any refunds[1] due to them, as though they had filed individually. These refunds are not simply split evenly between the spouses. The reason the refunds are not automatically commingled is because the filing of a joint return does not change the income of one spouse into the income of the other.

Sometimes, the IRS will use the refund owed to one spouse (the "injured spouse") to pay off a legally enforceable debt owed by the other spouse (the "debtor spouse"). In this case, the injured spouse may recover

---

1   Refunds may be owed to an injured spouse because of an overpayment of tax or a claimed refundable tax credit.

any money owed to her (her share of the refund) from the IRS by filing Form 8379: Injured Spouse Allocation.

There are some limitations to injured spouse relief, though. An injured spouse is entitled to relief if her refund was used to pay the debtor spouse's past-due federal or state income tax, child or spousal support, or federal non-tax debt, such as a student loan. In addition, the following are the types of refundable tax credits that may be repaid to the injured spouse:

- Making-work-pay credit
- Government retiree credit
- American opportunity credit
- First-time homebuyer credit
- Credit for federal tax paid on fuels
- Adoption credit
- Refundable prior year minimum tax
- Health coverage tax credit

What is Owed to the Injured Spouse?

To properly determine the amount of tax owed and the refund due to each spouse, a calculation must be made as if each spouse filed a separate tax return, instead of filing jointly. The spouses must allocate their separate wages, self-employment income and expenses, and credits to the spouse who would have shown the item(s) on his/her separate return. Other items that may not clearly belong to either spouse (for example, a penalty on early withdrawal of savings from a joint bank account) are equally divided. Using this information, the IRS determines the amount of money owed to the injured spouse, and refunds that amount to her.

Procedure For Seeking Relief

Form 8379: Injured Spouse Claim and Allocation, should be filed when the injured spouse becomes aware that all or part of her share of a refund was, or is expected to be, applied against the debtor spouse's legally enforceable past-due obligations. This form must be filed for each year the injured spouse is seeking relief and may be filed along with the original tax return or by itself after the IRS notifies the injured spouse that her refund was used to pay the debtor spouse's prior tax obligations.

To obtain injured spouse relief, the taxpayer must have filed a joint tax return. If one taxpayer on the joint return has an unpaid tax liability from a previous year, the IRS will seize the joint return refund in order to satisfy that debt. The reasoning by the IRS is that the IRS should not refund money to a taxpayer who owes the IRS money from a previous tax year. In other words, even if one person on the joint return did not have a tax liability from an earlier year, she can still be deprived of her refund from the current year's tax return because her spouse owes money from a previous tax year.

For example, a husband and wife file a joint return. The husband owes the IRS unpaid taxes from a previous year. The IRS then takes the entire refund, including the portion of the refund that belongs to the wife, and applies that money to the husband's unpaid tax debt. In this case, the wife would be considered an injured spouse because her portion of the tax refund was applied to a debt that was not hers.

Requests for injured spouse relief are filed on Form 8379. The form requires information from both taxpayers involved. With the information collected on the form, the IRS will make a calculation that will divide the refund between the spouses, so that the innocent spouse receives her share of the refund while the spouse who owes the tax debt does not receive his share of the refund. To qualify for the relief the injured spouse *must meet all of the following:*

1. She is not liable for the past due tax—only her spouse owes the IRS money; and
2. She reported income on a joint tax return; and
3. She made and reported payments on the joint return—payments include federal income tax withheld from wages, estimated tax payments, or refundable credits.

Form 8379 must be completed, signed, and sent to the service center for processing. There are two occasions when the injured spouse form needs to be filed. First, if the IRS has already taken the portion of the refund due to the non-liable spouse. Second, the taxpayer is filing a return and knows the spouse has a debt to the IRS and does not want her portion of the refund to be retained by IRS to reduce the spouse's debt to the IRS. In this situation, the taxpayer should attach Form 8379 to the return being filed and the IRS will calculate the portion due to the non-liable (injured) spouse.

CHAPTER 18

Audits

Audits in Brief

One of taxpayers' greatest fears is being audited by the IRS, ranking a close second to death itself. Receiving a notice from the IRS that you are going to be audited is enough to send a shiver down anyone's spine. Luckily, the idea of the dreaded audit is much worse than the actual experience. This chapter will demystify the audit experience and give you the skills and knowledge needed to take on an audit with confidence.

An audit is simply an examination of your return (or returns) by the IRS after it has been filed. Being selected to be audited does not necessarily mean that you will owe the IRS money. In fact, an audit can result in one of three outcomes. First, the IRS could determine that the return was filled out properly, and there are no tax consequences. Second, the IRS could decide that you filled out the return improperly and you owe money to the IRS. Finally, the IRS could determine that you filled out the return improperly, but money is actually owed to you.

There are a few reasons why a certain taxpayer may be chosen for an audit. First, you may be selected based on an IRS computer program that determines the likelihood that an audit would result in a change in tax liability (the more likely such a change would result, the more likely that you will be chosen). Second, you may be audited if certain third-party information, such as a Form 1099 or W-2, does not match the information on your return. Third, you may be audited based on other sources of information suggesting noncompliance, such as newspapers or public records. Finally, the IRS randomly selects taxpayers to audit, as well.

This chapter is intended to give a taxpayer a basic understanding of the audit process. This knowledge will undoubtedly make an audit a far less intimidating experience. However, because an audit could have serious consequences, you should contact an IRS-approved representative if notified of an audit (the next section will explain the role of this representative).

What to Expect

Once you receive notice that you are going to be audited by the IRS, you should hire a tax professional to represent or accompany you during the process. The following tax professionals are eligible to take on this role:

- an attorney,
- a certified public account,
- a person enrolled to practice before the IRS,
- an enrolled actuary, or
- any other person permitted to represent a taxpayer during a tax return examination.

This tax professional will ensure that the IRS does not violate your rights by overstepping its bounds and that your interests will be protected.

The audit can occur in one of many settings. First, it can be done entirely by mail. If not done by mail, the audit can take place at the your home, your place of business, an IRS office, or at your representative's office. While the logistics of the audit can be negotiated with the IRS, the decision of when, where, and how the audit will take place is ultimately made by the IRS.

The process begins with a notice from the IRS informing you that you are being audited. This notification should inform you of which records will be needed for the audit, through Form 4564: Information Document Request (IDR). If the IRS has chosen a face-to-face audit, you should try to gather these records before the interview. After the IRS has received all of the information it deems necessary, it makes a decision about your actual liability, compared to the liability it determined after its initial review of the tax return. The final section of this chapter will discuss your options for moving forward after this decision is rendered.

IRS Investigative Power and Limitations

The IRS has a lot of power to investigate whether or not taxpayers accurately fill out their federal income tax return. This broad power has been granted to the IRS because tax reporting is essentially done on the honor system, in that each taxpayer fills out his return as he sees fit. Therefore, if the IRS did not have the ability to closely examine each return, it would be too easy for fraudulent or inaccurate returns to be filed, resulting in a broken tax collection system.

While the IRS's investigative power is vast, it is not without limits set by the Internal Revenue Code (IRC), the Constitution, and other sources of law. This chapter will describe what the IRS can and cannot do in determining whether your return needs to be modified, thereby affecting your tax liability.

Under the IRC, the IRS has the power to determine the accuracy of a tax return by the following methods:

1. Examining records
2. Taking testimony under oath
3. Issuing administrative summonses to compel evidence, if necessary

Generally, the IRS initially will request that you voluntarily share any information it is seeking. The request is made through an information document request (IDR), which lists a description of all the documents the IRS needs from the taxpayer. There is a wide array of documents the IRS might request from you, including but not limited to bank statements, bills, employment and salary information, proof of other sources of income, and business records. More often than not, taxpayers comply with these requests, if possible, hoping to end the audit as quickly as possible.

However, you are not required to disclose any information simply at the request of the IRS. If there is certain information (such as records or testimony) you choose not share for any reason, the IRS must issue an administrative summons to compel you to produce said information. The IRS cannot enforce a summons on its own, though; it must get an order from the federal court to have you produce the information.

The Supreme Court has listed four necessary criteria for when a court should grant an enforcement order for an administrative summons.[1] If any of

---

1   US v. Powell, 379 US 48, 57-58 (1964).

the following requirements are not met, the summons should not be granted and you should not be compelled to produce the information in question:

1. The IRS investigation will be conducted pursuant to a legitimate purpose.
2. The inquiry may be relevant to the legitimate purpose.
3. The information sought is not already within the IRS's possession.
4. The administrative steps required by the IRC have been followed; in particular, that the IRS, after investigation, has determined the investigation to be necessary and has notified the taxpayer in writing of said necessity.

The four requirements listed above are not difficult for the IRS to meet while looking for information during an audit. The federal court has simplified these four requirements to essentially a test of "whether the inspection sought would throw light upon the correctness of the taxpayer's returns."[2] Therefore, if the IRS lacks information that it feels would further its investigation as to the accuracy of a tax return, it will likely be able to compel you to share said information.

If the federal court issues an enforcement order of an administrative summons, you must comply with the summons. Refusal to comply can have grave consequences, such as contempt proceedings or even criminal prosecution.

A Couple of Tricks For IDR Compliance

There are certain times when a taxpayer cannot comply with an IDR. If this is the case, then the taxpayer needs to let the IRS know that certain requested documents cannot be obtained. However, there are situations

---

2   US v. Ryan, 455 F.2d 728, 733 (9th Cir. 1971).

where even though the taxpayer might not think he has access to proof of information sought by the IRS, he actually is able to comply with the IDR. Below are a couple of examples of common IDR issues taxpayers face, and how the taxpayer can actually comply with the problematic requests.

Proof of Income

A common request during an audit is proof of income. This can become problematic for a taxpayer if the IRS is looking for a copy of a check (or checks) that the taxpayer has deposited at a bank and kept no copy for his records. Luckily, this problem can be easily solved.

Many taxpayers are unaware that banks keep records of all transactions, including every check that is deposited there. So, if you need to produce a copy of a check, you can get one from the bank where it was deposited. Your bank might be reluctant to get you a copy of the check, especially if it was an older deposit. However, if you inform the bank that the copy is needed to comply with an IRS audit, the bank should be very cooperative.

Proof of Travel

If you have claimed travel expenses as a deduction, the IRS could request proof of those travel expenses. Often, self-employed taxpayers fail to keep any proof of these costs (such as receipts and a travel log), though. If this is the case, your best bet is to calculate your yearly traveling distance, and submit proof of that calculation to the IRS.

Proving traveling distance is not very difficult. Assume you are self-employed and have an office in Location A. Commuting to your office in Location A is not deductible. Once a week, your job requires you to travel from Location A to Location B. This travel is deductible.

In order to calculate travel distance, there are many helpful websites, such as Google Maps or Mapquest. Using one of these sites, you can calculate the distance between Location A and Location B. Then, this distance should be doubled, for the weekly round trip, and multiplied by the number of workdays in the year in question that you were required to make this trip. This calculation should be sufficient proof of travel.

The Outcome: Agree or Disagree

If you agree with the outcome of the audit, you sign an agreement form and pays any additional taxes, with interest, that you might owe. You might not agree with the proposed changes, though. If there is no agreement, you could attempt to have the IRS reconsider the audit. Audit reconsideration is discussed in Chapter 19.

If you had a scheduled audit and did not attend, and did not call to reschedule, the revenue agent more likely than not denied every expense taken resulting in a significant increase in tax, penalties, and interest. This can be reviewed and lowered, ever many years later, by following the instructions in Chapter 19, Audit Reconsideration.

Yes, you can have a second bite of the apple. Who knew?

CHAPTER 19

Audit Reconsideration

Audit Reconsideration in Brief

The best-kept secret in audits is the audit reconsideration process. Did the IRS prepare substitutes for returns (tax returns you failed to file) with huge balances? Did you have a bad audit? Were you scared of the audit and just failed to show up? Maybe you couldn't locate all your tax records.

You may request that the IRS reconsider an audit of a tax return by filing an *amended* return, or that it reconsider an IRS-prepared substitute for return (SFR) by filing an *original* return. By following the audit reconsideration process, the IRS can reconsider your tax return many years later and resolve the case through this process.

If you have already paid the amount due, you can even claim a refund by filing Form 1040X or an amended return. Many people don't know this can be done. Read on and learn the process. You can do this!

When The IRS Will Accept an Audit Reconsideration Request

If you failed to attend an audit and the IRS made changes to your tax return that you believe are incorrect, you may file an amended return and seek audit reconsideration. If the IRS prepared a return for you, commonly called a substitute for return (SFR), you may file your original return and have it accepted through the audit reconsideration process. Most people never try this.

If you believe the IRS made a computation error or an error in processing or assessing your tax, you may seek audit reconsideration. The taxpayer may also seek audit reconsideration if a liability is unpaid or credits were denied.

However, if you have already agreed to pay the amount due by signing a formal agreement (such as a Closing Agreement, Form 906) that is final and closes the return, the IRS will not consider an audit reconsideration request. The IRS will not consider an audit reconsideration if you entered an agreement with the appeals office on Form 870-AD, an Offer in Compromise Agreement, a US Tax Court decision, or if any other court has issued a final determination on your tax liability. This is appropriate to the cases of tax protestors who seek to file their returns after the federal district court has issued a judgment against them.

The Audit Reconsideration Process

The general rule is that you do not have an unequivocal right to the audit reconsideration process. The Internal Revenue Code authorizes the IRS to reconsider tax liabilities where the amount is excessive, the tax is assessed subsequent to the expiration of the statute of limitations, or the tax deficiency was erroneously or illegally assessed.

Many tax professionals do not know that they may disagree with the findings of an original audit or an audit in which the taxpayer did not appear through the audit reconsideration process. If you were not notified of the examination appointment or could not appear due to a scheduling conflict, the IRS may reconsider the initial audit results through the audit reconsideration process. If you want to challenge the basis of an SFR or deductions or credits made, you may due so through the audit reconsideration process. See IRS Publication 3598.

When you request audit reconsideration you must send your request to the address of the IRS campus shown on your examination report, or Form 4549 (the Original Audit Report) or, in the case of an SFR, your notice of deficiency. I have found that if you do not have the address, you can call the IRS and they will provide the proper address and put a hold on your account while you submit the return information for audit reconsideration.

> *In submitting the request for audit reconsideration, the IRS does not have a specific audit reconsideration form. The best practice is to draft a cover letter with your name, address, Social Security number, and the tax year in which you seek audit reconsideration.*

For example, if there are multiple SFRs and you intend to file the original tax returns to replace the SFRs that show the large debt the IRS has assessed against you, each tax return would have a separate cover letter and be mailed to the relevant IRS campus in a separate envelope. Make a brief statement requesting audit reconsideration and mention any relevant facts and circumstances. Also, request that the failure to file penalty be removed, because it creates an economic hardship, and provide any background facts and circumstances.

It is in your best interest to provide complete information on each disputed issue. Each issue will be considered by the IRS separately and any information provided will help in receiving a change or adjustment. If you have extensive backup documentation, you may hold on to the documentation and advise the IRS that, if they need to review it, you can forward it to them. Generally, if a CPA or tax preparer prepares the tax return, the IRS will not request the documentation, but rely upon the preparer. Notwithstanding, the best practice is to be ready for a spot check of your records.

After the IRS receives the documentation, they may delay collection activity further than the initial 30-day hold. They may ask that you call back and get a new call-back date so that the ACS computer does not automatically send out a levy or wage garnishment. If the return and supporting documents are not sufficient, the collection activity will normally resume. Calling back is important so that the lines of communication are open and you are warned before collection action happens.

The IRS representative on your case will acknowledge acceptance of your information and of the tax assessed or reduced during the audit reconsideration process. This process normally takes 8–12 weeks and in the case of tax returns before the year 2000, the audit reconsideration process can take longer because of the retrieval time needed to obtain the records.

Because there is no specific Internal Revenue Code section related to audit reconsideration, few practitioners know the process exists. Most practitioners do not think that a closed audit can be reopened when a taxpayer did not produce documentation or did not attend the original audit or produce documentation requested during the audit. But as you now know, you are within your rights to request audit reconsideration, and you should include it in your arsenal if there's a chance it can help you out of your taxjam.

CHAPTER 20

Credit Card Debt

Credit Card Debt in Brief

These are the lessons we have learned and experienced from persons with too much credit card debt. If you are seriously underwater with your home mortgage, have huge credit card debt, and/or your financial situation is such that you are considering bankruptcy, then perhaps credit card settlement may be an option or solution for some of your money issues. If credit card settlement on one or more cards will allow you to move into your new and stronger financial future without filing for bankruptcy, then it will certainly be the lesser of two evils.

This chapter will provide you with the information you need to know whether you are a candidate for settlement. You will learn about the process of settlement and the increased tax liabilities you will incur. You will be able to map out a planned budget and follow that path to a debt-free future where you will not owe tax to the government or any state and you will not have any credit card debt.

Before I explain how to settle debt, I want to be certain that you understand that any financial settlements with banks or credit card companies (or individuals to whom you owe money) will seriously affect your credit score for a few years. When you settle debt, you must be able to prove that you have a financial hardship. This is not an easy way out for individuals or companies with assets or income high enough to cover their expenses. This is not a solution for people who have the ability to pay their debts. This is an option for those who can no longer continue on their downward spiral. You will know if you fall into this category. You must be aware of the following important information so that you can make a completely informed decision about whether you will settle any financial debt.

> *If you owe IRS money, they will not allow you to pay the high-interest credit card debt before they are paid in full.*

Credit card debt is unsecured debt. The credit card company does not have a lien on items purchased to protect itself from default, so the interest rate that it charges is high. Conversely, an auto loan is secured when the creditor files a security interest or lien on the car at the time of financing. Secured creditors can, and will, take the car (the security) if you do not pay the loan.

When you default, what is the process to settle this debt on your own?

- How do you do it?
- What should you pay?
- What is the process?

If you default on a credit card, you can settle the debt at a very low percentage of the balance due if you know about the default process and if you understand the ramifications of cancelling debt.

- If you default and settle your credit card debt then you will have a tax consequence. The forgiven debt, for tax purposes, will be considered income. You will be prepared and consider the tax consequences when you negotiate.
- Know how to settle credit card debt.

Credit Card Debt vs. Taxes

Please note that I am *not* advocating that you should default on your credit card debt. I am informing you of an option—other than bankruptcy—that you may not know is available to you, which could be a second chance to make things right. I have met too many people who are struggling to keep their homes and put food on the table for their family; all the while, they continue to make payments, mostly minimum payments, on their credit cards. The number of active cards people have, and how many have balances spent up to the credit limit, is shocking.

Do you find yourself skipping a payment here or there on a card because you need groceries or have to pay the electric bill? Do you receive a phone call that your payment is past due and you end up being "forced" to make a payment over the phone? Are you in this type of situation?

First of all, you need to set up a budget and prioritize your spending. You don't need me to tell you what the important things in life are, but I will remind you anyway. Shelter, food, and clothing are most important. The necessities must be met before you buy anything else. Forget about "keeping up with the Joneses." Commit to becoming financially secure. Have a family meeting and include everyone to help support and achieve the financial goals. Together you will come up with both a short-term and a long-term plan to move into the future.

If you try to do this without the help of your spouse or family, it will be extremely difficult. You must be honest with them and explain your financial situation. If you think they don't notice your stress, you're kidding yourself. Trust me when I tell you that this stress affects you both mentally and physically, and you are probably not the fun and loving individual that you used to be.

There is no shame in having financial difficulty, although it's not a topic people like to share with one another. I want you to know that you are not alone. Ten years ago, one in five individuals had an income tax problem. In today's economy, this number has mushroomed. People from all walks of life and all socio-economic classes have tax issues. You and your family can decide together your necessities and priorities, and what you can live without. Dismiss all of those hopeless feelings. I tell clients, "This is only money. Yes, we need it to live but we cannot pay what we do not have. We have the rest of our lives to earn a living, so let's move forward."

Learn from the past, but waste no more time looking over your shoulder. Move forward and purchase only what you need. Only after these bills have been paid can you take care of past bills. Remember, this is a new beginning—you're building a new future by taking responsibility, making lifestyle changes, and making sound and informed choices and decisions.

Budget

So, a budget?! Yes, a budget. If you want to become financially sound, you must be aware of your income and expenses. Your budget does not have to be complicated. You need to write down your monthly income on the top line of a piece of paper. Underneath, make a list of all your expenses. If bills are paid annually or semi-annually such as auto or home insurance, then divide accordingly to figure the monthly cost.

Now, subtract the expenses from the income. I find that most people either spend everything they earn or overspend with the help of their trusty credit cards. If you overextend yourself or live beyond your means, then you surely will find yourself in financial trouble. Perhaps that's how you find yourself in this hot water. Make the choice—right now—to improve your situation.

> *Next comes the difficult task of removing any, and all, excessive spending. Prioritize your expenses. If you are paying more than 25% of your gross income towards rent or mortgage then you need to move. You must live within your means.*

Open a new savings account and deposit *all* of the money that would have been earmarked for all of the credit card payments. It is extremely important that you do not spend this money, because you will need it in a few months to settle the credit card debt. Also, be sure to secure a debit card attached to your checking account or a different savings account.

The IRS will not permit credit card debt to be paid before their tax lien, because it is not part of the national standard. As discussed in Chapter 9, Collection Information Statements, the IRS does not allow a taxpayer who owes them significant debt ($50,000 or more) to pay credit card debt before the IRS tax liability. Therefore, the IRS can force you to default on your credit card debt; you may have to get a second job to pay the credit card company. If you default on the credit card debt you need to know the consequences of the default and what options you have to settle the debt.

You may not want or choose to default on your credit card debt. You have most likely been paying your credit card bills, on time, for years. You may fear losing your credit cards because you've become so accustomed to making purchases on credit—many of us feel the same way. We are extremely dependent on credit cards to allow us to purchase the things we desire *at this very moment.*

You want to make good on your entire obligation, but paying off a high-balance credit card without significant additional income could take forever, literally, because the credit card interest charged to your balance continues to grow *daily*, increasing the amount due. If you continue to use your card for purchases, and/or make only minimum or low payments, then it will be difficult to reduce the debt you owe; most likely you will pay for many years without reducing the principal, because the interest continues to grow daily even though you're paying something every month. And what's worse is, if you pay late, they will add a penalty to the account, making the balance even higher. If the balance rises above the credit limit, then you will be penalized and charged additional fees. This is an extremely stressful situation.

The credit card companies have had defaults before, and they have developed a repertoire of tricks to get you to keep paying them for as long as it takes for them to get their money. If you default, some companies have a department call you so you think you are settling the debt and you are getting the best deal ever offered to a customer. Typically this deal is the company freezes the credit card, the interest is lowered to two percent and you pay the balance due over five years—sixty payments. This is a great offer if you are paying very high interest, but they don't go back and lower all the interest that has accrued over the years.

Before you accept it, *think* about the deal they offer you.

- The credit card company is paid in full in this deal.
- You lose your credit card.

- Your credit is besmirched for five years with debt, and
- You are paying them for five years.

This may not be the best deal for you.

Another option may be that you stop using all of your credit cards. Perhaps you may choose to put one low balance or no balance card aside and continue making timely payments until it is paid in full. Keep this card in a safe place *for emergencies only*. But, be prepared: Once you begin missing payments on other cards, it is very possible that the credit limit on this paid card will be reduced each month so that the emergency card may quickly lose its value. Let's see what your options are.

Another way of looking at this is that you want the IRS to lower the tax bill that you owe, right? You want to ask them to cut you a break, remove the penalties, and remove the interest owed on the tax. Well, if you can negotiate with the IRS, you can certainly negotiate with the credit card companies.

Master Your Budget

If you remove the credit card debt payments from your monthly budget you will have more money available to pay bills and save to settle others. I find that many individuals spend less money when they pay with cash rather than pay with credit. By playing with the numbers, you will learn that low debt and eventually no debt is the best financial position. Lower debt or monthly obligations, such as credit card payments, allows you to save more money. You can pay off your home mortgage quicker, or perhaps purchase a home—the American dream. After you own your home you can save and invest your hard-earned money. This will take some time, but it will happen faster than you can imagine. The best part of this is that you will have learned a good lesson—you'll be sure you never fall into these circumstances again. And if your children are involved in the plan, they will become financially wiser.

Credit card debt can be a burden on your financial budget. The credit card companies want you to pay high interest, but if you make just the minimum payments, you will be paying them forever. As you can see, this prevents you from saving for retirement, or pay off your home, or just save money in the bank.

The credit card company wants you to owe them a lot of money and to pay high interest. This is how they make a profit. Regardless of how or why you find yourself in this position, if you are making minimum payments and the principal due to them continues to increase, then it's time to do something drastic!

To start the settlement process, *you must stop paying the credit card companies*. If you want to get a fresh start and build a financial empire for you and your family, there is simply no alternative. Their deal is another five years of payments. Your deal can be as simple as one to four monthly payments and you are done. Which will be best for you and your family?

The Settlement Process & The Tax Consequences

I know you are thinking this is going to be difficult and stressful, and you're right. It is. But in reality, you are going to fix your credit by reducing the debt to income ratio. The credit bureaus measure your debt (that is, the amount you owe), and compare it to your ability to pay the loan(s) based on your income. If you have high debt, your score is lower than if you have no debt, because people with high debt are more likely to default on the payment schedule. You could lose your job or get sick. Credit bureaus also track late payments. If you settle your debts, yes, it will damage your credit score in the short term. But in the long run (as little as a year) your credit score will recover to an even higher score because that old balance due is gone, and now you appear to be in a better position to pay monthly debt. One more thing to consider—when you have no debt the credit card companies charge you their lowest interest because you wouldn't borrow from them if they charged 15–20%.

Mr. & Mrs. Joe Taxpayer owed huge credit card debt. He is in insurance sales and she is not employed. Joe and his wife were still paying the interest instead of other necessary expenses, like taxes. This stopped! They have settled huge credit card debt for pennies on the dollar as well as other debts without filing bankruptcy. They have a fresh start.

The Settlement Process

You must follow the plan and save the money you usually pay the credit card company while you enter and pass through the default stages so that when you are negotiating a deal you will have the money or available funds immediately accessible to forward the payments and complete the settlement. You are not going into bankruptcy but you are fully planning to settle the credit card debt on very favorable terms.

The very first thing you must do is open a savings account designated specifically for the future settlements. Also, be sure you have a debit card for future purchases. The debit card will take the place of all credit cards. Sometimes a check or cash will not suffice and you will need a debit card to make a purchase. Be sure you have the debit card before you begin this process, because your credit will be in disarray until your settlements are complete. After completion of the settlements, your

FICO score will slowly increase and eventually be as high or higher than it has ever been. I have seen this process take place in as short as nine months. That is, of course, assuming that all other financial obligations are being paid on time.

1. After you have secured a debit card and a separate savings account, do not make any more payments on your credit cards. Call the card company and tell them you will not make further payments due to financial hardship. Ask the customer service representative whom you should speak to within their company to "settle" the debt. Get the contact information and write them a letter. Let them know you only want to be contacted by mail without phone calls. *Put this in writing* and mail it to the credit card company and the settlement representative. If you are contacted by phone, politely let the collection agent know you may only be contacted by mail and then hang up. This will remove much of the stress within the settlement period.

2. This next step is very important! *Do not spend the money* that would have paid the monthly credit card bills. You *must* put that money away in a separate account to make the settlement payments and subsequently the tax payments on the cancellation of debt.

3. Cut up the cards! You don't need them. If you need to make a purchase, use cash or your debit card. If you are no longer making credit card payments you will have funds available for necessary purchases.

4. Any debt settlement, specifically credit card settlement, is serious. It will affect your credit score (FICO) but that is probably already affected due to your debt-to-credit ratio.

5. Be patient during the settlement period. I'll say that one more time: *be patient during the settlement period.* The card company

will likely be more anxious to settle after a few months of not receiving payments. When they run your credit score and find a tax lien, they will be still more anxious to settle. Generally it takes 4–6 months to agree on an amount that you find affordable. Typically, a settlement is 30 percent of the debt. Don't be afraid to try to reduce it further. Inform them that you have a true financial hardship and be sure to make the credit card company aware that you have an IRS tax issue or tax lien. Remind them that you must pay your taxes before you can begin to pay the credit card debt. You may even want to inform them that you are a possible bankruptcy candidate. When both parties eventually agree upon an acceptable amount you can expect to make one payment in full or monthly payments to be made over three, four or five months. These may be done by advancing checks monthly or by auto-withdraw from a designated bank account. If you default anywhere in the process, the settlement will be null and void so be sure you will have the ability to pay the agreed amount. In other words, have the money in the savings account originally designated for depositing money for this settlement.

6.   On rare occasions, a credit card company will move forward to file a judgment against you in court. It is important that you open all mail that comes to you and be sure to sign for all certified mail. The fact that you ignore the notices does not mean they will go away. Be informed at all times!

7.   The Tax Issue: You will receive a 1099-C for the cancellation of debt for the tax year the debt was settled. This is the tax you will owe on the amount of the debt you did not pay. The debt not repaid is considered income to you for tax purposes.

By way of example, suppose you owe a credit card company $25,000 and make arrangements to settle for 30 % of the amount due or $7,500.

You will receive a 1099-C for the difference of the amount of debt which you did not pay or $17,500. Expect to owe tax on that amount of $17,500 in cancelled debt. If you are in the 30% tax bracket then you will owe approximately $5,300 in tax. Through the settlement you will have saved about $12,200. Remember to work out the numbers in advance of any agreement. You must be able to afford the deal.

Some crafty people have their withholding adjusted by their employer to compensate for this. Others use the designated money in savings so they can pay off the tax due when they file the tax return in April of the next year. There are numerous options but you have to be thinking of this issue ahead of the curve. Be prepared for the taxes on the cancelled debt.

You will most likely have to settle your various credit card debts at different times to allow yourself time to make each of the payments. Settle the card with the smallest balance first, because you will become a better negotiator with each settlement, and the cards with the highest balances will not disappear from your credit report when you are working with the other card companies. If you settled in reverse order the smallest balance credit card would not settle in the end because there was no other debt.

The credit card company does not want you to default and then try to settle your loan with them for a fraction of the balance due. You will only choose this path if you are facing budgetary issues that are much greater than the credit card debt itself.

CHAPTER 21

Mortgage Debt Forgiveness: How To Handle The Tax Consequences

Cancellation of Indebtedness Income in Brief

The IRS generally taxes all sources of income. What many taxpayers fail to realize is that income can come in many forms, not just cash. For example, if you owe a creditor $5,000, and the creditor decides that it will accept $3,000 from you to settle the debt, the $2,000 that you were not required to pay is seen by the IRS as income from the creditor to you. This is known as cancellation of indebtedness income.

A mortgage on a house is a debt owed to a bank or other lender. When a taxpayer is unable to pay the mortgage, it generally results in a foreclosure, where the lender will take ownership of the house. Mortgage forgiveness occurs when the lender takes possession of a taxpayer's home, and does not require the taxpayer to pay any additional money owed for the house. Mortgage forgiveness may also occur when a taxpayer keeps his home, but there is a modification of the terms of his mortgage, in which the amount of money owed by the taxpayer is reduced (known as mortgage restructuring). This mortgage forgiveness can have serious tax consequences for the taxpayer who just lost his house.

For example, Joe Taxpayer buys a house, and owes the bank $20,000. Over the course of six months, Joe reduces the amount owed to the bank to $15,000, through regular mortgage payments. However, at that point, Joe is no longer able to make payments, and the bank takes possession of the property. Joe still owes $15,000 to the bank, but the bank is not asking for that money to be repaid, because the bank has the house. That $15,000 is cancellation of indebtedness income, which could be taxed by the IRS in the year it was cancelled.

Based on the example above, it is clear that while having a mortgage forgiven by a bank can be helpful to you at first glance, the tax consequences can be quite substantial. Luckily for you, there are exceptions to the general rule that mortgage forgiveness will have tax consequences. The first two exceptions, insolvency and qualified principal residence indebtedness, are the most common, and I will explain both in detail. The remaining four exceptions, bankruptcy, qualified real property business indebtedness, qualified farm indebtedness, and qualified midwestern disaster area indebtedness, will also be mentioned and briefly described.

Insolvency[1]

If you are insolvent immediately before your mortgage is forgiven, then the IRS will not count that cancellation of indebtedness as income, and it will not be taxed. In order for you to be insolvent, your liabilities must exceed the fair market value of your assets. The IRS will only allow the amount of money by which you are insolvent to be excluded

---

1   IRC § 108(a)(1)(B).

as income if your mortgage is forgiven. The following example will clarify this insolvency rule.

Joe Taxpayer owes $50,000 in debts, and the fair market value of his assets is $10,000. That means he is insolvent to the extent of $40,000 ($50,000 of liability minus $10,000 of assets). He has a mortgage of $30,000, which he is no longer able to pay. If he loses his house and his $30,000 of mortgage debt is forgiven by the lender, that $30,000 would normally be considered income. However, since he was already insolvent, and his degree of insolvency ($40,000) was greater than the cancelled debt ($30,000), Joe can apply the insolvency exception, and the $30,000 that was forgiven would not be taxed by the IRS.

However, if all of Joe's $50,000 debt is his mortgage, and he had $10,000 in assets at the time the mortgage was forgiven, only $40,000 of the mortgage forgiveness would be excluded from being taxed because the IRS will only exclude cancellation of indebtedness income to the extent the taxpayer is insolvent (in Joe's case, $40,000, based on the calculations above). Therefore, Joe would still be taxed on $10,000 ($50,000 mortgage minus $40,000 excluded through the insolvency exception).

If you are using the insolvency exception to avoid paying tax of a forgiven mortgage, fill out Form 982: Reduction of Tax Attributes Due to Discharge of Indebtedness. To claim the exclusion, you must attach this form to your tax return. Check box 1b and, on line 2, include the smaller amount of

a. the debt cancelled or
b. the amount by which you were insolvent immediately prior to the mortgage forgiveness.

Then, you must fill out Part II of Form 982, which asks for a breakdown of the total amount excluded from gross income.

Qualified Principal Residence Indebtedness[2]

Under the Mortgage Debt Relief Act of 2007, a qualified principal residence indebtedness (QPRI) that is forgiven in the years 2007 through 2012 is not taxed as cancellation of indebtedness income. According to IRS Publication 4681, Cancelled Debts, Foreclosures, Repossessions, and Abandonments, a QPRI is any mortgage that you took out to buy, build, or substantially improve your main home. Your main home is the home where you ordinarily live most of the time, and you can only have one main home at any given time. Additionally, the mortgage must be secured by your main home, meaning that if you are unable to pay off the mortgage, the lender could take possession of your home. A QPRI also includes any debt secured by your main home that was used to *refinance* a mortgage taken out to buy, build, or substantially improve your main home, up to the amount of the original mortgage principal before the refinancing.

The following example helps clarify the QPRI exception to cancellation of indebtedness income:

In 2003, Joe Taxpayer bought his main home for $430,000. Joe took out a $400,000 mortgage loan to buy the home and made a down payment of $30,000. The loan was secured by the home. At this point, Joe's QPRI is $400,000.

In 2004, Joe took out a second mortgage loan in the amount of $75,000 that he used to add a bathroom to his home. At this point, Joe's QPRI is $475,000.

In 2009, when the remaining amount owed on the first and second mortgage was reduced to $350,000 total through Joe's monthly payments, he was in need of money, so he refinanced the two mortgage loans into one loan in the amount of $400,000. This refinancing gave

---

2   IRC § 108(a)(1)(E).

him an additional $50,000, which he spent on paying off his credits cards and his son's gambling debts. Even though Joe's current mortgage for his main home is now $400,000, his QPRI is only $350,000 because when a mortgage is refinanced, the maximum amount that can be QPRI is the amount of the original mortgage principal before the refinancing.

If Joe was unable to pay his mortgage at this point, and the bank foreclosed his house and forgave the $400,000 he still owed, $350,000 of that cancelled debt would not be taxed because it was QPRI. However, the $50,000 increase from the refinancing would be taxed as income at this point.

There is a limit to how much cancelled QPRI the IRS will allow you to avoid paying income tax on. Up to $2 million can be excluded as QPRI income for a taxpayer, unless the taxpayer is married filing separately, in which case the maximum is $1 million.

If a lender forgives your QPRI, the lender should send you Form 1099-C: Cancellation of Indebtedness. The amount of debt forgiven will be shown in box 2 of this form. If you wish to have this amount excluded as income, you must fill out Form 982 and attach it to your tax return. You must also check box 1e of Form 982. The amount of cancelled debt should be included on lines 2 and 10b of the form. However, line 10b only needs to be filled out if you kept ownership of your home and modification of the terms of your mortgage resulted in forgiveness of QPRI.

Bankruptcy[3]

Any debt cancelled in a Title 11 Bankruptcy is not included in your income. Therefore, if your mortgage is forgiven through Title 11 Bankruptcy proceedings, the IRS will not tax that cancelled debt.

---

3   IRC § 108(a)(1)(A).

For more information on the impact of bankruptcy on your income tax, see Chapter 13 on Bankruptcy.

Qualified Real Property Business Indebtedness[4]

The IRS will not apply income tax to cancelled qualified real property business indebtedness. In order for debt to fall into this category, it must meet all of the following requirements:

1. The debt was incurred or assumed in connection with real property used in a trade or a business.
2. The debt was secured by that real property.
3. The debt was incurred or assumed either:
    a. Before 1993, or
    b. After 1992, if the debt is either:
        i. Qualified acquisition indebtedness. Qualified acquisition indebtedness is debt incurred or assumed to acquire, construct, reconstruct, or substantially improve real property that is used in a trade or business and secures the debt, or debt resulting from the refinancing of qualified acquisition indebtedness, to the extent the amount of the debt does not exceed the amount of debt being refinanced.
        ii. Debt incurred to refinance qualified real property business debt incurred or assumed before 1993 (but only to the extent the amount of such debt does not exceed the amount of debt being refinanced)
4. The debt is debt to which you elect to apply these rules.

---

4   IRC § 108(a)(1)(D).

Qualified Farm Indebtedness[5]

The IRS will not apply income tax to cancelled qualified farm indebtedness. In order for debt to fall into this category, it must meet all of the following requirements:

1. The debt was incurred directly in connection with your operation of the trade or business of farming.
2. Fifty percent or more of your total gross receipts for 2006, 2007, and 2008 were from the trade or business of farming.
3. The cancellation was made by an individual or organization that is actively and regularly engaged in the business of lending money.

Qualified Midwestern Disaster Area Indebtedness[6]

This exception applies to cancelled non-business tax debts for taxpayers whose main home is located in a Midwestern disaster area. If you think this exception might apply to you, you should contact a local tax professional.

---

5   IRC § 108(a)(1)(C).
6   Heartland Disaster Tax Relief Act of 2008.

CHAPTER 22

Retaining a Representative: Power of Attorney

If you decide to hire a representative, you will have to authorize the IRS to speak to her or the IRS will not recognize the individual as your representative. To do this, you must complete an IRS Form 2848. This form is not a durable power of attorney. The power of attorney is limited and specific and the IRS will only allow the representative to discuss matters you have specifically identified in the form. This is for your privacy and protection.

Form 2848: Power of Attorney and Declaration of Representative

If you intend to hire or retain a representative you must sign Form 2848: Power of Attorney and Declaration of Representative, to permit the IRS to speak to the representative, permit the representative to participate in a conference or to file written response on your behalf. A power of attorney is your written authorization allowing an individual to represent you—in this case, in your tax matters. Generally, the power of attorney allows the representative to act on your behalf in all matters before the

IRS. Form 2848 is an IRS form, which you are required to sign before the representative may perform any of the following acts:

1. Represent you before any office of the IRS.
2. Record the interview.
3. Sign an offer, or a waiver of restriction on assessment or collection of a tax deficiency, or a waiver of notice of disallowance of claim for credit or refund.
4. Sign a consent to extend the statutory time period for assessment or collection of a tax.
5. Sign a closing agreement.
6. Receive, but not endorse or cash, a refund check. To permit a representative to endorse or cash a refund check, you must specifically initial a particular line to designate authority.

Generally, a representative may not sign a tax return unless you specifically authorized it due to a disease, injury, continuous absence from the United States for more than 60 days, or any other good cause shown, and agreed to, by the IRS.

Other non-IRS forms can be submitted, but the Form 2848 must be attached for the document to be accepted by the Centralized Authorization File System.

Who Can Represent You?

The following individuals can practice before the IRS. The recognized representative must be designated as the taxpayer's power of attorney and file a written authorization with the IRS stating that he is authorized and qualified to represent a taxpayer. Completing Form 2848 does this. Generally, an attorney who is a member in good standing of the bar of the highest court of any state, possession, territory, commonwealth, or the District of Columbia may practice before the IRS. A certified public accountant (CPA) who is duly qualified to practice as a CPA in any state, possession, territory, commonwealth, or the District of Columbia may practice before the IRS. Any enrolled agent in active status may practice before the IRS. Un-enrolled return preparers and public accountants my represent the taxpayer before customer service representatives, revenue agents, and examination officers with respect to an examination regarding the return they prepared. But they cannot represent a taxpayer before other IRS offices, such as Collections or Appeals, and this would include Automated Collection System (ACS).

There are other limited areas of practice for enrolled retirement plan agents and enrolled actuaries. Student attorneys, student CPAs, and other un-enrolled individuals can be permitted to represent an individual or entity before the IRS on a very limited basis. For example, a family member may represent an individual member of his or her immediate family because of the special relationship with the taxpayer. But before this can be done, he or she must present satisfactory identification to the IRS and proof of authority to represent the taxpayer.

Duties of the Practitioner

The practitioner must conform to IRS Circular 230. Practitioners must promptly submit records and information requested of them by employees and representatives of the IRS. Practitioners may not intentionally delay a case.

A tax practitioner must not knowingly, directly or indirectly, accept assistance from any person who is under disbarment from practice before the IRS or participate in disreputable conduct. Disreputable conduct includes but is not limited to: willfully failing to file tax returns or attempting to evade payment, knowingly giving false or misleading information in federal tax matters, being convicted of any criminal offense under the revenue laws or being involved in dishonesty or breach of trust, directly or indirectly attempting to influence official action of an IRS employee or by misappropriating funds from a client.

Practitioners must exercise due diligence when preparing or assisting in preparation, approving, and filing of returns, documents, affidavits, and other papers relating to tax matters. The practitioner has a duty to advise his client if he has not complied with revenue laws or has made an error or omission in any return, document, affidavit, or other paper. Practitioners must advise their client promptly of non-compliance and the consequences of non-compliance. A practitioner must not unreasonably delay the prompt disposition of any tax matter before the IRS.

Confidentiality and Privilege

Communications with an attorney are privileged and confidential. In limited circumstances, communications between a CPA, enrolled agent, and enrolled actuary are also privileged, but the rule applies *only* to tax advice given to the taxpayer by the individual who is federally authorized. The tax advice is in regard to a matter that is within the scope of the practitioner's authority to practice. It is also limited to non-criminal tax matters and proceedings brought in federal court. Thus, if a matter were to be initiated civilly and become criminal, the Justice Department could attempt to break down the privilege between a taxpayer and his accountant or tax preparer. The attorney-client privilege could not be broken down unless there was criminal activity between the two; crime or fraud committed by the two is the exception to the attorney-client privilege.

These are the basic tenants of a power of attorney.

How to Prepare the Power of Attorney

Generally, the practitioner prepares a Form 2848: Power of Attorney, pursuant to the instructions and has the client execute it. The client will sign the document after verifying the content and will send it to the practitioner for filing with the IRS. The practitioner will execute the power of attorney (POA) and fax it to the IRS, Central Authorization File Unit (CAF). Each taxpayer must be listed on a separate POA. This is Congress's way of saying each taxpayer has a right to a separate representative. But having two representatives is going to be very costly.

> *The best practice in completing the form is to be as broad as possible in the section concerning tax matters.*

Specifically identify the type of tax; for example, Income, then the tax form, Form 1040, and finally the tax periods covered by the POA, such as 2000 through 2013. By way of example, the POA is going back to cover periods before and after the current tax year so that it includes every possible tax period at issue and the IRS RO cannot circumvent the POA and go to your home or work to discuss something not covered by the POA. With respect to the preparation and filing of the form, see Publication 947: Practice Before the IRS and Power of Attorney.

How to Disengage Your Representative

The taxpayer or his representative can revoke the power of attorney by simply writing "REVOKE" across the top of Form 2848 and sending it to the CAF. In the case of the representative, he must sign his name next to the the taxpayer's signature on page two of Form 2848 and fax or mail the revoked POA to the Central Authorization File Unit. Often the taxpayer can rescind the POA by calling the IRS and telling the IRS to revoke the POA immediately so the representative cannot access his file.

LIST OF ACRONYMS

ACS	Automated Collection System
CAF	Central Authorization File Unit
CAP	Collection Appeals Program
CCC	Credit Card Company
CCD	Credit Card Debt
CDP	Collection Due Process
CI	Criminal Investigator
CIS	Collection Information Statement
CNC	Currently Not Collectible
CPA	Certified Public Account
CRFTL	Certificate of Release of the Federal Tax Lien
CSED	Collection Statute End/Expiration Date
FICA	Federal Insurance Contributions Act
IA	Installment Agreement
IDR	Information Document Request
IMF	Information Master File
IRA	Individual Retirement Account
IRC	Internal Revenue Code
IRMF	Information Return Master File
IRS	Internal Revenue Service
NFTL	Notice of Federal Tax Lien
NTA	National Taxpayer Advocate
OIC	Offer In Compromise
POA	Power of Attorney
QPRI	Qualified Principal Residence Indebtedness
RCP	Reasonable Collection Potential
RO	Revenue Officer
SFR	Substitute For Return
TAO	Taxpayer Assistance Order
TAS	Taxpayer Advocate Service
TBOR	Taxpayer Bill of Rights

GLOSSARY OF TERMS

Appeal—A formal challenge to an IRS determination of tax liability or action.

Assessment—The process by which the IRS imposes a tax liability.

Asset*—Anything owned by an individual or a business, which has cash, commercial, or exchange value.

Audit*—An IRS examination of your tax return.

Audit Reconsideration—The reevaluation of a tax return that was previously audited by the IRS.

Bankruptcy*—A person or company is considered bankrupt if they are unable to pay their bills and debts in a timely fashion. Under Chapter 11 (for businesses) and Chapter 13 (for wage earners) the bankrupt tries to reorganize his/its debts.

Budget*—An itemized listing of the amount of all estimated revenue and the amount of all estimated costs and expenses that will be incurred in obtaining the revenue during a given period of time for a business.

Cancellation of Debt*—Forgiveness of a debt without payment or consideration. Cancellation of debt is taxable as income to the debtor unless the creditor intended it as a gift or it meets certain exceptions relating to bankruptcy, insolvency, or farming.

Case Analysis—The thorough review of your current tax situation and tax history. This is the first step toward tax compliance.

Collection Financial Standards—The maximum costs the IRS deems necessary for certain living expenses.

Collection Information Statement—Either Form 433 A, B, or F, which informs the government of your complete financial condition.

Collection Statute End/Expiration Date—As a general rule the IRS has ten (10) years to collect taxes, which are assessed. The ten years term begins the date after the assessment or the date the C-21 is signed. This term refers to the date the tax liability expires due to the statute of limitations running its course.

Compliance—Conformity in fulfilling official requirements; b: the act or process of complying with a desire, demand, proposal, or regimen or the coercion.

Currently Not Collectible—This is the status in which you may be placed by the IRS if you are unable to pay a tax debt without suffering an undue hardship. While in currently not collectible status, you are not required to pay any tax debts.

Garnishment*—Money withheld from your pay and redirected to the IRS.

Income Tax*—Tax on both earned income, i.e. salaries, wages, tips, and commissions - and unearned income, i.e. interest from savings accounts, dividend, and rents, etc.

Innocent Spouse Rule*—An exception to the general rule that both signers of a joint return are individually liable for the entire tax due plus penalties and interest. Basically, if you can show that you didn't know and didn't have reason to know about an error that resulted in the underpayment of tax on a joint return you can be relieved of responsibility for that underpayment. Under the innocent spouse rule a spouse may claim to not be jointly liable if he or she did not know about the errors and did not benefit from them. You have two years from the time the IRS begins trying to collect the underpayment to petition for innocent spouse relief.

Injured Spouse Rule—Sometimes, the IRS will use the refund owed to one spouse (the "injured spouse") to pay off a legally enforceable debt owed by the other spouse (the "debtor spouse"). In this case, the injured spouse may recover any money owed to her (her share of the refund) from the IRS by filing Form 8379: Injured Spouse Allocation.

Installment Agreement—A plan agreed upon by both the IRS and the taxpayer, where the taxpayer is given a certain amount of time (usually no more than 60 months) to pay money owed to the IRS in set monthly increments.

Joint Return*—A return filed by a married couple reporting their combined income and deductions.

Lien—A claim, or an encumbrance, placed on property.

Levy—The actual seizure of property, claimed by the IRS in order to satisfy a tax debt.

Married Filing Jointly*—The filing status used by most married couples. When couples file jointly they combine their income and deductions on the same tax return.

Married Filing Separately*—A filing status a married couple can use if they are married as of the end of the tax year. Each spouse can file a separate income tax return with their own income and deductions.

Non-filer—An individual or entity that has not filed one or more tax returns timely.

Notice of Federal Tax Lien—A public notice that a tax lien in favor of the government has been placed against a taxpayer on all assets that he owns or will own in the future.

Offer in Compromise—An agreement between a taxpayer and the IRS, where a taxpayer satisfies a tax debt by only paying off a certain portion of it.

Penalty*—A fine charged by the IRS for various infractions including filing your tax return and/or paying your taxes late. The amount of the fine depends on the nature of the infraction. You may be charged interest in addition to penalties.

Penalty Abatement—The reduction or termination of tax penalties.

Power of Attorney*—A legal document authorizing one person to act in the name, place, and stead of another person as attorney or agent. You can give a specific power of attorney to someone such as your accountant or an enrolled agent to represent you on tax matters before the IRS.

Statute of Limitations (See also, Collection statute Expiration Date in glossary)—A statute prescribing a limitation to the period within which a certain right may be enforced [to collect money from the taxpayer] or declaring that no action may be taken after a specified date.

Subordination of a Tax Lien—The priority of a tax lien on a certain property is lowered by the IRS, in favor of some other lien against that same property.

Substitute for Return—A tax return prepared by examination and filed pursuant to the Internal Revenue Code because the taxpayer did not timely file after notice by IRS. SFRs are usually prepared with extraordinarily high tax liabilities to induce the non-filer/taxpayer to file the proper return.

Tax Year*—A period of 12 months for reporting income and expenses. Most individual taxpayers use the calendar year as their tax year.

Taxpayer Advocate*—The IRS official who is charged with helping individuals resolve their problems with the IRS, as well as identifying changes in IRS procedures that could make the agency more taxpayer friendly.

Tolling/Suspension—The statute of limitations is suspended or tolled (stopped), thereby extending the liability period. This occurs when one files an appeal, offer in compromise, bankruptcy or case in Tax Court, Collection Due Process Hearing Request (CDP), Application for a Taxpayer Assistance Order--Form 911, Tax Collection Waiver or Consent Form 872 or other action designed to delay collection.

*Definitions from http://www.wwwebtax.com/glossary/@_tax_glossary.htm

FORMS INDEX

Any forms not in the book can be found at www.taxjams.com.

FORM/EXHIBIT	CHAPTER(S)
Call to IRS Form	3
Certificate of Release of the Federal Tax Lien	4, 5
CP-2000	3
CP-504 (2 versions) Notice of Intent to Levy	4
Final Notice of Intent to Levy	4, 5, 7
Form 1127 Application for Extension of Time for Payment of Tax Due to Undue Hardship	4
Form 12153 Request for a Collection Due Process or Equivalent Hearing	4, 7, 15
Form 12507 Innocent Spouse Statement	16
Form 12508 Questionnaire for Non-Requesting Spouse	16

FORM/EXHIBIT	CHAPTER(S)
Form 12509 Statement of Disagreement	16
Form 13711 Request for Appeal of Offer in Compromise	14
Form 14134 Application for Certificate of Subordination of Federal Tax Lien	5
Form 2848 Power of Attorney and Declaration of Representative	1, 7, 22
Form 433-A Collection Information Statement for Wage Earners and Self-Employed Individuals	4, 6, 7, 8, 9, 10, 14
Form 433-B Collection Information Statement for Businesses	6, 7, 9, 10, 14
Form 433-F Collection Information Statement	6, 8, 9, 10, 11
Form 4549 Income Tax Examination Changes	19
Form 8379 Injured Spouse Allocation	17
Form 843 Claim for Refund and Request for Abatement	12
Form 870 Waiver of Restrictions on Assessment and Collection of Deficiency in Tax and Acceptance of Overassessment	19
Form 872 Consent to Extend the Time to Assess Tax	15
Form 872-T Notice of Termination of Special Consent to Extend the Time to Assess Tax	15
Form 8822 Change of Address	4

FORM/EXHIBIT	CHAPTER(S)
Form 8857 Request for Innocent Spouse Relief	16
Form 911 Request for Taxpayer Advocate Service Assistance	4, 6, 7
Form 9423 Collection Appeal Request	7
Form 9465 Installment Agreement Request	11
Form 9465-FS Installment Agreement Request	11
Form 982 Reduction of Tax Attributes Due to Discharge of Indebtedness	13, 21
IRS Account Transcript	13
Notice of Federal Tax Lien	5, 7, 13
Publication 1 Your Rights as a Taxpayer	1, 7
Substitute for Return	2, 3, 13, 15, 19
Summons	18

TAX JAMStm

CASE ANALYSIS: CALL TO IRS FORM

Revenue Person:
(have rep spell name)

ID Number:

Office Address:

Tax Year	Filed or SFR*	Amount Owed	CSED**
2000			
2001			
2002			
2003			
2004			
2005			
2006			
2007			
2008			
2009			
2010			
2011			
2012			

*SFR – Substitute for Return (prepared by IRS)
**CSED – Collection Statute Expiration Date

Form 668 (Z) (Rev. 10-2000)	▮	Department of the Treasury - Internal Revenue Service **Certificate of Release of Federal Tax Lien**

Area: SMALL BUSINESS/SELF EMPLOYED AREA #3 Lien Unit Phone: (800) 913-6050	Serial Number ▮	For Use by Recording Office

I certify that the following-named taxpayer, under the requirements of section 6325 of the Internal Revenue Code has satisfied the taxes listed below and all statutory additions. Therefore, the lien provided by Code section 6321 for these taxes and additions has been released. The proper officer in the office where the notice of internal revenue tax lien was filed on _____ March 09 _____,

_____ 2010 _____, is authorized to note the books to show the release of this lien for these taxes and additions.

Name of Taxpayer ▮

Residence ▮

COURT RECORDING INFORMATION:

Liber	Page	UCC No.	Serial No.
n/a	n/a	n/a	▮

Kind of Tax (a)	Tax Period Ended (b)	Identifying Number (c)	Date of Assessment (d)	Last Day for Refiling (e)	Unpaid Balance of Assessment (f)
1040	12/31/2005	▮	05/29/2006	06/28/2016	
1040	12/31/2005	▮	12/29/2008	01/28/2019	11744.59
1040	12/31/2005	▮	12/29/2008	01/28/2019	

Place of Filing

Recorder of Deeds
▮

Total   11744.59

This notice was prepared and signed at _____ BALTIMORE, MD _____, on this,

the _19th_ day of _May_, _2010_.

Signature ▮

Title
Director, Campus Compliance Operations

(NOTE: Certificate of officer authorized by law to take acknowledgements is not essential to the validity of Certificate of Release of Federal Tax Lien Rev. Rul. 71-466, 1971 - 2 C.D. 409

Part 2 - Taxpayer's Copy

Form **668 (Z)** (Rev. 10-2000)
CAT. NO 60026I

Department of Treasury
Internal Revenue Service
PO BOX 9038
ANDOVER, MA 01810-4544

AUR Control: ███████

Notice: CP2000
Notice Date: **June 13, 2011**

Social Security Number:
███████

Form: 1040
Tax Year: 2009

To call for assistance:
1-800-829-3009 Toll Free

between 7:00 AM - 8:00 PM

To FAX information:
1-877-477-9485 Fax

Contact: ███████

You Must Return the Response Form by July 13, 2011

1 | Why are you getting this notice?

The income and payment information (e.g., wages, miscellaneous income, interest, income tax withheld, earned income credit, etc.) that we have on file does not match entries on your **2009** Form **1040**.   If this information is correct, you will owe **$688**.

The proposed changes to your tax are listed below.

Summary of Proposed Changes		
2009 Tax Increase	$	670
Payment Increase	$	0
Penalties - may not include all applicable penalties	$	0
Interest - if paid by July 13, 2011	$	18
Proposed Balance Due	$	688

2 | What steps should you take?

Following these steps can help you understand this notice.

1. Review your **2009** tax return.
2. Compare your return to the information in the *Explanation Section* -- page 7.
3. Decide if the information in the *Explanation Section* is correct.
4. Check the answers to *Frequently Asked Questions* -- page 2.
5. Complete and return the *Response Form* in the enclosed envelope -- page 3.
6. Complete and return the *Installment Agreement Request* (enclosed) if you need to set up a payment plan.
7. Review your rights in *The Examination Process* Booklet (enclosed).

3 | What happens if you don't respond by July 13, 2011?

We will send you a final notice, followed by a bill. During this time, interest will increase and certain penalties may apply.

Frequently Asked Questions

Why did it take IRS so long to contact me?

Tax years generally end on December 31, but we may not receive complete information from employers, banks, businesses, and other payers until much later.

Will I need to file amended returns (federal/state/local) if I agree with some or all of the proposed changes?

1. You do not need to file an amended federal tax return to include the proposed changes shown on this notice. We will correct this tax year when we receive your response. If you choose to file an amended tax return, write "CP2000" along the top of the 1040X, attach it behind the Response Form page and send to the address shown on this notice.
2. If the changes on this notice apply to your state tax return, file an amended state/local tax return as soon as possible. We send information about changes based on this notice to your state and local tax agencies.
3. File amended returns for any prior or subsequent tax years in which the same error occurred. You'll limit the penalty and interest you owe.

What should I do if I am currently in bankruptcy?

If you filed for bankruptcy, please complete and return the response page, including any applicable supporting documentation if you checked Option 2 or Option 3. Please be sure to also include a copy of your bankruptcy petition.

What steps do I take if I do not agree?

We need you to tell us why you do not agree and send us information to support your statement. Please refer to *The Examination Process Booklet* (enclosed) for tips about what information you should send with your response.

What if I need more time to collect my supporting documentation?

If you cannot respond by July 13, 2011, please call us at 1-800-829-3009 to request an extension. *Remember: If the tax increase is correct, then we will add interest and penalties to your bill during the extension.*

Why do I have to pay interest and penalties?

We are required by law to charge interest and penalties, if applicable, on all tax owed that is not paid in full by its due date (usually April 15). By law, interest will continue to increase until you have fully paid the tax owed and certain penalties may apply.

How can I prevent an error in the future?

1. Include <u>all</u> income you've received during the year on your tax return.
2. Wait to file your return until you receive all income statements to be sure your return is complete. If you do not receive an income statement in time to meet the April 15th deadline, estimate the amount of income using pay stubs, bank statements, etc.
3. Check the records (for example, W-2s, 1098s, 1099s, etc.) you receive from your employer, mortgage company, bank, or other source of income to be sure the information they're reporting is correct. (Some states pay taxable unemployment benefits, so report that as income as well.)
4. If you receive any additional information after you filed your return, you should amend your return with the corrected information as soon as possible to avoid any interest or penalties.
5. Keep accurate and complete records. Normally, keeping your records for three years is sufficient.

What if I have more questions?

If we haven't answered your question here, you can find other Frequently Asked Questions on our website, www.irs.gov, or you can call 1-800-829-4477, topic 652, for pre-recorded responses.

Response Form #1 - Payment Enclosed

Use this form to respond ONLY if you are enclosing a FULL or PARTIAL payment. If you are NOT sending a payment please complete Response Form #2 located on the next page.

1. Review the Explanation Section to decide whether you agree or do not agree with IRS's proposed changes.
2. Complete and return the Response Form by July 13, 2011.
3. If you need additional time, call us at 1-800-829-3009.

STEP A | Check only one of the three options. Then go to Step B.

If you agree with the changes IRS is proposing, return this form with your FULL or PARTIAL payment along with the completed Installment Agreement Request for the remaining balance (if applicable).

☐ **OPTION 1| I Agree with all Changes**

I agree with the changes to my 2009   tax return.
I understand that I owe $ 688   in additional tax, penalties, and interest.
I understand that the law requires IRS to charge interest on taxes that are not paid in full by April 15, 2010.   In addition, I understand that the IRS will charge interest until I have paid the tax in full. Certain penalties may also apply.
I understand that I can challenge these changes in the U.S. Tax Court only if IRS determines after the date I sign this form that I owe additional taxes for 2009.
I understand that I can file for a refund at a later date.
I understand that both myself and my spouse must sign below.

_______________________   _____________   ____________________   __________
Signature   Date   Spouse's Signature   Date

If you do not agree with the changes IRS is proposing, return this form. When you return this form, include a signed statement that explains what you do not agree with. Also include copies of any documents, such as a corrected W-2, 1099, or missing forms, that support your statement.

☐ **OPTION 2| I Do Not Agree with Some of the Changes**
I've enclosed documentation to support the entries on my original return.

☐ **OPTION 3| I Do Not Agree with Any of the Changes**
I've enclosed documentation to support the entries on my original return.

STEP B | Check the applicable payment options. Then go to Step C.

Tip! Pay as much as you can now to keep penalty and interest charges low.
Make your check or money order payable to "United States Treasury." Write "Tax Year 2009 *CP2000," this Social Security Number* ███████████ *and your phone number on your check or money order.*

☐ **OPTION 1| I'm paying the proposed balance due of $ 688.**
Balance may not include all applicable penalties - refer to the Explanation Section.

☐ **OPTION 2| I'm making a payment of $ ________________ because either:**

   ☐ I'm paying the amount I agree with or
   ☐ I'm making a partial payment at this time and would like to request a payment plan for the balance. *Complete the Installment Agreement Request (Form 9465) and mail it along with this form. Please refer to Form 9465 instructions for applicable fees.*

ANDOVER IRS CENTER   06/13/2011   ▮▮▮▮▮

| STEP C | Contact Information |

1. Please verify your address and note any corrections in the space below. *(Print clearly.)*

Make any address corrections here.

2. Please list your phone numbers and the best time to call below.

| Home | Best Time to Call |
| Work | Best Time to Call |

3. If you would like to authorize someone, in addition to you and your Spouse, to contact IRS concerning this notice, please include the person's contact information and sign below.

Name   Phone

Address

I authorize the person listed above to discuss information with and provide information to IRS about this notice.

_________________________   __________   _________________________   __________
Signature   Date   Spouse's Signature   Date

The authority granted in Step C is limited as indicated by the statement above the signature line. The contact may not sign returns, enter into agreements, or otherwise represent you before the IRS. If you want to have a designee with expanded authorization, see IRS Publication 947, Practice Before the IRS and Power of Attorney.

| Before Mailing | Please make sure you have: |

☐ Completed Steps A, B, and C (both sides of this form).
☐ Included this form and your payment (if applicable) in the envelope provided.
☐ Included the *Installment Agreement Request* (if applicable) in the envelope provided.
☐ Made a copy for your records of the *Response Form* and the *Installment Agreement Request* if you used it.
☐ Checked that the IRS address shows through the envelope window.

Please Fold Here. Do not detach. Please be sure our address shows through the envelope window.

{RF04}   AUR Control Number: ▮▮▮▮▮

Notice Number: CP2000
Notice Date: 06/13/2011

INTERNAL REVENUE SERVICE
FRESNO, CA 93888-0415

ANDOVER IRS CENTER ███████ ███████ 06/13/2011

Response Form #2 - No Payment Enclosed

Use this form to respond ONLY if you are NOT enclosing a payment. If you are sending a payment please complete Response Form #1 located on the previous page.

1. Review the Explanation Section to decide whether you agree or do not agree with IRS's proposed changes.
2. Complete and return the Response Form by July 13, 2011.
3. If you need additional time, call us at 1-800-829-3009.

STEP A | Check only one of the three options. Then go to Step B.

If you agree with the changes IRS is proposing, but are unable to send a payment at this time check Option 1 below and proceed to Step B, Option 1.

☐ **OPTION 1|** I Agree with All Changes

I agree with the changes to my **2009** tax return.
I understand that I owe **$688** in additional tax, penalties, and interest.
I understand that the law requires IRS to charge interest on taxes that are not paid in full by **April 15, 2010.** In addition, I understand that the IRS will charge interest until I have paid the tax in full. Certain penalties may also apply.
I understand that I can challenge these changes in the U.S. Tax Court only if IRS determines after the date I sign this form that I owe additional taxes for **2009.**
I understand that I can file for a refund at a later date.
I understand that both myself and my spouse must sign below.

_______________________   _______________   **Spouse's Signature**   **Date**
Signature   *Date*

If you do not agree with the changes IRS is proposing, return this form. When you return this form, include a signed statement that explains what you do not agree with. Also include copies of any documents, such as a corrected W-2, 1099, or missing forms, that support your statement.

☐ **OPTION 2|** I Do Not Agree with Some of the Changes
I've enclosed documentation to support the entries on my original return.

☐ **OPTION 3|** I Do Not Agree with Any of the Changes
I've enclosed documentation to support the entries on my original return.

STEP B | Check the appropriate option below, and proceed to Step C.

☐ **OPTION 1|** I agree with ALL of the changes but am unable to pay the amount I owe. I'd like to request a payment plan for the full amount.

Complete the Installment Agreement Request (Form 9465) and mail it along with this form.

☐ **OPTION 2|** I agree with SOME of the changes but am unable to pay the amount I owe. I'd like to request a payment plan for $______________________.

Complete the Installment Agreement Request (Form 9465) and mail it along with this form.

☐ **OPTION 3|** I do NOT agree with ANY of the changes and am not making a payment at this time.

ANDOVER IRS CENTER   06/13/2011

STEP C | Contact Information

1. Please verify your address and note any corrections in the space below. *(Print clearly.)*

Make any address corrections here.

2. Please list your phone numbers and the best time to call below.

Home		Best Time to Call
Work		Best Time to Call

3. If you would like to authorize someone, in addition to you **and your Spouse,** to contact IRS concerning this notice, please include the person's contact information and sign below.

Name   Phone

Address

I authorize the person listed above to discuss information with and provide information to IRS about this notice.

_______________________   _________   _______________________   _________
Signature   Date   Spouse's Signature   Date

The authority granted in Step C is limited as indicated by the statement above the signature line. The contact may not sign returns, enter into agreements, or otherwise represent you before the IRS. If you want to have a designee with expanded authorization, see IRS Publication 947, Practice Before the IRS and Power of Attorney.

Before Mailing | Please make sure you have:

☐ Completed Steps A, B, and C (both sides of this form).
☐ Included this form and your payment (if applicable) in the envelope provided.
☐ Included the *Installment Agreement Request* (if applicable) in the envelope provided.
☐ Made a copy for your records of the *Response Form* and the *Installment Agreement Request* if you used it.
☐ Checked that the IRS address shows through the envelope window.

Please Fold Here. Do not detach. Please be sure our address shows through the envelope window.

{RF05}   AUR Control Number: ▮▮▮▮▮▮

Notice Number: CP2000
Notice Date: 06/13/2011

INTERNAL REVENUE SERVICE
ANDOVER IRS CENTER
PO BOX 9038
ANDOVER, MA 01810-4544

ANDOVER IRS CENTER   ███████   ███████   06/13/2011

Explanation Section

How to Review This Section

1. Compare your records with the records we received under **Information Reported to IRS.**
2. Review the **Reasons for the Changes** to see why we changed your return.
3. Proceed to **Changes to Your Return** to see how your new tax was calculated.
4. Once you have fully reviewed the **Explanation Section**, please complete and return the **Response Form** in the envelope provided.

1. Information Reported to IRS that differs from the amounts shown on your return.

This section tells you specifically what income information IRS has received about you from others (including your employers, banks, mortgage holders, etc.). The information listed below does not match the information you listed on your tax return. Use this table to compare the data IRS has received from others to the information you listed on your tax return to understand where the discrepancy, or difference, occurred. To assist you in reviewing your income amounts, the table may include both reported and unreported amounts from the same payer.

If this information is correct, your tax increase is **$ 670** plus all applicable penalties, **interest and payment adjustments such as federal tax withholding, excess social security tax withheld, etc.** If you pay in full by July 13, 2011 , you'll owe   **$ 688.**

NONEMPLOYEE COMPENSATION Account Information	Amount Reported to IRS by Others	Amount Included on Your Return	Difference
#001 SSN: ███████ Form 1099-MISC ACCT: ███ ███████████	$ 1,770	$ 0	$ 1,770
NONEMPLOYEE COMPENSATION Total	$ 1,770	$ 0	$ 1,770

 ████████ ████████ 06/13/2011

2. Reasons for the Changes

This section provides explanations to help you understand the proposed changes to your tax return.

The paragraphs that follow provide explanations for:

* the items listed in Section 1. *Information Reported to IRS*
* the changes to your tax computation listed in Section 3. *Changes to Your Return*
* the penalty and interest charges listed in Section 3. *Changes to Your Return*
* *Payment Instructions*
* *Additional Information* that will help you understand this notice and what action you need to take to resolve the tax discrepancy

Within each subsection below, the paragraphs are organized by topic to help you review them.

These paragraphs explain the items listed in Section 1. Information Reported to IRS.

Other Income

General

MISIDENTIFIED INCOME
If any of the income shown on this notice is not yours, send us the name, address, and social security number of the person who received the income. Please notify the payers to correct their records to show the name and social security number of the person who actually received the income, so that future reports to us are accurate.

FORM W-2 OR 1099 NOT RECEIVED
The law requires you to report your income correctly. If your payers did not send you a yearly income statement (Form W-2, Form 1099, etc.), you must use the information you have (pay stubs, monthly income statements, deposit slips, etc.) to estimate the total amount of income you received during the year.

Tax & Credits

Tax Computation

REFIGURED TAX BASED ON SCHEDULE D COMPUTATION
We refigured your tax using the Schedule D tax computation.

Tax Credits

POTENTIAL ADJUSTMENT OF NONREFUNDABLE CREDITS
You included unused nonrefundable credits on your tax return. Please review your tax return to determine if, based on our proposal, the IRS needs to adjust any of these credits. In order to claim additional unused nonrefundable credits, send us a signed statement showing the additional unused credits you want to use. If you have already applied the unused credits to another tax year, you need to file a Form 1040X, Amended U.S. Individual Tax Return for the other year with the appropriate Internal Revenue Service Center. If the tax return for the affected period has not yet been filed, confirm with a signed statement that your records have been corrected.

Other Taxes

Self-Employment Tax - Schedule SE

SELF-EMPLOYMENT TAX ON SELF-EMPLOYMENT (SE) INCOME
Self-Employment(SE) income generally includes nonemployee compensation and
other income from part-time or full-time work and is subject to
Self-Employment Tax. We figured the Self-Employment Tax on the net SE
income reported on your return and/or on the underreported SE income.
Self-Employment Tax consists of Social Security Tax of 12.4% and
Medicare Tax of 2.9%. (Even if you have paid the maximum amount of Social
Security Tax, you are still liable for additional Medicare Tax.) The
deduction for one-half of the Self-Employment Tax is based on the change
we made to your Self-Employment Tax. If you were an employee, you will be
liable for income tax and the employee's share of Social Security (6.2%)
and Medicare taxes (1.45%). Your social security account will be credited
with the amount of Self-Employment income shown on this notice.

Penalty & Interest Charges

Interest Charges

INTEREST PERIOD - IRC SECTION 6601
We are required by law to charge interest on unpaid tax from the due date
of the tax return to the date the tax is paid in full. The law requires
that interest continue to be charged on the unpaid balance, including
penalties, until paid in full.

For More Information about Your Penalty & Interest Charges

DETAILED PENALTY/INTEREST COMPUTATION
If you require a detailed penalty or interest computation for this notice,
please call the toll-free telephone number listed on page 1.

Additional Information

FORMS, SCHEDULES, OR ASSISTANCE AVAILABILITY
If you need forms or schedules to respond to this notice, you may get
them by:

* Visiting local offices and some public libraries,
* Calling 1-800-TAX-FORM (1-800-829-3676), or
* Visiting the IRS Web site at www.irs.gov

If you have questions about this notice you may:

* Call the telephone number provided on the notice,
* Visit your local Taxpayer Assistance Center or Low Income Clinic (refer
  to www.irs.gov for locations), or
* Obtain professional assistance (Attorney, Certified Public Accountant,
  Enrolled Agent, Tax Preparer/Practioner, etc).

POWER OF ATTORNEY
We sent a copy of this notice to your representative as indicated in your
Power of Attorney.

ANDOVER IRS CENTER 06/13/201█

3. Changes to your Return

Note: We only show the items that have been affected by the information we received in the following chart. All other items are correct as shown on your return. Unless noted, line numbers always refer to the line number on your tax return.

Changes to Your Income and Deductions	Shown on Return	Reported to IRS, or as Corrected	Difference
NONEMPLOYEE COMPENSATION	$ 0	$ 1,770	$ 1,770
Income Net Difference			$ 1,770
SELF-EMPLOYMENT TAX DEDUCTION	$ 0	$ 125	$ 125
(*1)Deductions Net Difference			$ 125
Total Change to Taxable Income			$ 1,645

Changes to Your Tax Computation	Shown on Return	As Corrected By IRS	Difference
Taxable Income, line 43	$ 67,627	$ 69,272	$ 1,645
Tax, line 44	$ 9,196	$ 9,616	$ 420
Foreign tax credit, line 47	$ 32	$ 32	$ 0
Self-Employment Tax, line 56	$ 0	$ 250	$ 250
Total Tax, line 60	$ 9,164	$ 9,834	$ 670
Making Work Pay and Government Retire Credit, line 63	$ 800	$ 800	$ 0
Net Tax Increase			$ 670

Summary of Proposed Changes		
Amount of Tax Increase		$ 670
Interest, IRC Section 6601, From 04/15/2010 To 07/13/2011		$ 18
Total Amount You Owe		$ 688

(*1)Increases to Deductions result in a decrease to Taxable Income.

CAF COPY

SBN

IRS Department of the Treasury
Internal Revenue Service
CINCINNATI, OH 45999-0025

Notice Number: CP 504
Notice Date: 01-24-2011
SSN/EIN:
Caller ID:

Urgent !!

We intend to levy on certain assets. Please respond NOW.

(To avoid additional penalty and interest, pay the amount you owe within ten days from the date of this notice.)

Our records indicate that you haven't paid the amount you owe. The law requires that you pay your tax at the time you file your return. This is your notice, as required by Internal Revenue Code Section 6331(d), of our intent to levy (take) any state tax refunds that you may be entitled to if we don't receive your payment in full. In addition, we will begin to search for other assets we may levy. We can also file a Notice of Federal Tax Lien, if we haven't already done so. **To prevent collection action, please pay the current balance now.** If you've already paid, can't pay, or have arranged for an installment agreement, it is important that you **call us immediately** at the telephone number shown below. Current balance may include Civil Penalty, if assessed.

Account Summary

Form: 1040	Tax Period: 12-31-2009

Current Balance: $124,461.27
Includes:
Penalty: $1,691.24
Interest: $858.02
Last Payment: $0.00

For information on your penalty & interest computations, you may call 1-800-829-8374

Questions? Call us at **1-800-829-8374**

See the enclosed Publication 594, *The IRS Collection Process*, and Notice 1219B, *Notice of Potential Third Party Contact*, for additional information

---

Please mail this part with your payment, payable to United States Treasury.

Notice Number: CP 504
Notice Date: 01-24-2011

write on your check:

1040	12-31-2009	

Find information about filing and paying taxes at: www.irs.gov
Enter Keyword: filing late (or) paying late

Amount Due:
$124,461.27

Internal Revenue Service
CINCINNATI, OH 45999-0025

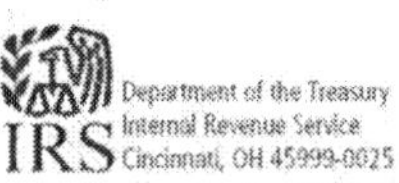

Department of the Treasury
Internal Revenue Service
Cincinnati, OH 45999-0025

RECEIVED
JUN 3 0 2011
BY:

Notice	CP504
Tax Year	2009
Notice date	June 27, 2011
Social Security number	
To contact us	Phone 1-800-829-8374
Page 1 of 4	

Notice of intent to levy

Intent to seize your property or rights to property
Amount due immediately: $131,962.60

As we notified you before, our records show you have unpaid taxes for the tax year ending December 31, 2009 (Form 1040). If you don't call us immediately or pay the amount due by July 7, 2011, we may seize ("levy") any state tax refund to which you're entitled and apply it to the $131,962.60 you owe.

If you still have an outstanding balance after we seize any state tax refund, we may take possession of your other property or your rights to property.

Billing Summary	
Amount you owed	$121,912.01
Failure-to-pay penalty	7,328.69
Interest charges	2,721.90
Amount due immediately	**$131,962.60**

What you need to do immediately

Pay immediately

- Send us the amount due of $131,962.60, or we may seize ("levy") your state tax refund on or after July 7, 2011.

Continued on back...

Notice	CP504
Notice date	June 27, 2011
Social Security number	

- Make your check or money order payable to the United States Treasury.
- Write your Social Security number [ ], the tax year (2009), and the form number (1040) on your payment and any correspondence.

Payment

INTERNAL REVENUE SERVICE
CINCINNATI, OH 45999-0025

Amount due immediately	$131,962.60

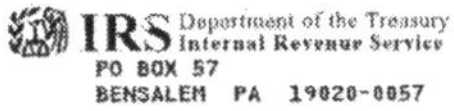

IRS Department of the Treasury
Internal Revenue Service
PO BOX 57
BENSALEM PA 19020-0057

Notice Number: CP   90
Notice Date: SEP. 20, 2010
Social Security Number:

Collection Assistance:
1-800-829-3903
(Asistencia en español disponible)
Caller ID:

Final Notice
Notice Of Intent To Levy And Notice Of Your Right To A Hearing
PLEASE RESPOND IMMEDIATELY

We previously asked you to pay the federal tax shown on the next page, but we haven't received your payment. This letter is your notice of our intent to levy under Internal Revenue Code (IRC) Section 6331 and your right to appeal under IRC Section 6330.

We may also file a Notice of Federal Tax Lien at any time to protect the government's interest. A lien is a public notice to your creditors that the government has a right to your current assets, including any assets you acquire after we file the lien.

If you don't pay the amount you owe, make alternative arrangements to pay, or request an appeals hearing within 30 days from the date of this letter, we may take your property, or rights to property. Property includes real estate, automobiles, business assets, bank accounts, wages, commissions, social security benefits, and other income. We've enclosed Publication 594, which has more information about our collection process; Publication 1660, which explains your appeal rights; and Form 12153, which you can use to request a Collection Due Process hearing with our Appeals Office. To preserve your right to contest Appeals' decision in the U.S. Tax Court, you must complete, sign, and return Form 12153 within 30 days from the date of this letter.

To prevent collection action, please send your full payment today.

- Make your check or money order payable to United States Treasury.
- Write your Social Security Number on your payment.
- Send your payment and the attached payment voucher to us in the enclosed envelope. The amount you owe is shown on the next page.

If you have recently paid this tax or you can't pay it, call us immediately at the above telephone number and let us know.

The assessed balance may include tax, penalties, and interest you still owe. It also includes any credits and payments we've received since we sent our last notice to you. Penalty and interest charges continue to accrue until you pay the total amount in full. We detail these charges, known as Statutory Additions, on the following pages.

Enclosures:
Copy of this notice
Pub 594, IRS Collection Process
Pub 1660, Collection Appeal Rights
Form 12153, Request for a Collection Due Process Hearing
Envelope

CP 90 (Rev. 07-2008)

ACCOUNT INFORMATION

Form Number	Tax Period	Assessed Balance	Statutory Additions		Amount You Owe
			Paying Late Penalty	Interest	
1040	DEC. 31, 2008	$95,182.16	$8,250.46	$3,267.38	$106,700.00

Payment Voucher   Cut below and use this voucher to send in your payment. This voucher is for payments only.

SB N   CP-90

Your Telephone Number: **Best Time to Call**

( ) ______ - ___________   _____ AM _____ PM

Amount you owe: $106,700.00
Less payments not included
Adjusted amount

Internal Revenue Service
PO BOX 219690
KANSAS CITY MO 64121-9690

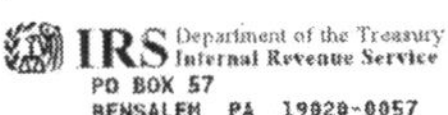

IRS Department of the Treasury
Internal Revenue Service
PO BOX 57
BENSALEM PA 19020-0057

Return the voucher on this page with Form 12153 to request a Collection Due Process (CDP) hearing.

Do not use the voucher below to send in a payment. Send payments only to the address shown on the voucher on the Account Information page of this notice.

If you would like to send in a payment and also request a CDP hearing, then you must mail them separately. Your CDP hearing request must be sent to the address below, and your payment must be sent to the address shown on the voucher on the Account Information page of this notice.

CDP Hearing Request

Cut below and return this voucher with Form 12153. Do not send in a payment with this voucher.

SB N   CP-90

Your Telephone Number:	Best Time to Call	
( ) ______-__________	_____ AM _____ PM	Amount you owe: $106,700.00
		Less payments not included
		Adjusted amount

Internal Revenue Service
PO BOX 57
BENSALEM PA 19020-0057

Form 1127: Application for Extension of Time for Payment of Tax Due to Undue Hardship

Form 1127
(Rev. February 2010)
Department of the Treasury
Internal Revenue Service

Application for Extension of Time for Payment of Tax Due to Undue Hardship

OMB No. 1545-2131

Before you begin: Use the chart on page 3 to see if you should file this form.

Name(s) shown on return

Identifying number

Number, street, and apt., room, or suite no. If you have a P.O. box, see instructions.

City, town, or post office, state, and ZIP code. If you have a foreign address, see instructions.

Part I — Request for Extension

I request an extension from _______________ , 20 _______ , to _______________ , 20 _______ to pay tax of $ _______________

This request is for (check only one box):

☐ The tax shown or required to be shown on Form _______________ .

☐ An amount determined as a deficiency on Form _______________ .

This request is for calendar year 20_______ , or fiscal year ending _______________ , 20 _______ .

Part II — Reason for Extension

Undue hardship. Enter below a detailed explanation of the undue hardship that will result if your application is denied. (If more space is required, please attach a separate sheet.) To establish undue hardship, you must show that you would sustain a substantial financial loss if forced to pay a tax or deficiency on the due date. For a complete definition of "undue hardship," see the instructions on page 3 under *Who Should File.*

____

____

____

____

Part III — Supporting Documentation

To support my application, I certify that I have attached (you must check both boxes or your application will not be accepted):

☐ A statement of my assets and liabilities at the end of last month (showing book and market values of assets and whether securities are listed or unlisted), and

☐ An itemized list of my income and expenses for each of the 3 months prior to the due date of the tax.

Signature and Verification

Under penalties of perjury, I declare that I have examined this application, including any accompanying schedules and statements, and to the best of my knowledge and belief, it is true, correct, and complete; and, if prepared by someone other than the taxpayer, that I am authorized to prepare this form.

Signature of taxpayer ▶ _______________________   Date ▶ _______________

Signature of spouse ▶ _______________________   Date ▶ _______________

Signature of preparer other than taxpayer ▶ _______________________   Date ▶ _______________

FOR IRS USE ONLY (Do not detach)

This application is   ☐ Approved   ☐ Denied   ☐ Returned:

Reason(s): ____

____

____

Signature of authorized official   Date

For Privacy Act and Paperwork Reduction Act Notice, see instructions.   Cat. No. 17238O   Form **1127** (Rev. 02-2010)

Request for a Collection Due Process or Equivalent Hearing

Use this form to request a Collection Due Process (CDP) or equivalent hearing with the IRS Office of Appeals if you have been issued one of the following lien or levy notices:

- Notice of Federal Tax Lien Filing and Your Right to a Hearing under IRC 6320,
- Notice of Intent to Levy and Notice of Your Right to a Hearing,
- Notice of Jeopardy Levy and Right of Appeal,
- Notice of Levy on Your State Tax Refund,
- Notice of Levy and Notice of Your Right to a Hearing.

Complete this form and send it to the address shown on your lien or levy notice. Include a copy of your lien or levy notice to ensure proper handling of your request.

Call the phone number on the notice or 1-800-829-1040 if you are not sure about the correct address or if you want to fax your request.

You can find a section explaining the deadline for requesting a Collection Due Process hearing in this form's instructions. If you've missed the deadline for requesting a CDP hearing, you must check line 6 (Equivalent Hearing) to request an equivalent hearing.

1. Taxpayer Name: (Taxpayer 1) ____________________

Taxpayer Identification Number ____________________

Current Address ____________________

City ____________________ State ______ Zip Code ____________________

2. Telephone Number and Best Time to Call During Normal Business Hours

				am.	pm.
Home	( ) ____ - ____ ____			☐ am.	☐ pm.
Work	( ) ____ - ____ ____			☐ am.	☐ pm.
Cell	( )			☐ am.	☐ pm.

3. Taxpayer Name: (Taxpayer 2) ____________________

Taxpayer Identification Number ____________________

Current Address ____________________
(If Different from Address Above) City ____________________ State ______ Zip Code ____________________

4. Telephone Number and Best Time to Call During Normal Business Hours

				am.	pm.
Home	( ) -			☐ am.	☐ pm.
Work	( ) -			☐ am.	☐ pm.
Cell	( ) -			☐ am.	☐ pm.

5. Tax Information as Shown on the Lien or Levy Notice *(If possible, attach a copy of the notice)*

Type of Tax (Income, Employment, Excise, etc. or Civil Penalty)	Tax Form Number (1040, 941, 720, etc)	Tax Period or Periods

Form **12153** (Rev. 3-2011)   Catalog Number 26685D   www.irs.gov   Department of the Treasury - Internal Revenue Service

Request for a Collection Due Process or Equivalent Hearing

6. Basis for Hearing Request (Both boxes can be checked if you have received both a lien and levy notice)

☐ Filed Notice of Federal Tax Lien   ☐ Proposed Levy or Actual Levy

7. Equivalent Hearing (See the instructions for more information on Equivalent Hearings)

☐ I would like an Equivalent Hearing - I would like a hearing equivalent to a CDP Hearing if my request for a CDP hearing does not meet the requirements for a timely CDP Hearing.

8. Check the most appropriate box for the reason you disagree with the filing of the lien or the levy. **See page 4 of this form for examples.** You can add more pages if you don't have enough space.

If, during your CDP Hearing, you think you would like to discuss a Collection Alternative to the action proposed by the Collection function it is recommended you submit a completed Form 433A (Individual) and/or Form 433B (Business), as appropriate, with this form. See www.irs.gov for copies of the forms.

Collection Alternative   ☐ Installment Agreement   ☐ Offer in Compromise   ☐ I Cannot Pay Balance

Lien   ☐ Subordination   ☐ Discharge   ☐ Withdrawal

Please explain:

My Spouse Is Responsible   ☐ Innocent Spouse Relief (Please attach Form 8857, *Request for Innocent Spouse Relief*, to your request.)

Other (*For examples, see page 4*)   ☐

Reason (*You must provide a reason for the dispute or your request for a CDP hearing will not be honored. Use as much space as you need to explain the reason for your request. Attach extra pages if necessary.*):

9. Signatures

I understand the CDP hearing and any subsequent judicial review will suspend the statutory period of limitations for collection action. I also understand my representative or I must sign and date this request before the IRS Office of Appeals can accept it. If you are signing as an officer of a company add your title (*president, secretary, etc.*) behind your signature.

SIGN HERE

Taxpayer 1's Signature	Date
Taxpayer 2's Signature (*if a joint request, both must sign*)	Date

☐ I request my CDP hearing be held with my authorized representative (*attach a copy of Form 2848*)

Authorized Representative's Signature	Authorized Representative's Name	Telephone Number

IRS Use Only

IRS Employee (Print)	Employee Telephone Number	IRS Received Date

---

Information You Need To Know When Requesting A Collection Due Process Hearing

---

What Is the Deadline for Requesting a Timely Collection Due Process (CDP) Hearing?

- Your request for a CDP hearing about a Federal Tax Lien filing must be postmarked by the date indicated in the *Notice of Federal Tax Lien Filing and Your Right to a Hearing under IRC 6320* (lien notice).

- Your request for a CDP hearing about a levy must be postmarked within 30 days after the date of the *Notice of Intent to Levy and Notice of Your Right to a Hearing* (levy notice) or Notice of Your Right to a Hearing After an Actual Levy.

Your timely request for a CDP hearing will prohibit levy action in most cases. A timely request for CDP hearing will also suspend the 10-year period we have, by law, to collect your taxes. Both the prohibition on levy and the suspension of the 10-year period will last until the determination the IRS Office of Appeals makes about your disagreement is final. The amount of time the suspension is in effect will be added to the time remaining in the 10-year period. For example, if the 10-year period is suspended for six months, the time left in the period we have to collect taxes will be extended by six months.

You can go to court to appeal the CDP determination the IRS Office of Appeals makes about your disagreement.

What Is an Equivalent Hearing?

If you still want a hearing with the IRS Office of Appeals after the deadline for requesting a timely CDP hearing has passed, you can use this form to request an equivalent hearing. <u>You must check the Equivalent Hearing</u> box on line 6 of the form to request an equivalent hearing. **An equivalent hearing request does not prohibit levy or suspend the 10-year period for collecting your taxes; also, you cannot go to court to appeal the IRS Office of Appeals' decision about your disagreement.** You must request an equivalent hearing within the following timeframe:

- Lien Notice-- one year plus five business days from the filing date of the Notice of Federal Tax Lien.

- Levy Notice-- one year from the date of the levy notice.

- Your request for a CDP levy hearing, whether timely or Equivalent, does not prohibit the Service from filing a Notice of Federal Tax Lien.

Where Should You File Your CDP or Equivalent Hearing Request?

File your request by mail at the address on your lien notice or levy notice. You may also fax your request. Call the telephone number on the lien or levy notice to ask for the fax number. **Do not send your CDP or equivalent hearing request directly to the IRS Office of Appeals, <u>it must be sent to the address on the lien or levy notice</u>. If you send your request directly to Appeals it may result in your request not being considered a timely request. Depending upon your issue the originating function may contact you in an attempt to resolve the issue(s) raised in your request prior to forwarding your request to Appeals.**

Where Can You Get Help?

You can call the telephone number on the lien or levy notice with your questions about requesting a hearing. The contact person listed on the notice or other representative can access your tax information and answer your questions.

In addition, you may qualify for representation by a low-income taxpayer clinic for free or nominal charge. Our Publication 4134, Low Income Taxpayer Clinic List, provides information on clinics in your area.

If you are experiencing economic harm, the Taxpayer Advocate Service (TAS) may be able to help you resolve your problems with the IRS. TAS cannot extend the time you have to request a CDP or equivalent hearing. See Publication 594, *The IRS Collection Process*, or visit <u>www.irs.gov/advocate/index-html.</u> You also can call 1-877-777-4778 for TAS assistance.

Note-- The IRS Office of Appeals will not consider frivolous requests. You can find examples of frivolous reasons for requesting a hearing or disagreeing with a tax assessment in Publication 2105, *Why do I have to Pay Taxes?*, or at <u>www.irs.gov</u> by typing "frivolous" into the search engine.

> **You can get copies of tax forms, schedules, instructions, publications, and notices at <u>www.irs.gov</u>, at your local IRS office, or by calling toll-free** *1-800-TAX-FORM (829-3676).*

Information You Need To Know When Requesting A Collection Due Process Hearing

What Are Examples of Reasons for Requesting a Hearing?

You will have to explain your reason for requesting a hearing when you make your request. Below are examples of reasons for requesting a hearing.

You want a collection alternative-- "I would like to propose a different way to pay the money I owe." Common collection alternatives include:

- Full payment-- you pay your taxes by personal check, cashier's check, money order, or credit card.
- Installment Agreement-- you pay your taxes fully or partially by making monthly payments.
- Offer in Compromise-- you offer to make a payment or payments to settle your tax liability for less than the full amount you owe.

"I cannot pay my taxes." Some possible reasons why you cannot pay your taxes are: (1) you have a terminal illness or excessive medical bills; (2) your only source of income is Social Security payments, welfare payments, or unemployment benefit payments; (3) you are unemployed with little or no income; (4) you have reasonable expenses exceeding your income; or (5) you have some other hardship condition. The IRS Office of Appeals may consider freezing collection action until your circumstances improve. Penalty and interest will continue to accrue on the unpaid balance.

You want action taken about the filing of the tax lien against your property-- You can get a Federal Tax Lien released if you pay your taxes in full. You also may request a lien subordination, discharge, or withdrawal. See www.irs.gov for more information.

When you request **lien subordination**, you are asking the IRS to make a Federal Tax Lien secondary to a non-IRS lien. For example, you may ask for a subordination of the Federal Tax Lien to get a refinancing mortgage on your house or other real property you own. You would ask to make the Federal Tax Lien secondary to the mortgage, even though the mortgage came after the tax lien filing. The IRS Office of Appeals would consider lien subordination, in this example, if you used the mortgage proceeds to pay your taxes.

When you request a **lien discharge**, you are asking the IRS to remove a Federal Tax Lien from a specific property. For example, you may ask for a discharge of the Federal Tax Lien in order to sell your house if you use all of the sale proceeds to pay your taxes even though the sale proceeds will not fully pay all of the tax you owe.

When you request a **lien withdrawal**, you are asking the IRS to remove the Notice of Federal Tax Lien (NFTL) information from public records because you believe the NFTL should not have been filed. For example, you may ask for a withdrawal of the filing of the NFTL if you believe the IRS filed the NFTL prematurely or did not follow procedures, or you have entered into an installment agreement and the installment agreement does not provide for the filing of the NFTL. A withdrawal does not remove the lien from your IRS records.

Your spouse is responsible-- "My spouse (or former spouse) is responsible for all or part of the tax liability." You may believe that your spouse or former spouse is the only one responsible for all or a part of the tax liability. If this is the case, you are requesting a hearing so you can receive relief as an innocent spouse. You should complete and attach Form 8857, *Request for Innocent Spouse Relief*, to your hearing request.

Other Reasons-- "I am not liable for (I don't owe) all or part of the taxes." You can raise a disagreement about the amount you owe only if you did not receive a deficiency notice for the liability (a notice explaining why you owe taxes-it gives you the right to challenge in court, within a specific timeframe, the additional tax the IRS says you owe), or if you have not had another prior opportunity to disagree with the amount you owe.

"I do not believe I should be responsible for penalties." The IRS Office of Appeals may remove all or part of the penalties if you have a reasonable cause for not paying or not filing on time. See Notice 746, Information About Your Notice, Penalty and Interest for what is reasonable cause for removing penalties.

"I have already paid all or part of my taxes." You disagree with the amount the IRS says you haven't paid if you think you have not received credit for payments you have already made.

> See Publication 594, *The IRS Collection Process*, for more information on the following topics: Installment Agreements and Offers in Compromise; Lien Subordination, Discharge, and Withdrawal; Innocent Spouse Relief; Temporarily Delay Collection; and belief that tax bill is wrong.

Form **12507** (December 1999)	**Innocent Spouse Statement**

Purpose of form: You can use this form to provide additional information to the Internal Revenue Service (IRS) to consider in determining relief of joint and several liability for the tax year(s) at issue in the letter you received with this form. ***Note:*** *You can use the back of this page or attach additional pages if you need more space.*

My Name	Social Security Number
Telephone Number	Best Time to Call

Innocent Spouse Statement

I, ________________________________ , residing at ________________________________

make the following statement to be used in the determination of innocent spouse relief
for Mr. / Mrs. ________________________________ ;

____

____

____

____

____

____

____

____

____

____

____

____

____

____

Under penalties of perjury, I declare that I have examined this statement, and to the best of
my knowledge and belief, it is true, correct and complete.

My Signature	Date

Form **12507** (12-1999)   Catalog Number 28728D   Department of the Treasury — **Internal Revenue Service**
www.irs.gov

Form **12508** (July 2008)	**Questionnaire for Non-Requesting Spouse**

We recognize that some of these questions involve sensitive subjects. However, we need this information to evaluate the circumstances of the claim and properly determine whether relief should be given. If this form is not completed and returned, the claim will be considered based on the information available to us.

Questions?
Call the IRS at 1-866-897-4270.

Part I   Tell us about yourself

1.

Your Current Name		Your Social Security Number	
Your Current Home Address (number & street)		Apt. No.	County
City, town or post office box, state and ZIP code		Best daytime phone number ( )	

2. What is the current status between you and your spouse for the years that relief was requested? (On this form we refer to your spouse for the years that relief was requested as *that individual.*)

☐ Married and living together

☐ Married living apart since _____ / _____ / _____
                      MM DD YYYY

☐ Legally separated since _____ / _____ / _____
                    MM DD YYYY

☐ Divorced since _____ / _____ / _____
              MM DD YYYY

☐ Widowed since _____ / _____ / _____
              MM DD YYYY

Note: A divorce decree stating you must pay all taxes does not necessarily mean that individual will qualify for relief.

Part II   Tell us about filing the returns and your financial situation for the years listed on the letter. If the information is not the same for all tax years, please explain. If you need more room to write your answer for any question, attach more pages. Be sure to write your name and social security number on the top of all pages you attach.

3. How were both of you involved with preparing the returns during those tax years? Check all that apply and explain, if necessary. If the answers are not the same for all the years, explain.

You	That Individual	
☐	☐	Prepared or helped prepare the returns.
☐	☐	Gathered receipts and canceled checks.
☐	☐	Gave tax documents (such as W-2s, 1099s, etc.) to the person who prepared the returns.
☐	☐	Asked the person who prepared the returns to explain any items or amounts.
☐	☐	Reviewed the returns before signing them.
☐	☐	Did not review the returns before signing them.
☐	☐	Other

Explain, if necessary

____

____

____

____

____

4. When you signed the returns, were any amounts owed to the IRS for those years?

☐ Yes. Explain how the amounts owed were to be paid.

____
____
____
____

☐ No

5. When that individual signed any of the returns, was he/she aware of any financial problems you were having (for example, bankruptcy or bills you could not pay)?

☐ Yes. Explain

____
____
____

☐ No
☐ Do not know

6. For those years, what kinds of accounts did you have? Check all that apply. Explain if the answers are not the same for all the years.

Joint	Separate	
☐	☐	Checking or money market
☐	☐	Savings or certificate of deposit

How did that individual use those accounts? Check all that apply.

Joint	Separate	
☐	☐	Made deposits
☐	☐	Reviewed bank statements or balanced the checkbook
☐	☐	Paid bills
☐	☐	Knew how much money was in the account
☐	☐	Made withdrawals from the account
☐	☐	Did not know about the account
☐	☐	Did not use the account
☐	☐	Was not involved in handling money for the household

Explain, if necessary

____
____
____
____

7. Did you ever transfer assets to that individual? (Did you put something of value, such as real estate or stocks, in that individual's name rather than in your own name?)

☐ Yes. List the assets and the dates they were transferred. Explain why the assets were transferred.

____
____
____

☐ No

8. During those tax years, were you self employed?

☐ Yes. Explain how that individual was involved in your business.

____
____
____

☐ No

9. If no tax year(s) in question were audited, what items, if any, changed? Were the changed items yours or that individual's? (For example, unreported income, disallowed deductions, unclaimed credits)

10. If the audit results changed your business income or deductions on your tax return, did that individual help you in the business? If so how? If not , did that individual know about your business affairs? Explain.

11. If the items changed by the audit were yours, did that individual benefit from them? (Example, unreported income paid for a family vacation, car, jewelry, etc.) Explain.

12. Do you have any other information you want us to consider?

SIGN HERE Under penalties of perjury, I declare that I have examined this statement and to the best of my knowledge it is true, correct, and complete.

____   ____________________
Signature   Date

Keep a copy for your records and return
the original in the enclosed envelope.

Form 12509: Statement of Disagreement

Form 12509 (January 2005)	**Statement of Disagreement**

Purpose of form: You can use this form to explain why you disagree with the Internal Revenue Service (IRS) Determination concerning relief from joint and several liability for a joint return under Internal Revenue Code sections 6013(e), 6015(b), 6015(c), or 6015(f) in the letter you received with this form.
Note: You can use the back of this page or attached additional pages if you need more space.

CHECK HERE IF YOU ALSO WISH TO GO TO APPEALS ☐

Taxpayer Name:	Social Security Number

Statement of Disagreement

I, _______________________, disagree with the Internal Revenue Service determination because

____

Under penalties of perjury, I declare that I have examined this statement, and to the best of my knowledge and belief, it is true, correct and complete.

My Signature	Date
Daytime phone number	Best time to Call

Form **12509** (Rev. 1-2005)   Catalog Number 28731A   Department of the Treasury-Internal Revenue Service
www.irs.gov

Request for Appeal of Offer in Compromise

Please provide the information required in the spaces below. Be sure to sign and date this form.

Taxpayer name(s)	Taxpayer Identification Number(s)
Taxpayer name(s)	Taxpayer Identification Number(s)
Mailing address	Tax form number
City / State / ZIP Code	Tax period(s) ended
Taxpayer's current daytime phone number	Tax period(s) ended

Identify the specific item(s) you don't agree with as shown on the Income and Expense Table and Asset and Equity Table you received with your rejection letter. In the space next to the disagreed item, provide a brief statement indicating why you don't agree with our determination (for example: incorrect valuation of real estate, omitted mileage from vehicle deduction, etc.). Attach supporting documents and indicate on the document which issue they apply to. Additional pages may be attached. If you do not agree with the Service's analysis of economic hardship or Effective Tax Administration, please provide an explanation with documentation.

Disagreed item — Reason for disagreement — Supporting documentation attached ☐ Yes ☐ No

Disagreed item — Reason for disagreement — Supporting documentation attached ☐ Yes ☐ No

Disagreed item — Reason for disagreement — Supporting documentation attached ☐ Yes ☐ No

Signature of Taxpayer(s)	Date signed
Signature of Taxpayer(s)	Date signed

If this application was prepared by someone other than the taxpayer, please fill in that person's name and address

Name

Mailing address	City	State	ZIP Code

Name and signature of authorized representative (If a representative is signing this form, please attach a copy of your completed Form 2848, Power of Attorney and Declaration of Representative.)

Name of authorized representative

Signature of authorized representative	Date signed
Telephone number of authorized representative	Best time to call

Form **13711** (Rev. 8-2009)　　Cat. No. 40992F　　www.irs.gov　　Department of the Treasury - **Internal Revenue Service**

Form **14134** (June 2010)	Department of the Treasury — Internal Revenue Service **Application for Certificate of Subordination of Federal Tax Lien**	OMB No. 1545-2174

Complete the entire application. Enter NA *(not applicable)*, when appropriate. Attachments and exhibits should be included as necessary. Additional information may be requested to clarify the details of the transaction(s).

1. Taxpayer Information *(Individual or Business named on the notice of lien)*

Name *(Individual First, Middle Initial, Last)* or *(Business)* as it appears on lien	Primary Social Security Number *(last 4 digits only)*
Name Continuation *(Individual First, Middle Initial, Last)* or *(Business d/b/a)*	Secondary Social Security Number *(last 4 digits only)*
Address *(Number, Street, P.O. Box)*	Employer Identification Number

City	State	ZIP Code
Telephone Number *(with area code)*	Fax Number *(with area code)*	

2. Applicant Information   ☐ Check if also the Taxpayer *(If not the taxpayer, attach copy of lien. See Sec.10)*

Name *(First, Middle Initial, Last)*	Relationship to taxpayer
Address *(Number, Street, P.O. Box)*	

City	State	ZIP Code
Telephone Number *(with area code)*	Fax Number *(with area code)*	

3. Property Owner   ☐ Check if also the Applicant

	Relationship to Taxpayer

4. Attorney/Representative Information   **Attached:** Form 8821 or Power of Attorney Form 2848   ☐ Yes   ☐ No

Name *(First, Middle Initial, Last)*	Interest Represented *(e.g. taxpayer, lender, etc.)*
Address *(Number, Street, P.O. Box)*	

City	State	ZIP Code
Telephone Number *(with area code)*	Fax Number *(with area code)*	

5. Lending/Finance Company

Company Name	Contact Name	Contact Phone Number

Type of transaction *(For example, loan consolidation, refinance, etc)*

6. Monetary Information

Amount of existing loan *(if refinancing)*	
Amount of new loan	
Amount to be paid to the United States *(6325(d)(1) applications only)*	

7. Basis for Subordination:
Check the box below that best addresses what you would like the United States to consider in your application for subordination. *(Publication 784 has additional descriptions of the Internal Revenue Code sections listed below.)*

☐ 6325(d)(1)   the United States will receive an amount equal to the lien or interest to which the certificate of subordination is issued *(provide amount in Section 6 above)*

☐ 6325(d)(2)   the issuance of the certificate of subordination will increase the government's interest and make collection of the tax liability easier. ***(Complete and attach a signed and dated statement describing how the amount the United States may ultimately realize will increase and how collection will be facilitated by the subordination.)***

       Statement   ☐ Attached   ☐ NA

8. Description of property
(For example, 3 bedroom rental house; 2002 Cessna twin engine airplane, serial number AT919000000000X00; etc.):

Address of real property *(If this is personal property list the address where the property is located):*

Address *(Number, Street, P.O. Box)*		
City	State	ZIP Code

Real Estate:
Legible copy of deed or title showing legal description   ☐ Attached   ☐ NA

9. Appraisal and Valuations

Appraisal: (Professional appraisal completed by a disinterested third party but it is not required for a subordination)	☐ Attached
OR ONE OF THE FOLLOWING VALUATIONS:	
County valuation of property *(real property)*	☐ Attached
Informal valuation of property by disinterested third party	☐ Attached
Proposed selling price *(for property being sold at auction)*	☐ Attached
Other: _________________________	☐ Attached

10. Copy of Federal Tax Lien(s) *(Complete if applicant and taxpayer differ)* ☐ Attached ☐ No

OR list the lien number(s) found near the top right corner on the lien document(s) *(if known)*

11. Copy of the proposed loan agreement *(if available)* ☐ Attached ☐ No

AND

Describe how subordination is in the best interests of the United States:

12. Copy of a current title report *(required for subordination)* ☐ Attached ☐ No

OR

List encumbrances with seniority over the Federal Tax Lien. Include name and address of the holder; description of the encumbrance, e.g., mortgage, state lien, etc.; date of agreement; original loan amount and interest rate; amount due at time of application; and family relationship, if applicable. Include any home equity line of credit (HELOCs) advances beginning the 46th day after the NFTL was filed, through the date you submit your application, and include expected advances through the date the certificate will be issued. *(Attach additional sheets as needed)*:

13. Copy of proposed closing statement *(aka HUD-1)* ☐ Attached ☐ No

OR

Itemize all proposed costs, commissions, and expenses of any transfer or sale associated with property *(Attach additional sheets as needed)*:

14. Additional information that may have a bearing on this request, such as pending litigation, explanations of unusual situations, etc., is attached for consideration ☐ Yes ☐ No

15. Declaration

Under penalties of perjury, I declare that I have examined this application, including any accompanying schedules, exhibits, affidavits, and statements and to the best of my knowledge and belief it is true, correct and complete.

_______________________________________ _____________________
Signature/Title   Date

_______________________________________ _____________________
Signature/Title   Date

Form **2848**	**Power of Attorney**	OMB No. 1545-0150

Form 2848
(Rev. October 2011)
Department of the Treasury
Internal Revenue Service

**Power of Attorney
and Declaration of Representative**

▶ Type or print. ▶ See the separate instructions.

OMB No. 1545-0150

For IRS Use Only
Received by:
Name _______________
Telephone _______________
Function _______________
Date ___ / ___ / ___

Part I   Power of Attorney

Caution: *Form 2848 will not be honored for any purpose other than representation before the IRS.*

1   Taxpayer information. Taxpayer must sign and date this form on page 2, line 7.

Taxpayer name and address

Identifying number

Daytime telephone number

Plan number (if applicable)

hereby appoints the following representative(s) as attorney(s)-in-fact:

2   Representative(s) must sign and date this form on page 2, Part II.

Name and address

CAF No. _______________
PTIN _______________
Telephone No. _______________
Fax No. _______________

Check if to be sent notices and communications ☐

Check if new: Address ☐   Telephone No. ☐   Fax No. ☐

Name and address

CAF No. _______________
PTIN _______________
Telephone No. _______________
Fax No. _______________

Check if to be sent notices and communications ☐

Check if new: Address ☐   Telephone No. ☐   Fax No. ☐

Name and address

CAF No. _______________
PTIN _______________
Telephone No. _______________
Fax No. _______________

Check if new: Address ☐   Telephone No. ☐   Fax No. ☐

to represent the taxpayer before the Internal Revenue Service for the following matters:

3   Matters

Description of Matter (Income, Employment, Excise, Whistleblower, PLR, FOIA, Civil Penalty, etc.) (see the instructions for line 3)	Tax Form Number (1040, 941, 720, etc.) (if applicable)	Year(s) or Period(s) (if applicable) (see the instructions for line 3)

4   Specific use not recorded on Centralized Authorization File (CAF). If the power of attorney is for a specific use not recorded on CAF, check this box. See the instructions for Line 4. **Specific Uses Not Recorded on CAF** . . . . ▶ ☐

5   Acts authorized. Unless otherwise provided below, the representatives generally are authorized to receive and inspect confidential tax information and to perform any and all acts that I can perform with respect to the tax matters described on line 3, for example, the authority to sign any agreements, consents, or other documents. The representative(s), however, is (are) not authorized to receive or negotiate any amounts paid to the client in connection with this representation (including refunds by either electronic means or paper checks). Additionally, unless the appropriate box(es) below are checked, the representative(s) are not authorized to substitute another representative or add additional representatives, to sign certain returns, or to execute a request for disclosure of tax returns or return information to a third party. See the line 5 instructions for more information.

☐ Disclosure to third parties;   ☐ Signing a return;   ☐ Substitute or add representatives;
☐ Other _______________________________________ (see instructions for more information)

Exceptions. An unenrolled return preparer cannot sign any document for a taxpayer and may only represent taxpayers in limited situations. An enrolled actuary may only represent taxpayers to the extent provided in section 10.3(d) of Treasury Department Circular No. 230 (Circular 230). An enrolled retirement plan agent may only represent taxpayers to the extent provided in section 10.3(e) of Circular 230. A registered tax return preparer may only represent taxpayers to the extent provided in section 10.3(f) of Circular 230. See the line 5 instructions for restrictions on tax matters partners. In most cases, the student practitioner's (level k) authority is limited (for example, they may only practice under the supervision of another practitioner).

List any specific deletions to the acts otherwise authorized in this power of attorney: _______________
____
____

For Privacy Act and Paperwork Reduction Act Notice, see the instructions.   Cat. No. 11980J   Form **2848** (Rev. 10-2011)

6   **Retention/revocation of prior power(s) of attorney.** The filing of this power of attorney automatically revokes all earlier power(s) of attorney on file with the Internal Revenue Service for the same matters and years or periods covered by this document. If you **do not** want to revoke a prior power of attorney, check here . . . . ▶ ☐
    YOU MUST ATTACH A COPY OF ANY POWER OF ATTORNEY YOU WANT TO REMAIN IN EFFECT.

7   **Signature of taxpayer.** If a tax matter concerns a year in which a joint return was filed, the husband and wife must each file a separate power of attorney even if the same representative(s) is (are) being appointed. If signed by a corporate officer, partner, guardian, tax matters partner, executor, receiver, administrator, or trustee on behalf of the taxpayer, I certify that I have the authority to execute this form on behalf of the taxpayer.

    ▶ **IF NOT SIGNED AND DATED, THIS POWER OF ATTORNEY WILL BE RETURNED TO THE TAXPAYER.**

Signature	Date	Title (if applicable)

Print Name	☐☐☐☐ PIN Number	Print name of taxpayer from line 1 if other than individual

Part II   Declaration of Representative

Under penalties of perjury, I declare that:

• I am not currently under suspension or disbarment from practice before the Internal Revenue Service;

• I am aware of regulations contained in Circular 230 (31 CFR, Part 10), as amended, concerning practice before the Internal Revenue Service;

• I am authorized to represent the taxpayer identified in Part I for the matter(s) specified there; and

• I am one of the following:

   a   Attorney—a member in good standing of the bar of the highest court of the jurisdiction shown below.

   b   Certified Public Accountant—duly qualified to practice as a certified public accountant in the jurisdiction shown below.

   c   Enrolled Agent—enrolled as an agent under the requirements of Circular 230.

   d   Officer—a bona fide officer of the taxpayer's organization.

   e   Full-Time Employee—a full-time employee of the taxpayer.

   f   Family Member—a member of the taxpayer's immediate family (for example, spouse, parent, child, grandparent, grandchild, step-parent, step-child, brother, or sister).

   g   Enrolled Actuary—enrolled as an actuary by the Joint Board for the Enrollment of Actuaries under 29 U.S.C. 1242 (the authority to practice before the Internal Revenue Service is limited by section 10.3(d) of Circular 230).

   h   Unenrolled Return Preparer - Your authority to practice before the Internal Revenue Service is limited. You must have been eligible to sign the return under examination and have signed the return. **See Notice 2011-6 and Special rules for registered tax return preparers and unenrolled return preparers in the instructions.**

   i   Registered Tax Return Preparer—registered as a tax return preparer under the requirements of section 10.4 of Circular 230. Your authority to practice before the Internal Revenue Service is limited. You must have been eligible to sign the return under examination and have signed the return. **See Notice 2011-6 and Special rules for registered tax return preparers and unenrolled return preparers in the instructions.**

   k   Student Attorney or CPA—receives permission to practice before the IRS by virtue of his/her status as a law, business, or accounting student working in LITC or STCP under section 10.7(d) of Circular 230. See instructions for Part II for additional information and requirements.

   r   Enrolled Retirement Plan Agent—enrolled as a retirement plan agent under the requirements of Circular 230 (the authority to practice before the Internal Revenue Service is limited by section 10.3(e)).

    ▶ **IF THIS DECLARATION OF REPRESENTATIVE IS NOT SIGNED AND DATED, THE POWER OF ATTORNEY WILL BE RETURNED. REPRESENTATIVES MUST SIGN IN THE ORDER LISTED IN LINE 2 ABOVE.** See the instructions for Part II.

Note: For designations d–f, enter your title, position, or relationship to the taxpayer in the "Licensing jurisdiction" column. See the instructions for Part II for more information.

Designation—Insert above letter **(a–r)**	Licensing jurisdiction (state) or other licensing authority (if applicable)	License/Bar or Enrollment Number (if applicable)	Signature	Date

<table>
<tr><td>Form 433-A
(Rev. January 2008)
Department of the Treasury
Internal Revenue Service</td><td colspan="2">Collection Information Statement for Wage
Earners and Self-Employed Individuals</td></tr>
</table>

Wage Earners Complete Sections 1, 2, 3, and 4, including signature line on page 4. *Answer all questions or write N/A.*
Self-Employed Individuals Complete Sections 1, 2, 3, 4, 5 and 6 and signature line on page 4. *Answer all questions or write N/A.*
For Additional Information, refer to Publication 1854, "How To Prepare a Collection Information Statement"
Include attachments if additional space is needed to respond completely to any question.

Name on Internal Revenue Service (IRS) Account	Social Security Number *SSN on IRS Account*	Employer Identification Number *EIN*

Section 1: Personal Information

1a Full Name of Taxpayer and Spouse (if applicable)	**1c** Home Phone ( )	**1d** Cell Phone ( )
1b Address (Street, City, State, ZIP code) (County of Residence)	**1e** Business Phone ( )	**1f** Business Cell Phone ( )
	2b Name, Age, and Relationship of dependent(s)	

2a Marital Status: ☐ Married ☐ Unmarried (Single, Divorced, Widowed)

	Social Security No. (SSN)	Date of Birth (mmddyyyy)	Driver's License Number and State
3a Taxpayer			
3b Spouse			

Section 2: Employment Information

If the taxpayer or spouse is self-employed or has self-employment income, also complete Business Information in Sections 5 and 6.

Taxpayer		Spouse	
4a Taxpayer's Employer Name		**5a** Spouse's Employer Name	
4b Address (Street, City, State, ZIP code)		**5b** Address (Street, City, State, ZIP code)	
4c Work Telephone Number ( )	**4d** Does employer allow contact at work ☐ Yes ☐ No	**5c** Work Telephone Number ( )	**5d** Does employer allow contact at work ☐ Yes ☐ No
4e How long with this employer (years) (months)	**4f** Occupation	**5e** How long with this employer (years) (months)	**5f** Occupation
4g Number of exemptions claimed on Form W-4	**4h** Pay Period: ☐ Weekly ☐ Bi-weekly ☐ Monthly ☐ Other	**5g** Number of exemptions claimed on Form W-4	**5h** Pay Period: ☐ Weekly ☐ Bi-weekly ☐ Monthly ☐ Other

Section 3: Other Financial Information *(Attach copies of applicable documentation.)*

6   **Is the individual or sole proprietorship party to a lawsuit** *(If yes, answer the following)*   Yes ☐   No ☐

☐ Plaintiff ☐ Defendant	Location of Filing	Represented by	Docket/Case No.
Amount of Suit $	Possible Completion Date (mmddyyyy)	Subject of Suit	

7   **Has the individual or sole proprietorship ever filed bankruptcy** *(If yes, answer the following)*   Yes ☐   No ☐

Date Filed (mmddyyyy)	Date Dismissed or Discharged (mmddyyyy)	Petition No.	Location

8   **Any increase/decrease in income anticipated** *(business or personal)* *(If yes, answer the following)*   Yes ☐   No ☐

Explain. (Use attachment if needed)	How much will it increase/decrease $	When will it increase/decrease

9   **Is the individual or sole proprietorship a beneficiary of a trust, estate, or life insurance policy**
(If yes, answer the following)   Yes ☐   No ☐

Place where recorded: EIN:

Name of the trust, estate, or policy	Anticipated amount to be received $	When will the amount be received

10   **In the past 10 years, has the individual resided outside of the United States for periods of 6 months or longer**
(If yes, answer the following)   Yes ☐   No ☐

Dates lived abroad: from (mmddyyyy)	To (mmddyyyy)

Form 433-A (Rev. 1-2008)   Page **2**

Section 4: Personal Asset Information for All Individuals

11   Cash on Hand. Include cash that is not in a bank.   **Total Cash on Hand** | $

Personal Bank Accounts. Include all checking, online bank accounts, money market accounts, savings accounts, stored value cards (e.g., payroll cards, government benefit cards, etc.) List safe deposit boxes including location and contents.

Type of Account	Full Name & Address *(Street, City, State, ZIP code)* of Bank, Savings & Loan, Credit Union, or Financial Institution.	Account Number	Account Balance As of ______ mmddyyyy
12a			
12b			$
			$

12c   Total Cash *(Add lines 12a, 12b, and amounts from any attachments)* | $

Investments. Include stocks, bonds, mutual funds, stock options, certificates of deposit, and retirement assets such as IRAs, Keogh, and 401(k) plans. **Include all corporations, partnerships, limited liability companies or other business entities in which the individual is an officer, director, owner, member, or otherwise has a financial interest.**

Type of Investment or Financial Interest	Full Name & Address *(Street, City, State, ZIP code)* of Company	Current Value	Loan Balance (if applicable) As of ______ mmddyyyy	Equity Value Minus Loan
13a				
	Phone	$	$	$
13b				
	Phone	$	$	$
13c				
	Phone	$	$	$

13d   Total Equity *(Add lines 13a through 13c and amounts from any attachments)* | $

Available Credit. List bank issued credit cards with available credit.

Full Name & Address *(Street, City, State, ZIP code)* of Credit Institution	Credit Limit	Amount Owed As of ______ mmddyyyy	Available Credit As of ______ mmddyyyy
14a			
Acct No.:	$	$	$
14b			
Acct No.:	$	$	$

14c   Total Available Credit *(Add lines 14a, 14b and amounts from any attachments)* | $

15a   Life Insurance. Does the individual have life insurance with a cash value (Term Life insurance does not have a cash value.)
☐ **Yes** ☐ **No**   If **Yes** complete blocks 15b through 15f for each policy:

15b Name and Address of Insurance Company(ies):			
15c Policy Number(s)			
15d Owner of Policy			
15e Current Cash Value	$	$	$
15f Outstanding Loan Balance	$	$	$

15g   Total Available Cash. *(Subtract amounts on line 15f from line 15e and include amounts from any attachments)* | $

16   **In the past 10 years, have any assets been transferred by the individual for less than full value** *(If yes, answer the following. If no, skip to 17a)*   Yes ☐   No ☐

List Asset	Value at Time of Transfer	Date Transferred *(mmddyyyy)*	To Whom or Where was it Transferred
	$		

Real Property Owned, Rented, and Leased. Include all real property and land contracts.

Property Description	Purchase/Lease Date *(mmddyyyy)*	Current Fair Market Value (FMV)	Current Loan Balance	Amount of Monthly Payment	Date of Final Payment *(mmddyyyy)*	**Equity** FMV Minus Loan
17a Property Description		$	$	$		$
Location *(Street, City, State, ZIP code)* and County			Lender/Lessor/Landlord Name, Address, *(Street, City, State, ZIP code)* and Phone			
17b Property Description		$	$	$		$
Location *(Street, City, State, ZIP code)* and County			Lender/Lessor/Landlord Name, Address, *(Street, City, State, ZIP code)* and Phone			

17c   **Total Equity** *(Add lines 17a, 17b and amounts from any attachments)* $

Personal Vehicles Leased and Purchased. Include boats, RVs, motorcycles, trailers, etc.

Description *(Year, Mileage, Make, Model)*		Purchase/Lease Date *(mmddyyyy)*	Current Fair Market Value (FMV)	Current Loan Balance	Amount of Monthly Payment	Date of Final Payment *(mmddyyyy)*	**Equity** FMV Minus Loan
18a Year	Mileage		$	$	$		$
Make	Model	Lender/Lessor Name, Address, *(Street, City, State, ZIP code)* and Phone					
18b Year	Mileage		$	$	$		$
Make	Model	Lender/Lessor Name, Address, *(Street, City, State, ZIP code)* and Phone					

18c   **Total Equity** *(Add lines 18a, 18b and amounts from any attachments)* $

Personal Assets. Include all furniture, personal effects, artwork, jewelry, collections *(coins, guns, etc.)*, antiques or other assets.

Property Description	Purchase/Lease Date *(mmddyyyy)*	Current Fair Market Value (FMV)	Current Loan Balance	Amount of Monthly Payment	Date of Final Payment *(mmddyyyy)*	**Equity** FMV Minus Loan
19a Property Description		$	$	$		$
Location *(Street, City, State, ZIP code)* and County			Lender/Lessor Name, Address, *(Street, City, State, ZIP code)* and Phone			
19b Property Description		$	$	$		$
Location *(Street, City, State, ZIP code)* and County			Lender/Lessor Name, Address, *(Street, City, State, ZIP code)* and Phone			

19c   **Total Equity** *(Add lines 19a, 19b and amounts from any attachments)* $

 Page **4**

If the taxpayer is self-employed, sections 5 and 6 must be completed before continuing.

Monthly Income/Expense Statement *(For additional information, refer to Publication 1854.)*

	Total Income			Total Living Expenses		IRS USE ONLY
	Source	Gross Monthly		Expense Items [5]	Actual Monthly	Allowable Expenses
20	Wages *(Taxpayer)* [1]	$	33	Food, Clothing, and Misc. [6]	$	
21	Wages *(Spouse)* [1]	$	34	Housing and Utilities [7]	$	
22	Interest - Dividends	$	35	Vehicle Ownership Costs [8]	$	
23	Net Business Income [2]	$	36	Vehicle Operating Costs [9]	$	
24	Net Rental Income [3]	$	37	Public Transportation [10]	$	
25	Distributions [4]	$	38	Health Insurance	$	
26	Pension/Social Security *(Taxpayer)*	$	39	Out of Pocket Health Care Costs [11]	$	
27	Pension/Social Security *(Spouse)*	$	40	Court Ordered Payments	$	
28	Child Support	$	41	Child/Dependent Care	$	
29	Alimony	$	42	Life insurance	$	
30	Other *(Rent subsidy, Oil credit, etc.)*	$	43	Taxes *(Income and FICA)*	$	
31	Other	$	44	Other Secured Debts *(Attach list)*	$	
32	**Total Income** *(add lines 20-31)*	$	45	**Total Living Expenses** *(add lines 33-44)*	$	

1 **Wages, salaries, pensions, and social security:** Enter gross monthly wages and/or salaries. Do not deduct withholding or allotments taken out of pay, such as insurance payments, credit union deductions, car payments, etc. To calculate the gross monthly wages and/or salaries:
  If paid weekly - multiply weekly gross wages by 4.3. Example: $425.89 x 4.3 = $1,831.33
  If paid biweekly (every 2 weeks) - multiply biweekly gross wages by 2.17. Example: $972.45 x 2.17 = $2,110.22
  If paid semimonthly (twice each month) - multiply semimonthly gross wages by 2. Example: $856.23 x 2 = $1,712.46

2 **Net Income from Business:** Enter monthly net business income. This is the amount earned after ordinary and necessary monthly business expenses are paid. **This figure is the amount from page 6, line 82.** If the net business income is a loss, enter "0". Do not enter a negative number. If this amount is more or less than previous years, attach an explanation.

3 **Net Rental Income:** Enter monthly net rental income. This is the amount earned after ordinary and necessary monthly rental expenses are paid. Do not include deductions for depreciation or depletion. If the net rental income is a loss, enter "0". Do not enter a negative number.

4 **Distributions:** Enter the total distributions from partnerships and subchapter S corporations reported on Schedule K-1, and from limited liability companies reported on Form 1040, Schedule C, D or E.

5 **Expenses not generally allowed:** We generally do not allow tuition for private schools, public or private college expenses, charitable contributions, voluntary retirement contributions, payments on unsecured debts such as credit card bills, cable television and other similar expenses. However, we may allow these expenses if it is proven that they are necessary for the health and welfare of the individual or family or for the production of income.

6 **Food, Clothing, and Misc.:** Total of clothing, food, housekeeping supplies, and personal care products for one month.

7 **Housing and Utilities:** For principal residence: Total of rent or mortgage payment. Add the average monthly expenses for the following: property taxes, home owner's or renter's insurance, maintenance, dues, fees, and utilities. Utilities include gas, electricity, water, fuel, oil, other fuels, trash collection, telephone, and cell phone.

8 **Vehicle Ownership Costs:** Total of monthly lease or purchase/loan payments.

9 **Vehicle Operating Costs:** Total of maintenance, repairs, insurance, fuel, registrations, licenses, inspections, parking, and tolls for one month.

10 **Public Transportation:** Total of monthly fares for mass transit (e.g., bus, train, ferry, taxi, etc.)

11 **Out of Pocket Health Care Costs:** Monthly total of medical services, prescription drugs and medical supplies (e.g., eyeglasses, hearing aids, etc.)

Certification: *Under penalties of perjury, I declare that to the best of my knowledge and belief this statement of assets, liabilities, and other information is true, correct, and complete.*

Taxpayer's Signature	Spouse's Signature	Date

Attachments Required for Wage Earners and Self-Employed Individuals:
Copies of the following items for the last 3 months from the date this form is submitted (check all attached items):

☐ Income - Earnings statements, pay stubs, etc. from each employer, pension/social security/other income, self employment income (commissions, invoices, sales records, etc.).

☐ Banks, Investments, and Life Insurance - Statements for all money market, brokerage, checking and savings accounts, certificates of deposit, IRA, stocks/bonds, and life insurance policies with a cash value.

☐ Assets - Statements from lenders on loans, monthly payments, payoffs, and balances for all personal and business assets. Include copies of UCC financing statements and accountant's depreciation schedules.

☐ Expenses - Bills or statements for monthly recurring expenses of utilities, rent, insurance, property taxes, phone and cell phone, insurance premiums, court orders requiring payments (child support, alimony, etc.), other out of pocket expenses.

☐ Other - credit card statements, profit and loss statements, all loan payoffs, etc.

☐ A copy of last year's Form 1040 with all attachments. Include all Schedules K-1 from Form 1120S or Form 1065, as applicable.

Form **433-A** (Rev. 1-2008)

Sections 5 and 6 must be completed only if the taxpayer is SELF-EMPLOYED.

Section 5: Business Information

46 Is the business a sole proprietorship (filing Schedule C) ☐ Yes. Continue with Sections 5 and 6. ☐ No. Complete Form 433-B.
All other business entities, including limited liability companies, partnerships or corporations, must complete Form 433-B.

47 Business Name	48 Employer Identification Number	49 Type of Business
		Federal Contractor ☐ Yes ☐ No
50 Business Website	51 Total Number of Employees	52a Average Gross Monthly Payroll
		52b Frequency of Tax Deposits

53 Does the business engage in e-Commerce (Internet sales) ☐ Yes ☐ No

Payment Processor (e.g., PayPal, Authorize.net, Google Checkout, etc.) Name & Address (Street, City, State, ZIP code)	Payment Processor Account Number
54a	
54b	

Credit Cards Accepted by the Business.

Credit Card	Merchant Account Number	Merchant Account Provider, Name & Address (Street, City, State, ZIP code)
55a		
55b		
55c		

56 **Business Cash on Hand.** Include cash that is not in a bank.   **Total Cash on Hand** $

Business Bank Accounts. Include checking accounts, online bank accounts, money market accounts, savings accounts, and stored value cards (e.g. payroll cards, government benefit cards, etc.) *Report Personal Accounts in Section 4.*

Type of Account	Full name & Address (Street, City, State, ZIP code) of Bank, Savings & Loan, Credit Union or Financial Institution.	Account Number	Account Balance As of ________ mmddyyyy
57a			$
57b			$

57c Total Cash in Banks (Add lines 57a, 57b and amounts from any attachments) $

Accounts/Notes Receivable. Include e-payment accounts receivable and factoring companies, and any bartering or online auction accounts. *(List all contracts separately, including contracts awarded, but not started.)* **Include Federal Government Contracts.**

Accounts/Notes Receivable & Address (Street, City, State, ZIP code)	Status (e.g., age, factored, other)	Date Due (mmddyyyy)	Invoice Number or Federal Government Contract Number	Amount Due
58a				$
58b				$
58c				$
58d				$

58e Total Outstanding Balance (Add lines 58a through 58d and amounts from any attachments) $

Business Assets. Include all tools, books, machinery, equipment, inventory or other assets used in trade or business. Include Uniform Commercial Code *(UCC)* filings. Include Vehicles and Real Property owned/leased/rented by the business, if not shown in Section 4.

	Purchase/Lease/Rental Date *(mmddyyyy)*	Current Fair Market Value *(FMV)*	Current Loan Balance	Amount of Monthly Payment	Date of Final Payment *(mmddyyyy)*	**Equity** FMV Minus Loan
59a Property Description		$	$	$		$
Location *(Street, City, State, ZIP code)* and County			Lender/Lessor/Landlord Name, Address *(Street, City, State, ZIP code)* and Phone			
59b Property Description		$	$	$		$
Location *(Street, City, State, ZIP code)* and County			Lender/Lessor/Landlord Name, Address *(Street, City, State, ZIP code)* and Phone			
59c Total Equity *(Add lines 59a, 59b and amounts from any attachments)*						$

Section 6 should be completed only if the taxpayer is SELF-EMPLOYED

Section 6: Sole Proprietorship Information *(lines 60 through 81 should reconcile with business Profit and Loss Statement)*

Accounting Method Used: ☐ Cash ☐ Accrual

Income and Expenses during the period *(mmddyyyy)* ________ to *(mmddyyyy)* ________

Total Monthly Business Income		Total Monthly Business Expenses *(Use attachments as needed.)*	
Source	Gross Monthly	Expense Items	Actual Monthly
60　Gross Receipts	$	70　Materials Purchased [1]	$
61　Gross Rental Income	$	71　Inventory Purchased [2]	$
62　Interest	$	72　Gross Wages & Salaries	$
63　Dividends	$	73　Rent	$
64　Cash	$	74　Supplies [3]	$
Other Income *(Specify below)*		75　Utilities/Telephone [4]	$
65	$	76　Vehicle Gasoline/Oil	$
66	$	77　Repairs & Maintenance	$
67	$	78　Insurance	$
68	$	79　Current Taxes [5]	$
		80　Other Expenses, including installment payments *(Specify)*	$
69　**Total Income** *(Add lines 60 through 68)*	$	81　**Total Expenses** *(Add lines 70 through 80)*	$
		82　**Net Business Income** *(Line 69 minus 81)* [6]	$

Enter the amount from line 82 on line 23, section 4. If line 82 is a loss, enter "0" on line 23, section 4.

Self-employed taxpayers must return to page 4 to sign the certification and include all applicable attachments.

[1] **Materials Purchased:** Materials are items directly related to the production of a product or service.

[2] **Inventory Purchased:** Goods bought for resale.

[3] **Supplies:** Supplies are items used in the business that are consumed or used up within one year. This could be the cost of books, office supplies, professional equipment, etc.

[4] **Utilities/Telephone:** Utilities include gas, electricity, water, oil, other fuels, trash collection, telephone and cell phone.

[5] **Current Taxes:** Real estate, excise, franchise, occupational, personal property, sales and employer's portion of employment taxes.

[6] **Net Business Income:** Net profit from Form 1040. Schedule C may be used if duplicated deductions are eliminated (e.g., expenses for business use of home already included in housing and utility expenses on page 4). Deductions for depreciation and depletion on Schedule C are not cash expenses and must be added back to the net income figure. In addition, interest cannot be deducted if it is already included in any other installment payments allowed.

FINANCIAL ANALYSIS OF COLLECTION POTENTIAL FOR INDIVIDUAL WAGE EARNERS AND SELF-EMPLOYED INDIVIDUALS		(IRS USE ONLY)
Cash Available (Lines 11, 12c, 13d, 14c, 15g, 56, 57c and 58e)	Total Cash	$
Distrainable Asset Summary (Lines 17c, 18c, 19c, and 59c)	Total Equity	$
Monthly Total Positive Income minus Expenses (Line 32 minus Line 45)	Monthly Available Cash	$

Privacy Act: The information requested on this Form is covered under Privacy Acts and Paperwork Reduction Notices which have already been provided to the taxpayer.

Form **433-F** (Rev. 6-2010)	Department of the Treasury — **Internal Revenue Service** **Collection Information Statement**

Name(s) and Address	Your Social Security Number or Individual Taxpayer Identification Number
	Your Spouse's Social Security Number or Individual Taxpayer Identification Number

☐ If address provided above is different than last return filed please check here.

County of Residence

Your Telephone Numbers	Spouse's Telephone Numbers
Home: ( )	Home: ( )
Work: ( )	Work: ( )
Cell: ( )	Cell: ( )

A. ACCOUNTS / LINES OF CREDIT (including Banking Institutions, Checking and Savings accounts, Credit Unions, Certificates of Deposit, Individual Retirement Accounts (IRAs), Keogh Plans, Simplified Employee Pensions, 401(k) Plans, Profit Sharing Plans, Mutual Funds and Stock Brokerage Accounts)

Name and Address of Institution	Type of Account	Current Balance / Value

Total number of dependents you will be claiming on next year's tax return ________ Over 65 ☐ Under 65 ☐

Total number of dependents you claimed on last year's tax return ________ Over 65 ☐ Under 65 ☐

B. REAL ESTATE (home, vacation property, timeshares and other real estate)

County / Description	Monthly Payment(s)	Financing		Current Value	Balance Owed	Equity
		Year Purchased	Purchase Price			
☐ Primary Residence ☐ Other		Year Refinanced	Refinance Amount			
		Year Purchased	Purchase Price			
☐ Primary Residence ☐ Other		Year Refinanced	Refinance Amount			
		Year Purchased	Purchase Price			
☐ Primary Residence ☐ Other		Year Refinanced	Refinance Amount			

C. OTHER ASSETS (cars, boats, recreational vehicles, whole life policies, etc.)

Description	Monthly Payment	Year Purchased	Final Payment (mo / yr)	Current Value	Balance Owed	Equity
			/			
			/			
			/			
			/			
			/			
			/			
			/			

D. CREDIT CARDS (Visa, MasterCard, American Express, Department Stores, etc.)

Type	Credit Limit	Balance Owed	Minimum Monthly Payment

E. WAGE INFORMATION (If you have more than one employer, include the information on another sheet of paper.)

Your current Employer (name and address)

Spouse's current Employer (name and address)

How often are you paid? (Check one)
☐ Weekly ☐ Biweekly ☐ Semi-monthly ☐ Monthly
Gross per pay period ___________
Taxes per pay period (Fed) _________ (State) _________ (Local) _________
How long at current employer ___________
Date of Birth ___________
Total Income from Last Year's 1040 Tax Return ___________

How often are you paid? (Check one)
☐ Weekly ☐ Biweekly ☐ Semi-monthly ☐ Monthly
Gross per pay period ___________
Taxes per pay period (Fed) _________ (State) _________ (Local) _________
How long at current employer ___________
Date of Birth ___________
Total Income from Last Year's 1040 Tax Return ___________

F. NON-WAGE HOUSEHOLD INCOME (List monthly amounts. For Self-Employment and Rental Income, list the monthly amount received after expenses or taxes.)

Alimony Income:		Net Rental Income:		Interest Income:	
Child Support Income:		Unemployment Income:		Social Security Income:	
Net Self Employment Income:		Pension Income:		Other: _________	

G. MONTHLY NECESSARY LIVING EXPENSES (List monthly amounts. For expenses paid other than monthly, see instructions.)

1. Food / Personal Care

Food:	
Housekeeping Supplies:	
Clothing and Clothing Services:	
Personal Care Products & Services:	
Misc. (Cable, Internet, etc.)*	
Total:	0.00

2. Transportation

Gas/Insurance/Licenses/Parking/ Maintenance etc.:	
Public Transportation:	

3. Housing & Utilities

Rent:	
Electric, Oil/Gas, Water/Trash:	
Telephone and/or Cell Phone:	
Real Estate Taxes and Insurance: (if not included in B above)	
Total:	0.00

4. Medical

Health Insurance:	
Out of Pocket Health Care Expenses:	

5. Other

Child / Dependent Care:	
Estimated Tax Payments:	
Term Life Insurance:	
Retirement (Employer Required):	
Retirement (Voluntary):	
Court Ordered Payments:	
Profit and Loss Statement:	

See the instructions for detailed information on how to complete the Monthly Necessary Living Expenses. IRS standard amounts are found on the internet at http://www.irs.gov/individuals/article/0,,id=96543,00.html. If you are required to send supporting documentation, please send copies and not the original documents.

H. ADDITIONAL INFORMATION

1. The IRS may establish a payment agreement for you based on the financial data you provided.

2. **We cannot consider an installment agreement unless all returns have been filed. Attach a signed copy of ALL unfiled return(s).**

3. Proposed Monthly Installment Agreement Payment Amount: ___________

4. Proposed Monthly Payment Date: ___________

5. Down Payment Amount: ___________

Under penalty of perjury, I declare to the best of my knowledge and belief this statement of assets, liabilities and other information is true, correct and complete.

Your Signature	Spouse's Signature	Date

Form **4549** (Rev. May 2008)	Department of the Treasury-Internal Revenue Service **Income Tax Examination Changes**		Page 1 of 3
Name and Address of Taxpayer ███████		**Taxpayer Identification Number** ███████	**Return Form No.:** 1040
		Person with whom examination changes were discussed.	Name and Title: ███████

1. Adjustments to Income	Period End 12/31/2007	Period End	Period End
a. Itemized Deductions	56,638.00		
b.			
c.			
d.			
e.			
f.			
g.			
h.			
i.			
j.			
k.			
l.			
m.			
n.			
o.			
p.			
2. Total Adjustments	56,638.00		
3. Taxable Income Per Return or as Previously Adjusted	(27,356.00)		
4. Corrected Taxable Income	29,282.00		
Tax Method	TAX TABLE		
Filing Status	Joint		
5. Tax	3,609.00		
6. Additional Taxes / Alternative Minimum Tax			
7. Corrected Tax Liability	3,689.00		
8. Less a. Child Tax Credit	1,000.00		
Credits b.			
c.			
d.			
9. Balance *(Line 7 less Lines 8a through 8d)*	2,689.00		
10. Plus a.			
Other b.			
Taxes c.			
d.			
11. Total Corrected Tax Liability *(Line 9 plus Lines 10a through 10d)*	2,689.00		
12. Total Tax Shown on Return or as Previously Adjusted	0.00		
13. Adjustments to: a.			
b.			
c. Addnl Child Tax Credit	(1,000.00)		
14. Deficiency-Increase in Tax or *(Overassessment-Decrease in Tax)* *(Line 11 less Line 12 adjusted by Lines 13a through 13c)*	3,689.00		
15. Adjustments to Prepayment Credits - Increase *(Decrease)*			
16. Balance Due or *(Overpayment)* - *(Line 14 adjusted by Line 15)* *(Excluding interest and penalties)*	3,689.00		

The Internal Revenue Service has agreements with state tax agencies under which information about federal tax, including increases or decreases, is exchanged with the states. If this change affects the amount of your state income tax, you should amend your state return by filing the necessary forms.

You may be subject to backup withholding if you underreport your interest, dividend, or patronage dividend income you earned and do not pay the required tax. The IRS may order backup withholding *(withholding of a percentage of your dividend and/or interest income)* if the tax remains unpaid after it has been assessed and four notices have been issued to you over a 120-day period.

Form **8379** (Rev. December 2010) Department of the Treasury Internal Revenue Service	**Injured Spouse Allocation** ▶ See instructions.	OMB No. 1545-0074 Attachment Sequence No. **104**

Part I **Should you file this form?** You must complete this part.

1 Enter the tax year for which you are filing this form. ▶ _____________ Answer the following questions for that year.

2 Did you (or will you) file a joint return?
- ☐ **Yes.** Go to line 3.
- ☐ **No.** **Stop here.** Do not file this form. You are not an injured spouse.

3 Did (or will) the IRS use the joint overpayment to pay any of the following legally enforceable past-due debt(s) owed only by your spouse? (see instructions)
- Federal tax • State income tax • Child support • Spousal support • Federal nontax debt (such as a student loan)
- ☐ **Yes.** Go to line 4.
- ☐ **No.** **Stop here.** Do not file this form. You are not an injured spouse.

  Note. If the past-due amount is for a joint federal tax, you may qualify for innocent spouse relief for the year to which the overpayment was applied. See *Innocent Spouse Relief*, in the instructions for more information.

4 Are you legally obligated to pay this past-due amount?
- ☐ **Yes.** **Stop here.** Do not file this form. You are not an injured spouse.

  Note. If the past-due amount is for a joint federal tax, you may qualify for innocent spouse relief for the year to which the overpayment was applied. See *Innocent Spouse Relief*, in the instructions for more information.
- ☐ **No.** Go to line 5.

5 Were you a resident of a community property state (Arizona, California, Idaho, Louisiana, Nevada, New Mexico, Texas, Washington, or Wisconsin) at any time during the tax year entered on line 1? (see instructions)
- ☐ **Yes.** Enter name(s) of community property states(s) _____________________________
  Skip lines 6 through 9 and **go to Part II** and complete the rest of this form.
- ☐ **No.** Go to line 6.

6 Did you make and report payments, such as federal income tax withholding or estimated tax payments?
- ☐ **Yes.** Skip lines 7 through 9 and **go to Part II** and complete the rest of this form.
- ☐ **No.** Go to line 7.

7 Did you have earned income, such as wages, salaries, or self-employment income?
- ☐ **Yes.** Go to line 8.
- ☐ **No.** Skip line 8 and go to line 9.

8 Did (or will) you claim the earned income credit or additional child tax credit?
- ☐ **Yes.** Skip line 9 and **go to Part II** and complete the rest of this form.
- ☐ **No.** Go to line 9.

9 Did (or will) you claim a refundable tax credit (see instructions)?
- ☐ **Yes.** **Go to Part II** and complete the rest of this form.
- ☐ **No.** **Stop here.** Do not file this form. You are not an injured spouse.

Part II **Information About the Joint Tax Return for Which This Form Is Filed**

10 Enter the following information exactly as it is shown on the tax return for which you are filing this form. The spouse's name and social security number shown first on that tax return must also be shown first below.

First name, initial, and last name shown first on the return	Social security number shown first	If Injured Spouse, check here ▶ ☐
First name, initial, and last name shown second on the return	Social security number shown second	If Injured Spouse, check here ▶ ☐

11 Check this box only if you are divorced or legally separated from the spouse with whom you filed the joint return and you want your refund issued in your name only . . . . ☐

12 Do you want any injured spouse refund mailed to an address different from the one on your joint return? ☐ Yes ☐ No
If "Yes," enter the address.

Number and street	City, town, or post office, state, and ZIP code

For Privacy Act and Paperwork Reduction Act Notice, see separate instructions.   Cat. No. 62474Q   Form **8379** (Rev. 12-2010)

Form 843: Claim for Refund and Request for Abatement

Form **843** (Rev. August 2011) Department of the Treasury Internal Revenue Service	**Claim for Refund and Request for Abatement** ▶ **See separate instructions.**	OMB No. 1545-0024

Use Form 843 if your claim or request involves:

  (a) a refund of one of the taxes (other than income taxes or an employer's claim for FICA tax, RRTA tax, or income tax withholding) or a fee, shown on line 3,

  (b) an abatement of FUTA tax or certain excise taxes, or

  (c) a refund or abatement of interest, penalties, or additions to tax for one of the reasons shown on line 5a.

Do not use Form 843 if your claim or request involves:

  (a) an overpayment of income taxes or an employer's claim for FICA tax, RRTA tax, or income tax withholding (use the appropriate amended tax return),

  (b) a refund of excise taxes based on the nontaxable use or sale of fuels, or

  (c) an overpayment of excise taxes reported on Form(s) 11-C, 720, 730, or 2290.

Name(s)	Your social security number
Address (number, street, and room or suite no.)	Spouse's social security number
City or town, state, and ZIP code	Employer identification number (EIN)
Name and address shown on return if different from above	Daytime telephone number

1 **Period.** Prepare a separate Form 843 for each tax period or fee year.
From ____ to ____

2 **Amount** to be refunded or abated:
$

3 **Type of tax or fee.** Indicate the type of tax or fee to be refunded or abated or to which the interest, penalty, or addition to tax is related.

☐ Employment   ☐ Estate   ☐ Gift   ☐ Excise   ☐ Income   ☐ Fee

4 **Type of penalty.** If the claim or request involves a penalty, enter the Internal Revenue Code section on which the penalty is based (see instructions). IRC section:

5a **Interest, penalties, and additions to tax.** Check the box that indicates your reason for the request for refund or abatement. (If none apply, go to line 6.)

☐ Interest was assessed as a result of IRS errors or delays.
☐ A penalty or addition to tax was the result of erroneous written advice from the IRS.
☐ Reasonable cause or other reason allowed under the law (other than erroneous written advice) can be shown for not assessing a penalty or addition to tax.

  b Date(s) of payment(s) ▶

6 **Original return.** Indicate the type of fee or return, if any, filed to which the tax, interest, penalty, or addition to tax relates.
☐ 706   ☐ 709   ☐ 940   ☐ 941   ☐ 943   ☐ 945
☐ 990-PF   ☐ 1040   ☐ 1120   ☐ 4720   ☐ Other (specify) ▶

7 **Explanation.** Explain why you believe this claim or request should be allowed and show the computation of the amount shown on line 2. If you need more space, attach additional sheets.

Signature. If you are filing Form 843 to request a refund or abatement relating to a joint return, both you and your spouse must sign the claim. Claims filed by corporations must be signed by a corporate officer authorized to sign, and the officer's title must be shown.

Under penalties of perjury, I declare that I have examined this claim, including accompanying schedules and statements, and, to the best of my knowledge and belief, it is true, correct, and complete. Declaration of preparer (other than taxpayer) is based on all information of which preparer has any knowledge.

Signature (Title, if applicable. Claims by corporations must be signed by an officer.)	Date
Signature (spouse, if joint return)	Date

Paid Preparer Use Only	Print/Type preparer's name	Preparer's signature	Date	Check ☐ if self-employed	PTIN
	Firm's name ▶			Firm's EIN ▶	
	Firm's address ▶			Phone no.	

For Privacy Act and Paperwork Reduction Act Notice, see separate instructions.   Cat. No. 10180R   Form **843** (Rev. 8-2011)

Form 870
Waiver of Restrictions on Assessment and Collection
of Deficiency in Tax and Acceptance of Overassessment

Form **870** (Rev. March 1992)	Department of the Treasury—Internal Revenue Service **Waiver of Restrictions on Assessment and Collection of Deficiency in Tax and Acceptance of Overassessment**	Date received by Internal Revenue Service

Names and address of taxpayers (*Number, street, city or town, State, ZIP code*)	Social security or employer identification number

Increase (Decrease) in Tax and Penalties

Tax year ended	Tax	Penalties		

(For instructions, see back of form)

Consent to Assessment and Collection

I consent to the immediate assessment and collection of any deficiencies (*increase in tax and penalties*) and accept any overassessment (*decrease in tax and penalties*) shown above, plus any interest provided by law. I understand that by signing this waiver, I will not be able to contest these years in the United States Tax Court, unless additional deficiencies are determined for these years.

YOUR SIGNATURE HERE ➤		Date
SPOUSE'S SIGNATURE ➤		Date
TAXPAYER'S REPRESENTATIVE HERE ➤		Date

CORPORATE NAME ➤			
CORPORATE OFFICER(S) SIGN HERE ➤		Title	Date
		Title	Date

Catalog Number 16894U   Form **870** (Rev. 3-1992)

<table>
<tr>
<td>Form 872
(Rev. October 2009)</td>
<td align="center">Department of the Treasury-Internal Revenue Service
Consent to Extend the Time to Assess Tax</td>
<td>In reply refer to:

TIN</td>
</tr>
</table>

____

____

(Name(s))

taxpayer(s) of ________________________________

____

(Address)

and the Commissioner of Internal Revenue consent and agree to the following:

(1) The amount of any Federal _______________________ tax due on any return(s) made by or

(Kind of tax)

for the above taxpayer(s) for the period(s) ended _______________________

may be assessed at any time on or before _______________________ . However, if

(Expiration date)

a notice of deficiency in tax or a notice of final partnership administrative adjustment for any such period(s) is sent to the taxpayer(s) on or before that date, then the time for assessing the tax will be further extended as provided by the Internal Revenue Code.

(2) The taxpayer(s) may file a claim for credit or refund and the Service may credit or refund the tax within 6 months after this agreement ends, except with respect to the items in paragraph (4).

(3) Paragraph (4) applies only to any taxpayer who holds an interest, **either directly or indirectly**, in any partnership subject to subchapter C of chapter 63 of the Internal Revenue Code.

(4) Without otherwise limiting the applicability of this agreement, this agreement also extends the period of limitations for assessing any tax (including additions to tax and interest) attributable to any partnership items (see section 6231 (a)(3)), affected items (see section 6231(a)(5)), computational adjustments (see section 6231(a)(6)), and partnership items converted to nonpartnership items (see section 6231(b)). This agreement extends the period for filing a petition for adjustment under section 6228(b) but only if a timely request for administrative adjustment is filed under section 6227. For partnership items which have converted to nonpartnership items, this agreement extends the period for filing a suit for refund or credit under section 6532, but only if a timely claim for refund is filed for such items.

(5) This Form contains the entire terms of the consent to extend the Time to Assess Tax. There are no representations, promises, or agreements between the parties except those found or referenced on this Form.

With respect to the returns listed in paragraph (1) above, if the three-year period for assessing tax, under Internal Revenue Code section 6501(a), ended prior to the date of this consent, then this consent serves to extend the time to assess tax under any other provision of section 6501 for which the period of time to assess tax has not ended as of the date of this consent.

This consent does not serve to shorten the statutory period of time to assess tax for any return.

Your Rights as a Taxpayer

You have the right to refuse to extend the period of limitations or limit this extension to a mutually agreed-upon issue(s) or mutually agreed-upon period of time. **Publication 1035, Extending the Tax Assessment Period**, provides a more detailed explanation of your rights and the consequences of the choices you may make. If you have not already received a Publication 1035, the publication can be obtained, free of charge, from the IRS official who requested that you sign this consent or from the IRS' web site at www.irs.gov or by calling toll free at 1-800-829-3676. Signing this consent will not deprive you of any appeal rights to which you would otherwise be entitled.

<table>
<tr>
<td>(Signature instructions are on the back of this form)</td>
<td>www.irs.gov</td>
<td>Catalog Number 20755I</td>
<td>Form 872 (Rev. 10-2009)</td>
</tr>
</table>

TIN	Period Ending		Expiration Date

SIGNING THIS CONSENT WILL NOT DEPRIVE THE TAXPAYER(S) OF ANY APPEAL RIGHTS TO WHICH THEY WOULD OTHERWISE BE ENTITLED.

YOUR SIGNATURE HERE ➤

I am aware that I have the right to refuse to sign this consent or to limit the extension to mutually agreed-upon issues and/or period of time as set forth in I.R.C. § 6501(c)(4)(B).　　*(Date signed)*

SPOUSE'S SIGNATURE ➤

I am aware that I have the right to refuse to sign this consent or to limit the extension to mutually agreed-upon issues and/or period of time as set forth in I.R.C. § 6501(c)(4)(B).　　*(Date signed)*

TAXPAYER'S REPRESENTATIVE

SIGN HERE ➤

I am aware that I have the right to refuse to sign this consent or to limit the extension to mutually agreed-upon issues and/or period of time as set forth in I.R.C. § 6501(c)(4)(B). In addition, the taxpayer(s) has been made aware of these rights.　　*(Date signed)*

If this document is signed by a taxpayer's representative, the Form 2848 must state that the acts authorized by the power of attorney include representation for the purposes of Subchapter C of Chapter 63 of the Internal Revenue Code in order to cover items in paragraph (4).

CORPORATE NAME ➤

CORPORATE OFFICER(S) SIGN HERE ➤

(Title)　　*(Date signed)*

➤

(Title)　　*(Date signed)*

I (we) am (we) aware that I (we) have the right to refuse to sign this consent or to limit the extension to mutually agreed-upon issues and/or period of time as set forth in I.R.C. § 6501 (c)(4)(B).

INTERNAL REVENUE SERVICE SIGNATURE AND TITLE

(Division Executive Name - see instructions)　　　　*(Division Executive Title - see instructions)*

BY

(Authorized Official Signature and Title - see instructions)　　*(Date signed)*

Instructions

If this consent is for:

- Income tax, self-employment tax, or FICA tax on tips and is made of any year (s) for which a joint return was filed, both husband and wife must sign the original and copy of this form unless one, acting under a power of attorney, signs as agent for the other. The signatures must match the names as they appear on the front of this form.

- Gift tax and the donor and the donor's spouse elected to have gifts to third persons considered as made one-half by each, both husband and wife must sign the original and copy of this form unless one, acting under a power of attorney, signs as agent for the other. The signatures must match the names as they appear on the front of this form.

- Chapter 41, 42, or 43 taxes involving a partnership or is for a partnership return, only one authorized partner need sign.

- Chapter 42 taxes, a separate Form 872 should be completed for each potential disqualified person, entity, or foundation manager that may be involved in a taxable transaction during the related tax year. See Revenue Ruling 75-391, 1975-2C B 446

If you are an attorney or agent of the taxpayer(s), you may sign the consent provided the action is specifically authorized by a power of attorney. If the power of attorney was not previously filed, you must include it with this form.

If you are acting as a fiduciary (such as executor, administrator, trustee, etc.) and you sign this consent, attach Form 56, Notice Concerning Fiduciary Relationship, unless it was previously filed.

If the taxpayer is a corporation, sign this consent with the corporate name followed by the signature and title of the officer(s) authorized to sign.

Instructions for Internal Revenue Service Employees

Complete the Division Executive's name and title depending upon your division:

- Small Business and Self-Employed Division = Area Director; Director, Examination; Director, Specialty Programs; Director, Compliance Services, etc.

- Wage and Investment Division = Area Director; Director, Field Compliance Services

- Large and Mid-Size Business Division = Director, Field Operations for your industry.

- Tax Exempt and Government Entities Division = Director, Exempt Organizations; Director, Employee Plans; Director, Federal, State and Local Governments; Director, Indian Tribal Governments; Director, Tax Exempt Bonds

- Appeals = Chief, Appeals.

The appropriate authorized official within your division must sign and date the signature and title line.

Form **872-T** (Rev. November 2011)	Department of the Treasury-Internal Revenue Service **Notice of Termination of Special Consent to Extend the Time to Assess Tax**	In reply refer to

Taxpayer(s) Name(s)

Termination by
☐ Taxpayer
☐ Internal Revenue Service

Taxpayer(s) Address

Taxpayer Identification Number

Office where
Form 872-A/Form 872-IA
Originated

Kind of Tax

Tax Period(s) Covered by this Notice

IRS Center Where Return Filed

This form is written notification of termination of: *(Check the appropriate box)*

☐ Form 872-A, Special Consent to Extend the Time to Assess Tax

☐ Form 872-IA, Special Consent to Extend the Time to Assess Tax As Well As Tax Attributable to Items of a Partnership

for the kind of tax and tax period(s) indicated above. This notice of termination of consent is provided under the terms of the agreement between the taxpayer(s) named above the Commissioner of Internal Revenue dated _______________.

See the back of this form for signature instructions.
Please note that signing this notice may alter the taxpayer(s) appeal rights.

YOUR SIGNATURE ▶ ___________________________ (Date signed)
____
(Type or print name)

SPOUSE'S SIGNATURE ▶ ___________________________ (Date signed)
(Type or print name)

TAXPAYER'S REPRESENTATIVE'S SIGNATURE
(Only needed if signing on behalf of the taxpayer.) ▶ ___________________________ (Date signed)
(Type or print name)
(You must also attach written authorization as stated in the instructions on the back of this form)

CORPORATE NAME

CORPORATE OFFICER(S) SIGNATURE ▶
(Name)   *(Title)*   *(Date signed)*
(Type or print name)

▶
(Name)   *(Title)*   *(Date signed)*
(Authorized Official Signature and Title - see instructions)
(Type or print name)

INTERNAL REVENUE SERVICE SIGNATURE AND TITLE

(IRS Official's Name - see instructions)   *(IRS Official's Title - see instructions)*

(IRS Official's Signature - see instructions)   *(Date signed)*

(Instructions are on the 2nd page of this form)   www.irs.gov   Catalog Number 20775A   Form **872-T** (Rev. 11-2011)

Form **8822**	**Change of Address**	
(Rev. January 2011) Department of the Treasury Internal Revenue Service	▶ Please type or print. ▶ **See instructions on back.** ▶ **Do not attach this form to your return.**	OMB No. 1545-1163

Before you begin: If you are changing both your home and business address, use a separate Form 8822 to report each change.

Part I   **Complete This Part To Change Your Home Mailing Address**

Check **all** boxes this change affects:

1 ☐ Individual income tax returns (Forms 1040, 1040A, 1040EZ, 1040NR, etc.)
　▶ If your last return was a joint return and you are now establishing a residence separate
　　from the spouse with whom you filed that return, check here . . . . ▶ ☐

2 ☐ Gift, estate, or generation-skipping transfer tax returns (Forms 706, 709, etc.)
　▶ For Forms 706 and 706-NA, enter the decedent's name and social security number below.
　▶ Decedent's name　　　　　　　　　　　　　　　　　　　　▶ Social security number

3a **Your name** (first name, initial, and last name)	**3b** **Your social security number**
4a **Spouse's name** (first name, initial, and last name)	**4b** **Spouse's social security number**

5a **Your prior name.** See instructions.

5b **Spouse's prior name.** See instructions.

6a **Old address** (no., street, apt no., city or town, state, and ZIP code). If a P.O. box or foreign address, see instructions.

6b **Spouse's old address, if different from line 6a** (no., street, apt no., city or town, state, and ZIP code). If a P.O. box or foreign address, see instructions.

7 **New address** (no., street, apt no., city or town, state, and ZIP code). If a P.O. box or foreign address, see instructions.

Part II   **Complete This Part To Change Your Business Mailing Address or Business Location**

Check **all** boxes this change affects:

8 ☐ Employment, excise, income, and other business returns (Forms 720, 940, 940-EZ, 941, 990, 1041, 1065, 1120, etc.)
9 ☐ Employee plan returns (Forms 5500, 5500-EZ, etc.)
10 ☐ Business location

11a **Business name**	**11b** **Employer identification number**

12 **Old mailing address** (no., street, room or suite no., city or town, state, and ZIP code). If a P.O. box or foreign address, see instructions.

13 **New mailing address** (no., street, room or suite no., city or town, state, and ZIP code). If a P.O. box or foreign address, see instructions.

14 **New business location, if different from mailing address** (no., street, room or suite no., city or town, state, and ZIP code). If a foreign address, see instructions.

Part III   **Signature**

Daytime telephone number of person to contact (optional) ▶

Sign Here ▶ Your signature	Date	▶ If Part II completed, signature of owner, officer, or representative	Date
▶ If joint return, spouse's signature	Date	▶ Title	

For **Privacy Act and Paperwork Reduction Act Notice, see back of form.**　　Cat. No. 12081V　　Form **8822** (Rev. 1-2011)

| Form **8857**
(Rev. September 2010)
Department of the Treasury
Internal Revenue Service (99) | **Request for Innocent Spouse Relief**

▶ **See separate instructions.** | OMB No. 1545-1596 |

Important things you should know

- **Do not file this form with your tax return.** See *Where To File* in the instructions.
- Answer all the questions on this form that apply, attach any necessary documentation, and sign on page 4. Do not delay filing this form because of missing documentation. See instructions.
- By law, the IRS must contact the person who was your spouse for the years you want relief. There are no exceptions, even for victims of spousal abuse or domestic violence. Your personal information (such as your current name, address, and employer) will be protected. However, if you petition the Tax Court, your personal information may be released, unless you ask the Tax Court to withhold it. See instructions for details.
- If you need help, see *How To Get Help* in the instructions.

Part I   **Should you file this form?** You **must** complete this part for each tax year.

		Tax Year 1		Tax Year 2		Tax Year 3*	
1	**Enter each tax year you want relief.** It is important to enter the correct year. For example, if the IRS used your 2009 income tax refund to pay a 2007 tax amount you jointly owed, enter tax year 2007, not tax year 2009 ▶ **1**						
	Caution. The IRS generally cannot collect the amount you owe until your request for each year is resolved. However, the time the IRS has to collect is extended. See *Collection Statute of Limitations* on page 3 of the instructions.						
2	**Check the box for each year you would like a refund if you qualify for relief.** You may be required to provide proof of payment. See instructions ▶ **2**	☐		☐		☐	
		Yes	No	Yes	No	Yes	No
3	**Did the IRS use your share of the joint refund to pay any of the following past-due debts of your spouse: federal tax, state income tax, child support, spousal support, or federal non-tax debt such as a student loan?**						
	• If "Yes," **stop here;** do not file this form for that tax year. Instead, file Form 8379, Injured Spouse Allocation. See instructions.						
	• If "No," go to line 4 ▶ **3**	☐	☐	☐	☐	☐	☐
4	**Was a return claiming married filing jointly status filed for the tax year listed on line 1?** See instructions. • If "Yes," skip line 5 and go to line 6. • If "No," go to line 5 ▶ **4**	☐	☐	☐	☐	☐	☐
5	**If a joint return for that tax year was not filed, were you a resident of Arizona, California, Idaho, Louisiana, Nevada, New Mexico, Texas, Washington, or Wisconsin?** • If "Yes," see *Community Property Laws* on page 2 of the instructions. • If "No" on both lines 4 and 5, **stop here.** Do not file this form for that tax year ▶ **5**	☐	☐	☐	☐	☐	☐

*If you want relief for more than 3 years, fill out an additional form.

Part II   **Tell us about yourself**

6	Your current name (see instructions)	**Your social security number**
	Your current mailing address (number and street).	Apt. no. **County**
	City, town or post office, state, and ZIP code. If a foreign address, see instructions.	Best daytime phone number

Part III   **Tell us about you and your spouse for the tax years you want relief**

7	**Who was your spouse for the tax years you want relief?** File a separate Form 8857 for tax years involving different spouses or former spouses.	
	That person's current name	**Social security number** (if known)
	Current home address (number and street) (if known). If a P.O. box, see instructions.	Apt. no.
	City, town or post office, state, and ZIP code. If a foreign address, see instructions.	Best daytime phone number

For Privacy Act and Paperwork Reduction Act Notice, see instructions.   Cat. No. 24647V   Form **8857** (Rev. 9-2010)

     Page **2**

Note. If you need more room to write your answer for any question, attach more pages. Be sure to write your name and social security number on the top of all pages you attach.

Part III   *(Continued)*

8   **What is the current marital status between you and the person on line 7?**

☐   Married and still living together

☐   Married and living apart since _______________
                                      MM   DD   YYYY

☐   Widowed since _______________   Attach a photocopy of the death certificate and will (if one exists).
                             MM   DD   YYYY

☐   Legally separated since _______________   Attach a photocopy of your entire separation agreement.
                                  MM   DD   YYYY

☐   Divorced since _______________   Attach a photocopy of your entire divorce decree.
                         MM   DD   YYYY

Note. A divorce decree stating that your former spouse must pay all taxes does not necessarily mean you qualify for relief.

9   **What was the highest level of education you had completed when the return(s) were filed?** If the answers are **not** the same for all tax years, explain.

☐   High school diploma, equivalent, or less
☐   Some college
☐   College degree or higher. List any degrees you have ▶ ___________________________________
List any college-level business or tax-related courses you completed ▶ _______________________

Explain ▶ ____

10   **Were you a victim of spousal abuse or domestic violence during any of the tax years you want relief?** If the answers are **not** the same for all tax years, explain.

☐   Yes. **Attach a statement** to explain the situation and **when** it started. Provide photocopies of any documentation, such as police reports, a restraining order, a doctor's report or letter, or a notarized statement from someone who was aware of the situation.

☐   No.

11   **Did you (or the person on line 7) incur any large expenses, such as trips, home improvements, or private schooling, or make any large purchases, such as automobiles, appliances, or jewelry, during any of the years you want relief or any later years?**

☐   Yes. **Attach a statement** describing (a) the types and amounts of the expenses and purchases and (b) the years they were incurred or made.

☐   No.

12   **Did you sign the return(s)?** If the answers are **not** the same for all tax years, explain.

☐   Yes. If you were forced to sign under duress (threat of harm or other form of coercion), check here ▶ ☐ . See instructions.
☐   No. Your signature was forged. See instructions.

13   **When any of the returns were signed, did you have a mental or physical health problem or do you have a mental or physical health problem now?** If the answers are **not** the same for all tax years, explain.

☐   Yes. **Attach a statement** to explain the problem and **when** it started. Provide photocopies of any documentation, such as medical bills or a doctor's report or letter.

☐   No.

Part IV   **Tell us how you were involved with finances and preparing returns for those tax years**

14   **How were you involved with preparing the returns?** Check all that apply and explain, if necessary. If the answers are **not** the same for all tax years, explain.

☐   You filled out or helped fill out the returns.
☐   You gathered receipts and cancelled checks.
☐   You gave tax documents (such as Forms W-2, 1099, etc.) to the person who prepared the returns.
☐   You reviewed the returns before they were signed.
☐   You did not review the returns before they were signed. Explain below.
☐   You were not involved in preparing the returns.
☐   Other ▶ ____

Explain how you were involved ▶ ____

____

____

____

Note. If you need more room to write your answer for any question, attach more pages. Be sure to write your name and social security number on the top of all pages you attach.

Part IV *(Continued)*

15 **When the returns were signed, what did you know about any incorrect or missing information?** Check all that apply and explain, if necessary. If the answers are **not** the same for all tax years, explain.

- ☐ You knew something was incorrect or missing, but you said nothing.
- ☐ You knew something was incorrect or missing and asked about it.
- ☐ You did not know anything was incorrect or missing.

Explain ▶ ____

16 **When any of the returns were signed, what did you know about the income of the person on line 7?** Check all that apply and explain, if necessary. If the answers are **not** the same for all tax years, explain.

- ☐ You knew that person had income.

List each type of income on a separate line. (Examples are wages, social security, gambling winnings, or self-employment business income.) Enter each tax year and the amount of income for each type you listed. If you do not know any details, enter "I don't know."

Type of income	Who paid it to that person	Tax Year 1	Tax Year 2	Tax Year 3
		$	$	$
		$	$	$
		$	$	$

- ☐ You knew that person was self-employed and you helped with the books and records.
- ☐ You knew that person was self-employed and you did not help with the books and records.
- ☐ You knew that person had no income.
- ☐ You did not know if that person had income.

Explain ▶ ____

17 **When the returns were signed, did you know any amount was owed to the IRS for those tax years?** If the answers are **not** the same for all tax years, explain.

- ☐ Yes. Explain when and how you thought the amount of tax reported on the return would be paid ▶ ______________________

- ☐ No.

Explain ▶ ____

18 **When any of the returns were signed, were you having financial problems** (for example, bankruptcy or bills you could not pay)? If the answers are **not** the same for all tax years, explain.

- ☐ Yes. Explain ▶ ____

- ☐ No.
- ☐ Did not know.

Explain ▶ ____

19 **For the years you want relief, how were you involved in the household finances?** Check all that apply. If the answers are **not** the same for all tax years, explain.

- ☐ You knew the person on line 7 had separate accounts.
- ☐ You had joint accounts but you had limited use of them or did not use them. Explain below.
- ☐ You used joint accounts. You made deposits, paid bills, balanced the checkbook, or reviewed the monthly bank statements.
- ☐ You made decisions about how money was spent. For example, you paid bills or made decisions about household purchases.
- ☐ You were not involved in handling money for the household.
- ☐ Other ▶

Explain anything else you want to tell us about your household finances ▶ ______________________

20 **Has the person on line 7 ever transferred assets (money or property) to you?** (Property includes real estate, stocks, bonds, or other property that you own.) See instructions.

- ☐ Yes. List the assets, the dates they were transferred, and their fair market values on the dates transferred. Explain why the assets were transferred ▶ ______________________

____

- ☐ No.

Part V **Tell us about your current financial situation**

21 Tell us the number of people currently in your household.   Adults ________________   Children ________________

22 **Tell us your current average monthly income and expenses for your entire household.** If family or friends are helping to support you, include the amount of support as gifts under **Monthly income.** Under **Monthly expenses,** enter all expenses, including expenses paid with income from gifts.

Monthly income	Amount	Monthly expenses	Amount
		Federal, state, and local taxes deducted from your paycheck	
Gifts		Rent or mortgage	
Wages (Gross pay)		Utilities	
Pensions		Telephone	
Unemployment			
Social security			
Government assistance, such as housing, food stamps, grants		Food	
Alimony		Car expenses, payments, insurance, etc.	
		Medical expenses, including medical insurance	
Child support		Life insurance	
Self-employment business income . .		Clothing	
Rental income		Child care	
Interest and dividends		Public transportation	
Other income, such as disability payments, gambling winnings, etc.		Other expenses, such as real estate taxes, child support, etc.	
List the type below:		List the type below:	
Type _______________________		Type _______________________	
Type _______________________		Type _______________________	
Type _______________________		Type _______________________	
Total . . . . ▶		Total . . . . ▶	

23 **Tell us about your assets.** Your assets are your money and property. Property includes real estate, motor vehicles, stocks, bonds, and other property that you own. Tell us the amount of cash you have on hand and in your bank accounts. Also give a description of each item of property, the fair market value of each item, and the balance of any outstanding loans you used to acquire each item. Do not list any money or property you listed on line 20. If you need more room, attach more pages. Write your name and social security number on the top of all pages you attach.

____

____

____

24 **Please provide any other information you want us to consider in determining whether it would be unfair to hold you liable for the tax.** If you need more room, attach more pages. Write your name and social security number on the top of all pages you attach.

____

____

____

Caution

By signing this form, you understand that, by law, we must contact the person on line 7. See instructions for details.

Sign Here

Under penalties of perjury, I declare that I have examined this form and any accompanying schedules and statements, and to the best of my knowledge and belief, they are true, correct, and complete. Declaration of preparer (other than taxpayer) is based on all information of which preparer has any knowledge.

Keep a copy for your records.   ▶ Your signature ________________________________   Date ________________

Paid Preparer's Use Only

Preparer's signature ▶	Date	Check if self-employed ☐	Preparer's SSN or PTIN
Firm's name (or yours if self-employed), address, and ZIP code ▶		EIN	
		Phone no.	

OMB No. 1545-1504

Department of the Treasury - Internal Revenue Service

Request for Taxpayer Advocate Service Assistance

(And Application for Taxpayer Assistance Order)

Form **911**
(Rev. 5-2011)

Section I – Taxpayer Information *(See Pages 3 and 4 for Form 911 Filing Requirements and Instructions for Completing this Form.)*

1a. Your name as shown on tax return

1b. Taxpayer Identifying Number (SSN, ITIN, EIN)

2a. Spouse's name as shown on tax return *(if applicable)*

2b. Spouse's Taxpayer Identifying Number (SSN, ITIN)

3a. Your current street address *(Number, Street, & Apt. Number)*

3b. City

3c. State *(or Foreign Country)*

3d. ZIP code

4. Fax number *(if applicable)*

5. Email address

6. Tax form(s)

7. Tax period(s)

8. Person to contact

9a. Daytime phone number

9b. ☐ Check here if you consent to have confidential information about your tax issue left on your answering machine or voice message at this number.

10. Best time to call

☐ Check if Cell Phone

11. Indicate the special communication needs you require *(if applicable)*

☐ TTY/TDD Line   ☐ Interpreter - Specify language other than English *(including sign language)* _______________

☐ Other *(please specify)*

12a. Please describe the tax issue you are experiencing and any difficulties it may be creating
(If more space is needed, attach additional sheets.)

12b. Please describe the relief/assistance you are requesting *(If more space is needed, attach additional sheets.)*

I understand that Taxpayer Advocate Service employees may contact third parties in order to respond to this request and I authorize such contacts to be made. Further, by authorizing the Taxpayer Advocate Service to contact third parties, I understand that I will not receive notice, pursuant to section 7602(c) of the Internal Revenue Code, of third parties contacted in connection with this request.

13a. Signature of Taxpayer or Corporate Officer, and title, if applicable

13b. Date signed

14a. Signature of spouse

14b. Date signed

Section II – Representative Information *(Attach Form 2848 if not already on file with the IRS.)*

1. Name of authorized representative

2. Centralized Authorization File (CAF) number

3. Current mailing address

4. Daytime phone number

☐ Check if Cell Phone

5. Fax number

6. Signature of representative

7. Date signed

Catalog Number 16965S

www.irs.gov

Form **911** (Rev. 5-2011)

Section III – Initiating Employee Information *(Section III is to be completed by the IRS only)*

Taxpayer name			Taxpayer Identifying Number *(TIN)*	
1. Name of employee	2. Phone number	3a. Function	3b. Operating division	4. Organization code no.

5. How identified and received *(Check the appropriate box)*

IRS Function identified issue as meeting Taxpayer Advocate Service (TAS) criteria

☐ (r) Functional referral (Function identified taxpayer issue as meeting TAS criteria).

☐ (x) Congressional correspondence/inquiry not addressed to TAS but referred for TAS handling.

   Name of Senator/Representative ______________________________

Taxpayer or Representative requested TAS assistance

☐ (n) Taxpayer or representative called into a National Taxpayer Advocate (NTA) Toll-Free site.

☐ (s) Functional referral (taxpayer or representative specifically requested TAS assistance).

6. IRS received date

7. TAS criteria *(Check the appropriate box. **NOTE: Checkbox 9 is for TAS Use Only**)*

☐ (1) The taxpayer is experiencing economic harm or is about to suffer economic harm.

☐ (2) The taxpayer is facing an immediate threat of adverse action.

☐ (3) The taxpayer will incur significant costs if relief is not granted (including fees for professional representation).

☐ (4) The taxpayer will suffer irreparable injury or long-term adverse impact if relief is not granted.

(if any items 1-4 are checked, complete Question 9 below)

☐ (5) The taxpayer has experienced a delay of more than 30 days to resolve a tax account problem.

☐ (6) The taxpayer did not receive a response or resolution to their problem or inquiry by the date promised.

☐ (7) A system or procedure has either failed to operate as intended, or failed to resolve the taxpayer's problem or dispute within the IRS.

☐ (8) The manner in which the tax laws are being administered raise considerations of equity, or have impaired or will impair the taxpayer's rights.

☐ (9) The NTA determines compelling public policy warrants assistance to an individual or group of taxpayers **(TAS Use Only)**

8. What action(s) did you take to help resolve the issue? **(This block MUST be completed by the initiating employee)**
   If you were unable to resolve the issue, state the reason why (if applicable)

9. Provide a description of the Taxpayer's situation, and where appropriate, explain the circumstances that are creating the economic burden and how the Taxpayer could be adversely affected if the requested assistance is not provided
   (This block MUST be completed by the initiating employee)

10. How did the taxpayer learn about the Taxpayer Advocate Service

☐ IRS Forms or Publications   ☐ Media   ☐ IRS Employee   ☐ Other *(please specify)* ______________________

Collection Appeal Request

1. Taxpayer's Name	2. Representative: (Form 2848, Power of Attorney Attached)

3. SSN/EIN	4. Taxpayer's Business Phone	5. Taxpayer's Home Phone	6. Representative's Phone

7. Taxpayer's Street Address

8. City	9. State	10. Zip Code

11. Type of Tax (Tax Form)	12. Tax Periods Being Appealed	13. Tax Due

Collection Action(s) Appealed

14. Please Check the Collection Action(s) You're Appealing:

☐ Federal Tax Lien   ☐ Denial of Installment Agreement

☐ Levy or Notice of Levy   ☐ Termination of Installment Agreement

☐ Seizure

Explanation

15. Please explain why you disagree with the collection action(s) you checked above and explain how you would resolve your tax problem. Attach additional pages if needed. Attach copies of any documents that you think will support your position.

Under penalties of perjury, I declare that I have examined this request and the attached documents, and to the best of my knowledge and belief, they are true, correct and complete. A submission by a representative, other than the taxpayer, is based on all information of which preparer has any knowledge.

16. Taxpayer's or Authorized Representative's Signature	17. Date
18. Collection Manager's Signature	19. Date Received

Form 9465: Installment Agreement Request

<table>
<tr>
<td>Form 9465
(Rev. December 2009)
Department of the Treasury
Internal Revenue Service</td>
<td>Installment Agreement Request
▶ If you are filing this form with your tax return, attach it to the
front of the return. Otherwise, see instructions.</td>
<td>OMB No. 1545-0074</td>
</tr>
</table>

Caution: *Do not file this form if you are currently making payments on an installment agreement or can pay your balance due in full within 120 days. Instead, call 1-800-829-1040. If you are in bankruptcy or we have accepted your offer-in-compromise, see* **Bankruptcy or offer-in-compromise** *on page 2.*

This request is for Form(s) (for example, Form 1040) ▶   and for tax year(s) (for example, 2008 and 2009) ▶

1 Your first name and initial   Last name   Your social security number

If a joint return, spouse's first name and initial   Last name   Spouse's social security number

Current address (number and street). If you have a P.O. box and no home delivery, enter your box number.   Apt. number

City, town or post office, state, and ZIP code. If a foreign address, enter city, province or state, and country. Follow the country's practice for entering the postal code.

2 If this address is new since you filed your last tax return, check here . . . . ▶ ☐

3 Your home phone number   Best time for us to call   **4** Your work phone number   Ext.   Best time for us to call

5 Name of your bank or other financial institution:

Address

City, state, and ZIP code

6 Your employer's name:

Address

City, state, and ZIP code

7 Enter the total amount you owe as shown on your tax return(s) (or notice(s)) **7**

8 Enter the amount of any payment you are making with your tax return(s) (or notice(s)). See instructions **8**

9 Enter the amount you can pay each month. **Make your payments as large as possible to limit interest and penalty charges.** The charges will continue until you pay in full **9**

10 Enter the day you want to make your payment each month. **Do not** enter a day later than the 28th ▶

11 If you want to make your payments by electronic funds withdrawal from your checking account, see the instructions and fill in lines 11a and 11b. This is the most convenient way to make your payments and it will ensure that they are made on time.

▶ **a** Routing number ☐☐☐☐☐☐☐☐☐

▶ **b** Account number ☐☐☐☐☐☐☐☐☐☐☐☐☐☐☐☐☐

I authorize the U.S. Treasury and its designated Financial Agent to initiate a monthly ACH electronic funds withdrawal entry to the financial institution account indicated for payments of my federal taxes owed, and the financial institution to debit the entry to this account. This authorization is to remain in full force and effect until I notify the U.S. Treasury Financial Agent to terminate the authorization. To revoke payment, I must contact the U.S. Treasury Financial Agent at **1-800-829-1040** no later than 10 business days prior to the payment (settlement) date. I also authorize the financial institutions involved in the processing of the electronic payments of taxes to receive confidential information necessary to answer inquiries and resolve issues related to the payments.

Your signature   Date   Spouse's signature. If a joint return, **both** must sign.   Date

General Instructions

Section references are to the Internal Revenue Code.

Purpose of Form

Use Form 9465 to request a monthly installment plan if you cannot pay the full amount you owe shown on your tax return (or on a notice we sent you). Generally, you can have up to 60 months to pay. In certain circumstances, you can have longer to pay or your agreement can be approved for an amount that is less than the amount of tax you owe. However, before requesting an installment agreement, you should consider other less costly alternatives, such as getting a bank loan or using available credit on a credit card. If you have any questions about this request, call 1-800-829-1040.

Do not use Form 9465 if:

● You can pay the full amount you owe within 120 days (see page 2), or

● You want to request an online payment agreement. See *Applying online for a payment agreement* on page 2.

Guaranteed installment agreement. Your request for an installment agreement cannot be turned down if the tax you owe is not more than $10,000 and all three of the following apply.

● During the past 5 tax years, you (and your spouse if filing a joint return) have timely filed all income tax returns and paid any income tax due, and have not entered into an installment agreement for payment of income tax.

● The IRS determines that you cannot pay the tax owed in full when it is due and you give the IRS any information needed to make that determination.

● You agree to pay the full amount you owe within 3 years and to comply with the tax laws while the agreement is in effect.

Form **9465-FS**	**Installment Agreement Request**	
(December 2011) Department of the Treasury Internal Revenue Service	▶ **If your balance due is greater than $25,000 but not more than $50,000, complete Parts I and II.** ▶ **If you are filing this form with your tax return, attach it to the front of the return.** ▶ **See separate instructions.**	OMB No. 1545-0074

Caution: *Do not file this form if you are currently making payments on an installment agreement or can pay your balance in full within 120 days. Instead, call 1-800-829-1040. If you are in bankruptcy or we have accepted your offer-in-compromise, see* **Bankruptcy or offer-in-compromise** *in the instructions.*

Note. If you are filing Form 9465-FS to request an installment agreement for a business tax liability and the business is no longer a functioning enterprise, complete line 2 in addition to 1a.

This request is for Form(s) (for example, Form 1040 or Form 941) ▶ _______ and for tax year(s) (for example, 2010 and 2011) ▶ _______

Part I	**General Information**

1a Your first name and initial | Last name | **Your social security number**

If a joint return, spouse's first name and initial | Last name | **Spouse's social security number**

Current address (number and street). If you have a P.O. box and no home delivery, enter your box number. | Apt. number

City, town or post office, state, and ZIP code. If a foreign address, enter city, province or state, and country. Follow the country's practice for entering the postal code.

b If this address is new since you filed your last tax return, check here . . . . ▶ ☐

2 Business name | **Employer Identification Number**

3 _______ | **4** _______

Your phone number | Best time for us to call | Your work phone number | Ext. | Best time for us to call

5 Name of your bank or other financial institution: | **6** Your employer's name:

Address | Address

City, state, and ZIP code | City, state, and ZIP code

7 Enter the total amount you owe as shown on your tax return(s) (or notice(s)) . . . . | **7** |
Note. If the amount on line 7 is greater than $25,000 but not more than $50,000, you **must** complete line 11 and Part II on page 2. See instructions. | |

8 Enter the amount of any payment you are making with your tax return(s) (or notice(s)). See instructions | **8** |

9 Enter the amount you can pay each month. **Make your payments as large as possible to limit interest and penalty charges.** The charges will continue until you pay in full. If a payment amount is not listed on line 9, one will be determined for you by dividing the balance due by 72 months . | **9** |

10 Enter the date you want to make your payment each month. **Do not** enter a date later than the 28th ▶ _______

11 If you want to make your payments by electronic funds withdrawal from your checking account, see the instructions and fill in lines 11a and 11b. This is the most convenient way to make your payments and it will ensure that they are made on time.

▶ **a** Routing number ☐☐☐☐☐☐☐☐☐

▶ **b** Account number ☐☐☐☐☐☐☐☐☐☐☐☐☐☐☐☐☐

I authorize the U.S. Treasury and its designated Financial Agent to initiate a monthly ACH debit (electronic withdrawal) entry to the financial institution account indicated for payments of my Federal taxes owed, and the financial institution to debit the entry to this account. This authorization is to remain in full force and effect until I notify the U.S. Treasury Financial Agent to terminate the authorization. To revoke payment, I must contact the U.S. Treasury Financial Agent at **1-800-829-1040** no later than 14 business days prior to the payment (settlement) date. I also authorize the financial institutions involved in the processing of the electronic payments of taxes to receive confidential information necessary to answer inquiries and resolve issues related to the payments.

Your signature | Date | Spouse's signature. If a joint return, **both** must sign. | Date

---

For Privacy Act and Paperwork Reduction Act Notice, see instructions. | Cat. No. 58656E | Form **9465-FS** (12-2011)

Form 9465-FS: Installment Agreement Request — page 2

Part II   **Additional information.** Complete this part only if your answer on line 7 is greater than $25,000 but not more than $50,000.

12   In which county is your primary residence? _______________________________

13a Marital status:
- ☐ Single. Skip question 13a and go to question 14.
- ☐ Married. Go to question 13b.

  b Do you share household expenses with your spouse?
- ☐ Yes.
- ☐ No.

14   How many dependents will you be able to claim on this year's tax return? . . . . **14** _______________

15   How many people in your household are 65 or older? . . . . **15** _______________

16   How often are you paid?
- ☐ Once a week.
- ☐ Once every two weeks.
- ☐ Once a month.
- ☐ Twice a month.

17   What is your net income per pay period (take home pay)? . . . . **17** $ _______________

18   How often is your spouse paid?
- ☐ Once a week.
- ☐ Once every two weeks.
- ☐ Once a month.
- ☐ Twice a month.

19   What is your spouse's net income per pay period (take home pay)? . . . . . . **19** $ _______________

20   How many vehicles do you own? . . . . **20** _______________

21   How many car payments do you have each month? . . . . **21** _______________

22a Do you have health insurance?
- ☐ Yes. Go to question 22b.
- ☐ No. Skip question 22b and go to question 23a.

  b Are your premiums deducted from your paycheck?
- ☐ Yes. Skip question 22c and go to question 23a.
- ☐ No. Go to question 22c.

  c How much are your monthly premiums? . . . . **22c** $ _______________

23a Do you make court-ordered payments?
- ☐ Yes. Go to question 23b.
- ☐ No. Go to question 24.

  b Are your court-ordered payments deducted from your paycheck?
- ☐ Yes. Go to question 24.
- ☐ No. Go to question 23c.

  c How much are your court-ordered payments each month? . . . . **23c** $ _______________

24   Not including any court-ordered payments for child and dependent support, how much do you pay for child or dependent care each month? . . . . **24** $ _______________

Form 982: Reduction of Tax Attributes Due to Discharge of Indebtedness

Form **982** (Rev. February 2011) Department of the Treasury Internal Revenue Service	**Reduction of Tax Attributes Due to Discharge of Indebtedness (and Section 1082 Basis Adjustment)** ▶ Attach this form to your income tax return.	OMB No. 1545-0046 Attachment Sequence No. **94**

Name shown on return	Identifying number

Part I   **General Information** (see instructions)

1	Amount excluded is due to (check applicable box(es)):	
a	Discharge of indebtedness in a title 11 case	☐
b	Discharge of indebtedness to the extent insolvent (not in a title 11 case)	☐
c	Discharge of qualified farm indebtedness	☐
d	Discharge of qualified real property business indebtedness	☐
e	Discharge of qualified principal residence indebtedness	☐
2	Total amount of discharged indebtedness excluded from gross income	**2**	
3	Do you elect to treat all real property described in section 1221(a)(1), relating to property held for sale to customers in the ordinary course of a trade or business, as if it were depreciable property?	☐ Yes ☐ No

Part II   **Reduction of Tax Attributes.** You must attach a description of any transactions resulting in the reduction in basis under section 1017. See Regulations section 1.1017-1 for basis reduction ordering rules, and, if applicable, required partnership consent statements. (For additional information, see the instructions for Part II.)

Enter amount excluded from gross income:

4	For a discharge of qualified real property business indebtedness applied to reduce the basis of depreciable real property	**4**	
5	That you elect under section 108(b)(5) to apply first to reduce the basis (under section 1017) of depreciable property	**5**	
6	Applied to reduce any net operating loss that occurred in the tax year of the discharge or carried over to the tax year of the discharge	**6**	
7	Applied to reduce any general business credit carryover to or from the tax year of the discharge	**7**	
8	Applied to reduce any minimum tax credit as of the beginning of the tax year immediately after the tax year of the discharge	**8**	
9	Applied to reduce any net capital loss for the tax year of the discharge, including any capital loss carryovers to the tax year of the discharge	**9**	
10a	Applied to reduce the basis of nondepreciable and depreciable property if not reduced on line 5. *DO NOT use in the case of discharge of qualified farm indebtedness*	**10a**	
b	Applied to reduce the basis of your principal residence. *Enter amount here ONLY if line 1e is checked*	**10b**	
11	For a discharge of qualified farm indebtedness applied to reduce the basis of:		
a	Depreciable property used or held for use in a trade or business or for the production of income if not reduced on line 5	**11a**	
b	Land used or held for use in a trade or business of farming	**11b**	
c	Other property used or held for use in a trade or business or for the production of income	**11c**	
12	Applied to reduce any passive activity loss and credit carryovers from the tax year of the discharge	**12**	
13	Applied to reduce any foreign tax credit carryover to or from the tax year of the discharge	**13**	

Part III   **Consent of Corporation to Adjustment of Basis of Its Property Under Section 1082(a)(2)**

Under section 1081(b), the corporation named above has excluded $ ______________________ from its gross income for the tax year beginning ______________________ and ending ______________________ . Under that section, the corporation consents to have the basis of its property adjusted in accordance with the regulations prescribed under section 1082(a)(2) in effect at the time of filing its income tax return for that year. The corporation is organized under the laws of ______________________ .

(State of incorporation)

Note. *You must attach a description of the transactions resulting in the nonrecognition of gain under section 1081.*

For Paperwork Reduction Act Notice, see page 5 of this form.   Cat. No. 17066E   Form **982** (Rev. 2-2011)

Internal Revenue Service
United States Department of the Treasury

This Product Contains Sensitive Taxpayer Data

Account Transcript

Request Date: 01-25-2012
Response Date: 01-25-2012
Tracking Number: [REDACTED]

FORM NUMBER: 1040　　　　　　　　　　　　　　TAX PERIOD: Dec. 31, 2003

TAXPAYER IDENTIFICATION NUMBER:
SPOUSE TAXPAYER IDENTIFICATION NUMBER:

<<<POWER OF ATTORNEY/TAX INFORMATION AUTHORIZATION (POA/TIA) ON FILE>>>>

--- ANY MINUS SIGN SHOWN BELOW SIGNIFIES A CREDIT AMOUNT ----

```
ACCOUNT BALANCE:                              46,694.24
ACCRUED INTEREST:                            182,592.02    AS OF: Feb. 06, 2012
ACCRUED PENALTY:                                  0.00    AS OF: Feb. 06, 2012

ACCOUNT BALANCE PLUS ACCRUALS
(this is not a payoff amount):               229,286.26
```

** INFORMATION FROM THE RETURN OR AS ADJUSTED **

```
EXEMPTIONS:                                       06
FILING STATUS:                    Married Filing Separate
ADJUSTED GROSS INCOME:                     1,329,286.00
TAXABLE INCOME:                            1,324,536.00
TAX PER RETURN:                              471,942.00
SE TAXABLE INCOME TAXPAYER:                   97,000.00
SE TAXABLE INCOME SPOUSE:                          0.00
TOTAL SELF EMPLOYMENT TAX:                    20,751.00

RETURN DUE DATE OR RETURN RECEIVED DATE (WHICHEVER IS LATER)     Oct. 18, 2004
PROCESSING DATE                                                 Nov. 22, 2004
```

TRANSACTIONS

CODE	EXPLANATION OF TRANSACTION	CYCLE	DATE	AMOUNT
150	Tax return filed	20044508	11-22-2004	$471,942.00
460	Extension of time to file ext. Date 08-15-2004		04-15-2004	$0.00
460	Extension of time to file ext. Date 10-15-2004		08-13-2004	$0.00
170	Penalty for not pre-paying tax	20044508	11-22-2004	$11,059.00
276	Penalty for late payment of tax	20044508	11-22-2004	$18,877.68

Code	Explanation of Transaction	Cycle / Date	Amount
196	Interest charged for late payment	20044508 11-22-2004	$13,243.81
420	Examination of tax return	11-09-2004	$0.00
971	Collection due process Notice of Intent to Levy -- issued	11-03-2005	$0.00
582	Lien placed on assets due to balance owed	11-11-2005	$0.00
960	Appointed representative	02-06-2006	$0.00
971	Pending installment agreement	02-06-2006	$0.00
971	Installment agreement established	03-24-2006	$0.00
971	Installment agreement established	04-10-2006	$0.00
670	Payment	05-07-2007	-$50,000.00
971	Installment agreement established	09-28-2007	$0.00
706	Credit transferred in from 1040 200212	10-29-2007	-$21,219.43
706	Credit transferred in from 1040 200212	11-30-2007	-$25,000.00
971	Installment agreement established	10-10-2006	$0.00
706	Credit transferred in from 1040 200212	12-31-2007	-$25,000.00
706	Credit transferred in from 1040 200212	02-01-2008	-$25,000.00
706	Credit transferred in from 1040 200212	03-03-2008	-$25,000.00
706	Credit transferred in from 1040 200212	04-01-2008	-$25,000.00
971	No longer in installment agreement status	05-05-2008	$0.00
706	Credit transferred in from 1040 200212	04-28-2008	-$50,000.00
670	Payment	06-02-2008	-$50,000.00
670	Payment	07-08-2008	-$50,000.00
670	Payment	08-18-2008	-$50,000.00
670	Payment	09-08-2008	-$50,000.00
971	Notice issued CP 071C	12-15-2008	$0.00
276	Penalty for late payment of tax	20084908 12-15-2008	$97,636.18
960	Appointed representative	04-06-2009	$0.00
480	Offer in compromise received	03-22-2010	$0.00
670	Payment	03-16-2010	-$150.00
481	Denied offer in compromise	05-21-2010	$0.00
971	Installment agreement established	11-09-2010	$0.00
971	Installment agreement established	11-09-2010	$0.00
670	Payment	12-27-2010	-$9,895.00
670	Payment	02-02-2011	-$10,000.00

670	Payment		02-27-2011	-$10,000.00
672	Removed payment CIVIL PENALTY 201101		12-27-2010	$105.00
673	Payment		12-27-2010	-$105.00
670	Payment		03-30-2011	-$10,000.00
670	Payment		04-27-2011	-$10,000.00
673	Payment		05-27-2011	-$10,000.00
670	Payment		06-13-2011	-$10,000.00
671	Bad check for payment		05-27-2011	$10,000.00
280	Penalty for bad check	20112508	07-04-2011	$200.00
670	Payment		06-30-2011	-$20,000.00
670	Payment		08-08-2011	-$20,000.00
670	Payment		09-08-2011	-$20,000.00

Jn 28 11 09:20p

p.3

| Form 668 (Y)(c)
(Rev. February 2004) | 1872 | Department of the Treasury - Internal Revenue Service
Notice of Federal Tax Lien |

Area:
SMALL BUSINESS/SELF EMPLOYED AREA #1
(800) 913-6050

Serial Number

For Optional Use by Recording Office

As provided by section 6321, 6322, and 6323 of the Internal Revenue Code, we are giving a notice that taxes (including interest and penalties) have been assessed against the following-named taxpayer. We have made a demand for payment of this liability, but it remains unpaid. Therefore, there is a lien in favor of the United States on all property and rights to property belonging to this taxpayer for the amount of these taxes, and additional penalties, interest, and costs that may accrue.

- This Notice of Federal Tax Lien has been filed as a matter of public record.
- IRS will continue to charge penalty and interest until you satisfy the amount you owe.
- Contact the Area Office Collection Function for information on the amount you must pay before we can release this lien.
- See the back of this page for an explanation of your Administrative Appeal rights.

Name of Taxpayer

Residence

IMPORTANT RELEASE INFORMATION: For each assessment listed below, unless notice of the lien is refiled by the date given in column (e), this notice shall, on the day following such date, operate as a certificate of release as defined in IRC 6325(a).

Kind of Tax (a)	Tax Period Ending (b)	Identifying Number (c)	Date of Assessment (d)	Last Day for Refiling (e)	Unpaid Balance of Assessment (f)
1040	12/31/2009		11/15/2010	12/15/2020	121912.01

Place of Filing

Prothonotary
Chester County
West Chester, PA 19380

Total   121912.01

This notice was prepared and signed at ____DETROIT, MI____________________, on this,

the __10th__ day of __June__________, __2011__.

Signature

Title
CASE PROC MGR

(NOTE: Certificate of officer authorized by law to take acknowledgment is not essential to the validity of Notice of Federal Tax Lien (Rev. Rul. 71-466, 1971-2 C.B. 409)

Part 3 - Taxpayer's Copy

CAT. NO. 60025X

Department of the Treasury
Internal Revenue Service

Publication 1

(Rev. May 2005)

Catalog Number 64731W

www.irs.gov

Your Rights as a Taxpayer

The first part of this publication explains some of your most important rights as a taxpayer. The second part explains the examination, appeal, collection, and refund processes. This publication is also available in Spanish.

Declaration of Taxpayer Rights

I. Protection of Your Rights

IRS employees will explain and protect your rights as a taxpayer throughout your contact with us.

II. Privacy and Confidentiality

The IRS will not disclose to anyone the information you give us, except as authorized by law. You have the right to know why we are asking you for information, how we will use it, and what happens if you do not provide requested information.

III. Professional and Courteous Service

If you believe that an IRS employee has not treated you in a professional, fair, and courteous manner, you should tell that employee's supervisor. If the supervisor's response is not satisfactory, you should write to the IRS director for your area or the center where you file your return.

IV. Representation

You may either represent yourself or, with proper written authorization, have someone else represent you in your place. Your representative must be a person allowed to practice before the IRS, such as an attorney, certified public accountant, or enrolled agent. If you are in an interview and ask to consult such a person, then we must stop and reschedule the interview in most cases.

You can have someone accompany you at an interview. You may make sound recordings of any meetings with our examination, appeal, or collection personnel, provided you tell us in writing 10 days before the meeting.

V. Payment of Only the Correct Amount of Tax

You are responsible for paying only the correct amount of tax due under the law—no more, no less. If you cannot pay all of your tax when it is due, you may be able to make monthly installment payments.

VI. Help With Unresolved Tax Problems

The Taxpayer Advocate Service can help you if you have tried unsuccessfully to resolve a problem with the IRS. Your local Taxpayer Advocate can offer you special help if you have a significant hardship as a result of a tax problem. For more information, call toll free 1-877-777-4778 (1-800-829-4059 for TTY/TDD) or write to the Taxpayer Advocate at the IRS office that last contacted you.

VII. Appeals and Judicial Review

If you disagree with us about the amount of your tax liability or certain collection actions, you have the right to ask the Appeals Office to review your case. You may also ask a court to review your case.

VIII. Relief From Certain Penalties and Interest

The IRS will waive penalties when allowed by law if you can show you acted reasonably and in good faith or relied on the incorrect advice of an IRS employee. We will waive interest that is the result of certain errors or delays caused by an IRS employee.

THE IRS MISSION

PROVIDE AMERICA'S TAXPAYERS TOP QUALITY SERVICE BY HELPING THEM UNDERSTAND AND MEET THEIR TAX RESPONSIBILITIES AND BY APPLYING THE TAX LAW WITH INTEGRITY AND FAIRNESS TO ALL.

Examinations, Appeals, Collections, and Refunds

Examinations (Audits)

We accept most taxpayers' returns as filed. If we inquire about your return or select it for examination, it does not suggest that you are dishonest. The inquiry or examination may or may not result in more tax. We may close your case without change; or, you may receive a refund.

The process of selecting a return for examination usually begins in one of two ways. First, we use computer programs to identify returns that may have incorrect amounts. These programs may be based on information returns, such as Forms 1099 and W-2, on studies of past examinations, or on certain issues identified by compliance projects. Second, we use information from outside sources that indicates that a return may have incorrect amounts. These sources may include newspapers, public records, and individuals. If we determine that the information is accurate and reliable, we may use it to select a return for examination.

Publication 556, Examination of Returns, Appeal Rights, and Claims for Refund, explains the rules and procedures that we follow in examinations. The following sections give an overview of how we conduct examinations.

By Mail

We handle many examinations and inquiries by mail. We will send you a letter with either a request for more information or a reason why we believe a change to your return may be needed. You can respond by mail or you can request a personal interview with an examiner. If you mail us the requested information or provide an explanation, we may or may not agree with you, and we will explain the reasons for any changes. Please do not hesitate to write to us about anything you do not understand.

By Interview

If we notify you that we will conduct your examination through a personal interview, or you request such an interview, you have the right to ask that the examination take place at a reasonable time and place that is convenient for both you and the IRS. If our examiner proposes any changes to your return, he or she will explain the reasons for the changes. If you do not agree with these changes, you can meet with the examiner's supervisor.

Repeat Examinations

If we examined your return for the same items in either of the 2 previous years and proposed no change to your tax liability, please contact us as soon as possible so we can see if we should discontinue the examination.

Appeals

If you do not agree with the examiner's proposed changes, you can appeal them to the Appeals Office of IRS. Most differences can be settled without expensive and time-consuming court trials. Your appeal rights are explained in detail in both Publication 5, Your Appeal Rights and How To Prepare a Protest If You Don't Agree, and Publication 556, Examination of Returns, Appeal Rights, and Claims for Refund.

If you do not wish to use the Appeals Office or disagree with its findings, you may be able to take your case to the U.S. Tax Court, U.S. Court of Federal Claims, or the U.S. District Court where you live. If you take your case to court, the IRS will have the burden of proving certain facts if you kept adequate records to show your tax liability, cooperated with the IRS, and meet certain other conditions. If the court agrees with you on most issues in your case and finds that our position was largely unjustified, you may be able to recover some of your administrative and litigation costs. You will not be eligible to recover these costs unless you tried to resolve your case administratively, including going through the appeals system, and you gave us the information necessary to resolve the case.

Collections

Publication 594, The IRS Collection Process, explains your rights and responsibilities regarding payment of federal taxes. It describes:

- What to do when you owe taxes. It describes what to do if you get a tax bill and what to do if you think your bill is wrong. It also covers making installment payments, delaying collection action, and submitting an offer in compromise.

- IRS collection actions. It covers liens, releasing a lien, levies, releasing a levy, seizures and sales, and release of property.

Your collection appeal rights are explained in detail in Publication 1660, Collection Appeal Rights.

Innocent Spouse Relief

Generally, both you and your spouse are each responsible for paying the full amount of tax, interest, and penalties due on your joint return. However, if you qualify for innocent spouse relief, you may be relieved of part or all of the joint liability. To request relief, you must file Form 8857, Request for Innocent Spouse Relief no later than 2 years after the date on which the IRS first attempted to collect the tax from you. For example, the two-year period for filing your claim may start if the IRS applies your tax refund from one year to the taxes that you and your spouse owe for another year. For more information on innocent spouse relief, see Publication 971, Innocent Spouse Relief, and Form 8857.

Potential Third Party Contacts

Generally, the IRS will deal directly with you or your duly authorized representative. However, we sometimes talk with other persons if we need information that you have been unable to provide, or to verify information we have received. If we do contact other persons, such as a neighbor, bank, employer, or employees, we will generally need to tell them limited information, such as your name. The law prohibits us from disclosing any more information than is necessary to obtain or verify the information we are seeking. Our need to contact other persons may continue as long as there is activity in your case. If we do contact other persons, you have a right to request a list of those contacted.

Refunds

You may file a claim for refund if you think you paid too much tax. You must generally file the claim within 3 years from the date you filed your original return or 2 years from the date you paid the tax, whichever is later. The law generally provides for interest on your refund if it is not paid within 45 days of the date you filed your return or claim for refund. Publication 556, Examination of Returns, Appeal Rights, and Claims for Refund, has more information on refunds.

If you were due a refund but you did not file a return, you generally must file your return within 3 years from the date the return was due (including extensions) to get that refund.

Tax Information

The IRS provides the following sources for forms, publications, and additional information.

- *Tax Questions:* 1–800–829–1040 (1–800–829–4059 for TTY/TDD)

- *Forms and Publications:* 1–800–829–3676 (1–800–829–4059 for TTY/TDD)

- *Internet: www.irs.gov*

- *Small Business Ombudsman:* A small business entity can participate in the regulatory process and comment on enforcement actions of IRS by calling 1-888-REG-FAIR.

- *Treasury Inspector General for Tax Administration:* You can confidentially report misconduct, waste, fraud, or abuse by an IRS employee by calling 1–800–366–4484 (1–800–877–8339 for TTY/TDD). You can remain anonymous.

Printed on recycled paper

Internal Revenue Service
Small Business and Self-Employed
850 Trafalgar Court
Suite 200
Maitland FL 32751

Date: September 1, 2011

Department of the Treasury

Taxpayer Identification Number:
███████████

Form:
1040

Tax Period(s) Ended:
201012

Person to Contact:
███████████

Contact Telephone Number:
███████████

Contact Fax Number:
███████████

Employee Identification Number:
███████████

Refer Reply to:
SBSE

Last Date to Respond to this Letter:
October 1, 2011

Dear ███████████:

On August 8, 2011, we asked you to send us your federal income tax return(s) for the tax period(s) shown above. Since we don't have a record of receiving a response from you, we calculated your tax and proposed penalties based on the information your employers, banks, and other payers reported on Forms W-2, 1099, etc.

See the attached Form 4549-A, *Income Tax Discrepancy Adjustments,* and *Explanation of Changes,* which explain the tax and penalties we calculated on your behalf as allowed by Internal Revenue Code Section 6020(b).

If you agree with the tax and penalties shown in the report, please sign, date, and return one copy of the enclosed Form 870, *Waiver of Restrictions on Assessment and Collection of Deficiency in Tax and Acceptance of Overassessment,* along with payment for the total amount due. It is to your advantage to pay the total amount now since we will continue to charge interest on any unpaid balance until you pay the amount you owe in full. If you can't pay the full amount at this time, pay as much as you can and contact us to discuss how you can pay the balance owed.

If you decide to file a return at this time, send it to the above address. To help us identify your case, include a copy of this letter with your return. Be sure to include copies of all supporting records. We have enclosed a copy of this letter for your records and an envelope for your convenience.

If you do not agree with the tax and penalties shown on the report, you may request an appeals conference. This is done by filing a small case request or a formal written protest (depending upon the amount we show you owe) at the above mailing address within 30 calendar days of the date of this letter. See the enclosed Publication 3498, *The Examination Process,* **if you don't agree.** This publication describes the procedures needed to request an appeals conference.

Letter 3391 (Rev. 8-2007)
Catalog Number 29973S

If you do not wish to have an appeals conference, but you still wish to dispute our decision, you must pay the full amount owed and file a claim with the Internal Revenue Service. Under Section 6511 of the Internal Revenue Code, you must file your claim within 3 years from the date you filed your original return, or within two years from the date you paid the tax, whichever is later. If no return was filed, you must file your claim within 2 years from the date you paid the tax.

If you do not respond within 30 days, the Internal Revenue Service will process your case based on the enclosed report. We will send you a Statutory Notice of Deficiency that allows you 90 days to petition the United States Tax Court. If you allow the 90-day period to expire without petitioning the Tax Court, we will bill you for tax, interest, and penalties.

If you have any questions, contact the person whose name and number is shown in the heading of this letter.

Thank you for your cooperation.

Sincerely,

█████████████████

Examination Technician

Enclosures:
Publication 3498
Form 4549-A (original and copy)
Form 870 (original and copy)
Form 9465
Envelope

Letter 3391 (Rev. 8-2007)
Catalog Number 29973S

Form **4549** (Rev. May 2008)	Department of the Treasury-Internal Revenue Service **Income Tax Examination Changes**		Page __1__ of __2__	
Name and Address of Taxpayer		Taxpayer Identification Number	Return Form No.: 1040	
▉		Person with whom examination changes were discussed.	Name and Title:	

	1. Adjustments to Income	Period End 12/31/2010	Period End	Period End
a.	Gambling Winnings	7,522.00		
b.	Sch C1 - Gross Receipts or Sales	100,750.00		
c.	SE AGI Adjustment	(7,118.00)		
d.	Standard Deduction	(5,700.00)		
e.	Exemptions	(3,650.00)		
f.				
g.				
h.				
i.				
j.				
k.				
l.				
m.				
n.				
o.				
p.				
2.	**Total Adjustments**	91,804.00		
3.	Taxable Income Per Return or as Previously Adjusted	0.00		
4.	**Corrected Taxable Income**	91,804.00		
	Tax Method	TAX TABLE		
	Filing Status	Married Separate		
5.	**Tax**	19,833.00		
6.	Additional Taxes / Alternative Minimum Tax			
7.	Corrected Tax Liability	19,833.00		
8.	**Less** a.			
	Credits b.			
	c.			
	d.			
9.	**Balance** *(Line 7 less Lines 8a through 8d)*	19,833.00		
10. Plus	a. Self Employment Tax	14,236.00		
Other	b.			
Taxes	c.			
	d.			
11.	Total Corrected Tax Liability *(Line 9 plus Lines 10a through 10d)*	34,069.00		
12.	Total Tax Shown on Return or as Previously Adjusted	0.00		
13.	Adjustments to: a.			
	b.			
	c.			
14.	Deficiency-Increase in Tax or *(Overassessment-Decrease in Tax)* *(Line 11 less Line 12 adjusted by Lines 13a through 13c)*	34,069.00		
15.	Adjustments to Prepayment Credits - Increase *(Decrease)*			
16.	Balance Due or *(Overpayment)* - *(Line 14 adjusted by Line 15)* *(Excluding interest and penalties)*	34,069.00		

The Internal Revenue Service has agreements with state tax agencies under which information about federal tax, including increases or decreases, is exchanged with the states. If this change affects the amount of your state income tax, you should amend your state return by filing the necessary forms.

You may be subject to backup withholding if you underreport your interest, dividend, or patronage dividend income you earned and do not pay the required tax. The IRS may order backup withholding *(withholding of a percentage of your dividend and/or interest income)* if the tax remains unpaid after it has been assessed and four notices have been issued to you over a 120-day period.

Catalog Number 23105A	www.irs.gov	Form **4549** (Rev. 5-2008)

Form **4549** (Rev. May 2008)	Department of the Treasury-Internal Revenue Service **Income Tax Examination Changes**		Page____2____ of ____2____
Name of Taxpayer █████████	Taxpayer Identification Number █████████		Return Form No.: 1040

17. **Penalties/ Code Sections**	Period End 12/31/2010	Period End	Period End
a. Delq-IRC 6651(a)(2)	851.73		
b. Delq-IRC 6651(a)(1)	7,665.53		
c. Estimated Tax-IRC 6654	730.63		
d.			
e.			
f.			
g.			
h.			
i.			
j.			
k.			
l.			
m.			
n.			
18. **Total Penalties**	9,247.89		
Underpayment attributable to negligence: *(1981-1987)* *A tax addition of 50 percent of the interest due on the* *underpayment will accrue until it is paid or assessed.*			
Underpayment attributable to fraud: *(1981-1987)* *A tax addition of 50 percent of the interest due on the* *underpayment will accrue until it is paid or assessed.*			
Underpayment attributable to Tax Motivated Transactions *(TMT)*. The interest will accrue and be assessed at 120% of the under- payment rate in accordance with IRC §6621(c)	0.00		
19. **Summary of Taxes, Penalties and Interest:**			
a. Balance due or *(Overpayment)* Taxes - *(Line 16, Page 1)*	34,069.00		
b. Penalties *(Line 18)* - computed to 08/31/2011	9,247.89		
c. Interest *(IRC § 6601)* - computed to 09/30/2011	775.45		
d. TMT interest - computed to 09/30/2011 *(on TMT underpayment)*	0.00		
e. Amount due or *(refund)* - *(sum of Lines a, b, c and d)*	44,092.34		

Other Information:

Examiner's Signature: █████████	Employee ID: █████	Office: Maitland, FL	Date: 08/31/2011

Consent to Assessment and Collection- I do not wish to exercise my appeal rights with the Internal Revenue Service or to contest in the United States Tax Court the findings in this report. Therefore, I give my consent to the immediate assessment and collection of any increase in tax and penalties, and accept any decrease in tax and penalties shown above, plus additional interest as provided by law. It is understood that this report is subject to acceptance by the Area Director, Area Manager, Specialty Tax Program Chief, or Director of Field Operations.

PLEASE NOTE: *If a joint return was filed,* **BOTH** *taxpayers must sign*

Signature of Taxpayer	Date:	Signature of Taxpayer	Date:
By:		Title:	Date:

Catalog Number 23105A	www.irs.gov	Form **4549** (Rev. 5-2008)

Name of Taxpayer: ███████		08/31/2011
Identification Number: ███████	Total	12.20.00

2010 - Form 6251 - Alternative Minimum Tax Computation

1. If filing Schedule A, enter taxable income before exemptions;
   otherwise, enter adjusted gross income   101,154.00
2. Total adjustment and preferences (excluding any NOL deduction)   0.00
3. Net operating loss deduction   0.00
4. Alternative tax net operating loss deduction   0.00
5. Alternative minimum taxable income (combine lines 1 thru 4)   101,154.00
6. Exemption amount   29,686.00
7. Subtract line 6 from line 5 (if zero or less, enter zero)   71,468.00
8. If capital gains are reported, see line 19 from continuation page
   (If FEIT worksheet for AMT is used, enter amount from line 6 of that worksheet instead)
   All others:
   If line 7 is $175,000 or less ($87,500 if MFS) multiply
   line 7 by 26%. Otherwise, multiply line 7 by 28% and
   subtract $3,500 ($1,750 if MFS) from the result   18,582.00
9. Alternative minimum tax foreign tax credit   0.00
10. Tentative minimum tax (line 8 less line 9)   18,582.00
11. Regular tax before credits (If Schedule J was used to figure tax,
    use the refigured amounts for lines 44 and 47 of Form 1040
    without using Schedule J)   19,833.00
12. Alternative minimum tax   0.00

Exemption Worksheet (line 6 above)

A. Exemption amount based on filing status   36,225.00
B. Alternative minimum taxable income   101,154.00
C. Enter $112,500 ($150,000 if married filing jointly or
   qualifying widow(er), $75,000 if married filing separately)   75,000.00
D. Subtract line C from line B   26,154.00
E. Multiply line D by 25%   6,539.00
F. Subtract line E from line A (if zero or less, enter zero)   29,686.00

Name of Taxpayer: ███████ 08/31/2011
Identification Number: ███████ Total 12.20.00

2010 - Form 6251 - Continuation, Tax Computation Using Maximum Capital Gain Rates

1. Amount from Form 6251 report, line 7	71,468.00
(If FEIT worksheet for AMT was used, enter amount from line 3 of that worksheet instead)	
2. Amount from line 6 Qualified Dividends and Capital Gain Tax Worksheet	
or line 13 Schedule D Tax Worksheet (refigured for AMT)	0.00
3. Amount from Schedule D line 19 (refigured for AMT)	0.00
4. Amount from line 2 if no Schedule D worksheet; otherwise, the smaller of	
the sum of line 2 and line 3 or Schedule D worksheet line 10 (refigured for AMT)	0.00
5. Smaller of line 1 or line 4	0.00
6. Subtract line 5 from line 1	71,468.00
7. If line 6 is $175,000 or less ($87,500 if MFS) multiply line 6 by 26%;	
otherwise, multiply line 6 by 28% and subtract $3,500 ($1,750 if MFS)	
from the result	18,582.00
8. Enter:	
$68,000 if married filing jointly or qualifying widow(er)	
$34,000 if single or married filing separately	34,000.00
$45,550 if head of household	
9. Amount from line 7 Qualified Dividends and Capital Gain Tax Worksheet	
or line 14 Schedule D Tax Worksheet	0.00
10. Subtract line 9 from line 8 (if zero or less, enter zero)	34,000.00
11. Smaller of line 1 or line 2	0.00
12. Smaller of line 10 or line 11	0.00
13. Subtract line 12 from line 11	0.00
14. Multiply line 13 by 15%	0.00
15. Subtract line 11 from line 5	0.00
16. Multiply line 15 by 25%	0.00
17. Total of lines 7, 14 and 16	18,582.00
18. If line 1 is $175,000 or less ($87,500 if MFS) multiply line 1 by 26%;	
otherwise, multiply line 1 by 28% and subtract $3,500 ($1,750 if MFS)	
from the result	18,582.00
19. Smaller of line 17 or line 18. Enter here and on line 8 of Form 6251 report	18,582.00

| Name of Taxpayer: ▮▮▮▮▮▮ | | 08/31/2011 |
| Identification Number: ▮▮▮▮▮▮ | Total | 12.20.00 |

EXPLANATION OF THE DELINQUENCY PENALTY

Since your income tax return was not filed within the time limit prescribed by law and/or the tax was not paid, and you have not shown that such failure was due to reasonable cause, an addition to the tax is charged as shown below, in accordance with Section 6651(a)(1) and/or Section 6651(a)(2) of the Internal Revenue Code.

2010 - DELINQUENCY PENALTY

1. Delinquency penalty abated		0.00
2. Date return due	04/15/2011	
3. Date return filed	08/31/2011	
4. Failure to File penalty rate	0.225	
5. Failure to Pay penalty rate	0.025	
6. Total corrected tax liability		34,069.00
7. Allowable payments on or prior to due date of return		0.00
8. Net Amount Due (line 6 less line 7)		34,069.00
9. Failure to File Penalty - line 8 multiplied by line 4		7,665.53
10. Minimum penalty if over 60 days delinquent		135.00
11. Failure to File Penalty - Greater of line 9 or line 10		7,665.53
12. Previously assessed/previously agreed Failure to File Penalty		0.00
13. Net Failure to File Penalty - line 11 less line 12		7,665.53
14. Failure to Pay Penalty - line 8 multiplied by line 5		851.73
15. Previously assessed/previously agreed Failure to Pay Penalty		0.00
16. Net Failure to Pay Penalty - line 14 less line 15 *		851.73
17. Total Delinquency Penalty - Sum of line 13 and 16		8,517.26

* If an amount appears as the Failure to Pay Penalty, the amount only reflects the addition to tax under Internal Revenue Code section 6651(a)(2) through the date of this notice. The addition to tax will continue to accrue from the due date of the return at a rate of 0.5 percent each month, or fraction thereof, of nonpayment, not exceeding 25 percent.

Name of Taxpayer: ████████
Identification Number: ████████

Total

08/31/2011
12.20.00

2010 - EXPLANATION OF THE ESTIMATED TAX PENALTY

Since you did not pay sufficient estimated tax, addition to the tax is charged as shown below, in accordance with Section 6654(a) of the Internal Revenue Code.

1. Total corrected tax liability, Form 4549, line 11 (Tax Per Return, if a return was filed)	34,069.00
2. Refundable Credits	0.00
3. Withholding taxes	0.00
4. Line 1 less sum of lines 2 & 3 (if less than $1000, estimated penalty does not apply)	34,069.00
5. 90% of the sum of line 1 less line 2	30,662.10
6. Prior year tax liability (100% of prior year tax except*)	0.00
7. The smaller of line 5 or 6 (as adjusted)	30,662.10

	Apr 15, 2010	Jun 15, 2010	Sep 15, 2010	Jan 15, 2011
8. Payment Due Date	Apr 15, 2010	Jun 15, 2010	Sep 15, 2010	Jan 15, 2011
9. Payment Required	7,665.53	7,665.53	7,665.53	7,665.53
10. Payments & Credits	0.00	0.00	0.00	0.00
11. Overpayment from line 17		0.00	0.00	0.00
12. Total of lines 10 & 11		0.00	0.00	0.00
13. Previous Qtr Underpayment		7,665.53	15,331.06	22,996.59
14. Line 12 less line 13	0.00	0.00	0.00	0.00
15. Remaining Underpayment		7,665.53	15,331.06	
16. Underpayment	7,665.53	7,665.53	7,665.53	7,665.53
17. Overpayment	0.00	0.00	0.00	0.00
18. Penalty	284.57	233.32	156.04	56.70
19. Previously Assessed/Previously Agreed Estimated Tax Penalty				0.00
20. Estimated Tax Penalty				730.63

* If the prior year AGI was >$150,000 ($75,000 if MFS): use 110% of prior year tax.

Name Of Taxpayer: ███████████   08/31/2011
Identification Number: ███████████   Total   12.20.00

2010 TAX YEAR INTEREST COMPUTATION

Interest computed to   09/30/2011

Total Tax Deficiency $34,069.00

Plus Penalties*
    Failure to File - IRC 6651 $7,665.53
    Accuracy Related Penalty - IRC 6662 $.00
    Accuracy Related Penalty - IRC 6662A $.00
    Civil Fraud - IRC 6663 $.00
    Manually Computed Penalty $.00

Total Penalties Subject to Interest $7,665.53

Tax Deficiency and Penalties Subject to Interest $41,734.53

Type	Effective Dates	Days	Rate	Interest
Compound	04/15/2011~09/30/2011	168	4%	$775.45

Total Interest $775.45

Interest on penalties is computed from the due date of the return (including extensions) until the date of payment. The interest shown on this report is estimated. Interest is computed from the due date of the return (including extensions) and will continue to accrue until the date paid in full. Interest on the failure to pay penalty is computed from the date of assessment and is therefore not considered in this report.

Name of Taxpayer: ███████		08/31/2011
Identification Number: ███████	Total	12.20.00

2010 · STANDARD DEDUCTION

1. Filing status amount	5,700.00
2. If taxpayer (or spouse if married filing jointly) can be claimed as a dependent, enter earned income amount (if earned income is less than $ 650 , enter $ 950); otherwise, skip this line and enter amount from line 1 on line 3	
3. Smaller of line 1 or line 2 (if applicable)	5,700.00
4. Multiply number of age/blind exemptions by $ 1,100	0.00
5. Net disaster loss included in standard deduction	0.00
6. Deductible portion of vehicle taxes paid	0.00
7. Adjusted gross income	101,154.00
8. Excluded foreign earned income	0.00
9. Add lines 7 and 8	101,154.00
10. Enter $125,000 ($250,000 if married filing jointly)	125,000.00
11. If line 9 is greater than line 10, subtract line 10 from line 9; otherwise, skip lines 11 through 13 and enter amount from line 6 on line 14	
12. Divide line 11 by $10,000 and enter result as decimal rounded to at least three places (no more than 1.000)	
13. Multiply line 6 by line 12	
14. Subtract line 13 from line 6	0.00
15. Standard deduction. Add lines 3, 4, 5, and 14	5,700.00

<table>
<tr><td>Form 886-A
(Rev. January
1994)886-A</td><td align="center">EXPLANATION OF ITEMS</td><td>Schedule number or exhibit</td></tr>
<tr><td>Name of Taxpayer
■■■■■■■■</td><td>Taxpayer Identification Number
■■■■■■■</td><td>Year/Period Ended
2010</td></tr>
</table>

Self-Employment Tax

	Tax Period	Per Return	Per Exam	Adjustment
	2010	$0.00	$14,235.52	$14,235.52

We have classified your non-employee compensation income as self-employment income. Therefore, you are subject to self-employment tax.

Gambling Winnings

	Tax Period	Per Return	Per Exam	Adjustment
	2010	$0.00	$7,522.00	$7,522.00

We have adjusted your income to include the amounts shown on Form W-2G from Dover Downs INC and Day At The Track INC.

Sch C1 - Gross Receipts or Sales

	Tax Period	Per Return	Per Exam	Adjustment
	2010	$0.00	$100,750.00	$100,750.00

We have included the amounts reported on forms 1099-Misc. These are as follows:

2009 Adesa US Central Office $40,850		2007 Manheim Services Corporation $42,975	
2009 Manheim New Jersey 58,000		2007 Adesa US Central Office 44,375	
		2007 Rons Auction and Realty Co 3,850	
2008 Manheim Services Corporation $ 825		2007 National Auto Dealers Exchange 54,880	
2008 Adesa US Central Office 44,625		2007 Insurance Auto Auctions 3,250	
2008 Rons Auction and Realty Co 1,925			
2008 National Auto Dealers Exchange 57,420		2006 Manheim Services Corporation $35,350	
2008 Insurance Auto Auctions Inc 650		2006 Adesa New Jersey 44,200	
		2006 National Auto Dealers Exchange 56,160	

Exemptions-Self/Spouse

	Tax Period	Per Return	Per Exam	Adjustment
	2010	0	1	-1

Since the interest expense was not incurred during the taxable year, no deduction is allowed. Yourself.

<table>
<tr><td>Form 886-A
(Rev. January
1994)886-A</td><td>EXPLANATION OF ITEMS</td><td>Schedule number or exhibit</td></tr>
<tr><td>Name of Taxpayer
█████████</td><td>Taxpayer Identification Number
█████████</td><td>Year/Period Ended
2010</td></tr>
</table>

Filing Status

	Tax Period	Per Return	Per Exam	Adjustment
	2010	$0.00	$0.00	$0.00

Since you were married during the tax year but did not elect to file a joint income tax return, we figured your tax using the rates that apply to married individuals filing separately.

Statutory-SE AGI Adjustment

	Tax Period	Per Return	Per Exam	Adjustment
	2010	$0.00	$7,118.00	($7,118.00)

Your self-employment tax has changed as a result of adjustments made to your net earnings from self-employment as shown in this report. The self-employment tax deduction has been adjusted to one-half of the recomputed amount.

Statutory-Self Employment Tax

	Tax Period	Per Return	Per Exam	Adjustment
	2010	$0.00	$14,236.00	$14,236.00

We have adjusted your self-employment tax due to a change in your net earnings from self-employment.

Form **886-A** (1-1994)   Department of the Treasury - Internal Revenue Service

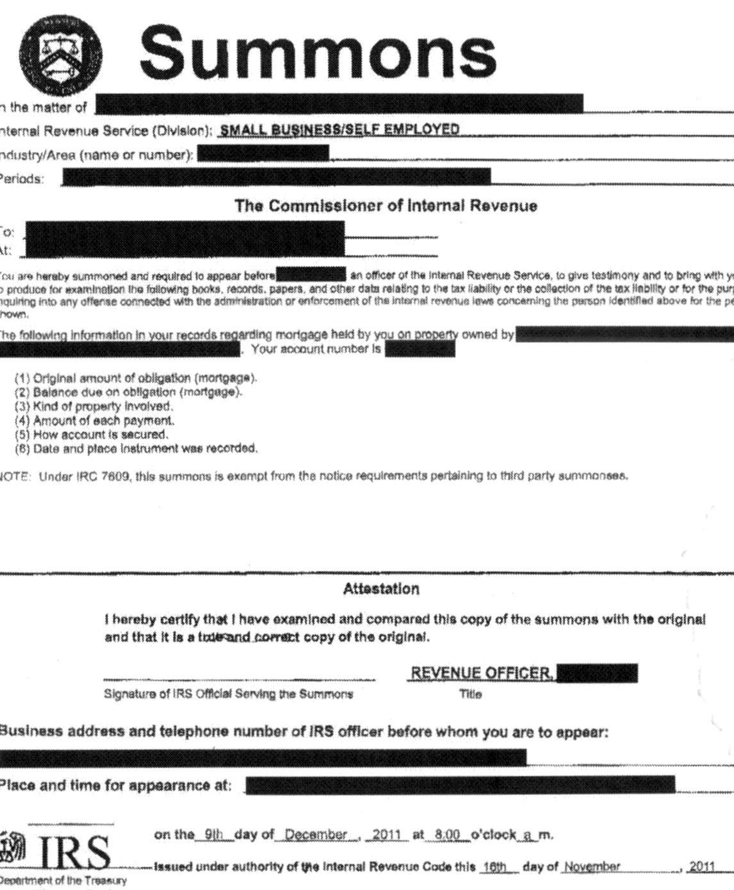

Summons

In the matter of ▮▮▮▮▮▮▮▮▮▮▮▮▮▮▮▮▮▮▮▮▮▮▮▮▮▮▮

Internal Revenue Service (Division): **SMALL BUSINESS/SELF EMPLOYED**

Industry/Area (name or number): ▮▮▮▮▮▮▮

Periods: ▮▮▮▮▮▮▮▮▮▮▮▮▮

The Commissioner of Internal Revenue

To: ▮▮▮▮▮▮▮▮▮▮▮

At: ▮▮▮▮▮▮▮▮▮

You are hereby summoned and required to appear before ▮▮▮▮▮ an officer of the Internal Revenue Service, to give testimony and to bring with you and to produce for examination the following books, records, papers, and other data relating to the tax liability or the collection of the tax liability or for the purpose of inquiring into any offense connected with the administration or enforcement of the internal revenue laws concerning the person identified above for the periods shown.

The following information in your records regarding mortgage held by you on property owned by ▮▮▮▮▮▮▮▮▮▮▮▮▮▮▮▮▮▮▮▮▮. Your account number is ▮▮▮▮▮▮

    (1) Original amount of obligation (mortgage).
    (2) Balance due on obligation (mortgage).
    (3) Kind of property involved.
    (4) Amount of each payment.
    (5) How account is secured.
    (6) Date and place instrument was recorded.

NOTE: Under IRC 7609, this summons is exempt from the notice requirements pertaining to third party summonses.

Attestation

I hereby certify that I have examined and compared this copy of the summons with the original and that it is a true and correct copy of the original.

_______________________________   **REVENUE OFFICER,** ▮▮▮▮▮▮
Signature of IRS Official Serving the Summons   Title

Business address and telephone number of IRS officer before whom you are to appear:

▮▮▮▮▮▮▮▮▮▮▮▮▮▮▮▮▮▮▮▮▮

Place and time for appearance at: ▮▮▮▮▮▮▮▮▮▮▮▮▮▮▮▮

IRS

on the __9th__ day of __December__, __2011__ at __8:00__ o'clock __a__ m.

Issued under authority of the Internal Revenue Code this __16th__ day of __November__, __2011__

Department of the Treasury
Internal Revenue Service

www.irs.gov   ▮▮▮▮▮▮▮▮   **REVENUE OFFICER**
           Signature of Issuing Officer   Title

Form 2039(Rev. 10-2010)
Catalog Number 21405J   _______________________________   **GROUP MANAGER**
          Signature of Approving Officer (if applicable)   Title

Part A -- to be given to person summoned

Made in United States
Orlando, FL
13 September 2023